The Sporting Life

The Punter's Friend

A guide to betting

The Sporting Life
The Punter's Friend
A guide to betting

JACK WATERMAN

Macdonald
Queen Anne Press

A *Queen Anne Press* BOOK

© Jack Waterman 1987

First published in Great Britain in 1987 by
Queen Anne Press, a division of
Macdonald & Co (Publishers) Ltd
3rd Floor
Greater London House
Hampstead Road
London NW1 7QX

A BPCC plc Company

British Library Cataloguing in Publication Data

Waterman, Jack
    The punter's friend.
    1. Horse race betting—Great Britain
    I. Title
    798.4'01'0941   SF333.G7

    ISBN 0-356-12107-0

Typeset by Leaper & Gard Limited, Bristol
Printed and bound in Great Britain by
Hazell, Watson & Viney Limited
Aylesbury, Bucks

A Member of the BPCC Group

CONTENTS

*This book is dedicated to the memory of Maxie Read,
the best friend on a racecourse that ever was.*

INTRODUCTION

The English believe that racing is sinful . . . Perhaps that is the secret of its appeal. I fail to see the sin myself, in watching a marvellous horse perform deeds of wonder. People also believe that gambling is sinful. It is not even enjoyable. It is winning that is enjoyable. Mostly, gambling is an exciting way of making yourself depressed.

I had already written this introduction when I read in *The Times* Simon Barnes's rave notice of *Dancing Brave*'s astonishing and wonderful performance in the 1986 Prix de l'Arc de Triomphe. The words he wrote, and quoted above, express exactly my thoughts about racing and betting, and tie in perfectly with what I wish to make clear about *The Punter's Friend*. It is *not* a gospel for the gone gambler. There is quite enough evidence on the sad fact and incidence of compulsive gambling to dissuade anything that might be construed as encouragement in that direction. This book, therefore, nowhere suggests that there is a copperbottom, unsinkable method of finding winners all the time. Equally, those who consider they know everything about racing are excused all further reading beyond this point.

What I have attempted to do is largely for the benefit of those who would like to go racing, and have an occasional bet either on the racecourse or in the local betting shop, but are so put off by the mystique surrounding the whole business and its impenetrable terminology, that they find the effort is beyond them. At the same time, experienced racegoers will also find certain sections of interest and use. From them, however, a certain amount of indulgence is asked for, when what to their eyes appears self-evident is given a basic explanation.

Chapter One, therefore, is devoted at much greater length than is usual in a 'Glossary' section, to de-mystifying the Turf as far as possible. I have also tried to take a fresh look at the way certain statistics are presented. In the case of breeding, the yardstick of success for a sire is normally the amount of prize money won by his progeny in a given season. This is based on the sound principle that the most prize money is won by the best horses, hence the best sires can also be so judged. In the National Hunt field, because of increases in prize money, statistics viewed that way can now be somewhat lop-sided, so I have attempted to indicate the most prolific National Hunt sires.

Above all, I have tried to suggest that horses should not be treated simply as names in a newspaper, or, worse, as a kind of homogeneous breed of racing Daleks, running their races like automata. A few examples will suffice to show that horses are as different in personality and characteristics as human beings, and this fairly naturally affects their racecourse performances: *St Paddy* was scared of birds, and *Silver Buck* a bundle of nerves until solaced by a Trebor Mint; and *Mandarin* was always more amenable after a pint of Guinness. A horse called *Woodburn* was so spoilt and almost ruined when very young that he used to take it out of other horses round him on the racecourse, to the extent of biting a bit of the rump of the horse in front (which did not have the effect *Woodburn* desired — it simply made the other horse go faster). *Hyperion* when at home on the gallops used to decide not to do any work and would stand stock still for as much as half an hour. When he was at stud he was fascinated by aeroplanes crossing the Newmarket sky. Another great horse, *Le Moss*, had to be fooled into working by Henry Cecil. Many horses like a travelling companion, and 'peerless' *Pretty Polly* was only one who had a pony to keep her company. Strangest of all, perhaps, that good old jumper *Pelican's Pay* had a telly installed in his box to keep him amused. And not all horses like to be retired from the racing scene: one of the greatest of Grand National winners, *Freebooter*, was put out in a paddock away from Bobby Renton's Yorkshire stables where he used regularly to get out and swim a canal; back in the yard he just used to stand looking at the door of his old box.

Finally, my acknowledgements, first to Toby Roxburgh who originally approached me with the idea of doing the book for Queen Anne Press. Next to some other old friends: George Ennor, formerly of *The Sporting Life*, now of the *Racing Post* who has been unstinting of time and encouragement, information and loan of material, and his daughter Charlotte who, with Theo Barr, gave great help with the statistical side; to Doug Newton, senior *Sporting Life* man on the racecourse, and to John Sharratt, senior race reader for *Raceform* who both gave their time and knowledge generously. Richard Lancelyn Green very kindly loaned the 1879 copy of the *The Times*, while Ian Clark of the *Manchester Evening News*, Jane McKerron, Tony Fairbairn, former Director of the Racing Information Bureau, and Geoffrey Webster of the Tote must be thanked for supplying invaluable material. Specimen pages *Raceform*, *Chaseform*, the *Notebook* and *Private Handicap* are reproduced by kind permission of their publishers, Raceform Ltd, and the kind help of Timeform in reprinting material and giving permission for use is also gratefully acknowledged. In making clear one or two difficult settlements for the 'Compendium of Bets' section, I am indebted to Max Thomas bookmakers of Archway Road. Lastly, thanks must go to my wife, Penny, on whom the ideas were first tried, and who undertook the arduous task of helping to proof-read the race statistics in Chapter Nine.

Jack Waterman
June 1987

CHAPTER ONE
An Alphabet of Racing Terms

Acceptor   *See ENTRIES*

Added money   *See PRIZE-MONEY*

Age   All horses share the same birthday irrespective of the exact date of their foaling. This is fixed to facilitate the framing of races according to age groups, and is 1 January each year. Until 1834, the fixed date was 1 May, in line with the end, more or less, of the foaling season. In that year the official date was shifted, for Newmarket horses, to the present one, which occurs before the foaling season has properly got under way. It was not until nearly a quarter of a century later that the rest of the country followed suit.

The majority of races on the Flat are for two-year-olds (2-y-o) only or three-year-olds (3-y-o) only, with a fair proportion also confined to three-year-olds and four-year-olds only, or three-year-olds and upwards. A horse of either sex, before its first birthday, is known as a foal; between that date and its next birthday, a yearling. (*See also COLT, FILLY, GELDING, MARE and WEIGHT FOR AGE*)

Aged   A term not as insulting as it might be when applied to human beings. Past the age of five, all racehorses are officially 'aged'. Because of the use of this description in early records, it is often impossible to determine exactly how old a horse was when he or she won a particular contest, say, in the late 18th, or for much of the 19th century. Vagueness as to precise age in contemporary accounts compounds the difficulty. Today, however, exact ages are used for the purpose of records, whether or not the horse is officially 'aged'.

Most horses have finished their careers on the Flat by the time they are rising five-year-olds, and often earlier in the case of winners of Classics and other important races, and in the case of fillies. Many horses go to stud; others continue racing over hurdles and fences. But a proportion of race-horses on the Flat continue long after becoming officially 'aged', and when assessing the runners for a race, a horse should by no means be overlooked solely because it is (literally) long in the tooth (or, more accurately, has a full set of teeth). *Predominate* was eight years old when, in 1960, he won his third Goodwood Stakes (an important long distance event, over 2 miles 3 furlongs) in as many successive summers. The following year, at nine, he won an even more important staying race at the same meeting, the Goodwood Cup, and only then was honourably retired. In the 1985 season, no fewer than 119 horses of eight years old and upwards ran on the Flat, and, although some of them were hurdlers having a run to get fit before jumping in the autumn, they won 38 races between them. The oldest winner on the Flat that year was 12-year-old *Belle Vue*, and the most consistent 'golden oldie' was the eight-year-old *Ballydurrow* who ran 11 times, winning five races and being placed in a further three (and, as this book went to press, had already won a race in 1986 as a nine-year-old). Another eight-year-old, *Morgan's Choice* beat all his younger contempories for the tough staying race, the Chester Cup. (See also Chapter Six, which deals with the exploits of the most remarkable old horse of all, *Brown Jack*.)

As far as jumping is concerned, a good chaser is usually not mature for his kind of racing until the age of eight or nine (*Red Rum* won the Grand National when he was eight, nine, and twelve; the triumphs of *Arkle* over fences were between the age of seven and nine). There are many jumpers who stay around for a long time after that, too, and win good races. In recent years, *Sea Pigeon* in 1979, when a 9-year-old, was runner-up for the second time in the Champion Hurdle as well as winning the highly competitive Ebor Handicap on the Flat, carrying a record high weight, then won the Champion Hurdle in the two following years. The Queen Mother's *Special Cargo* won the Whitbread Gold Cup, one of the most important chasing prizes, in 1984, when he was 11; 10 years earlier, *The Dikler* had won it at the same age; both horses being trained by Fulke Walwyn. At the age of 13, *Certain Justice* was recording his 25th victory, more than half of them round the figure-of-eight fences at Fontwell Park; while several horses have won at the advanced age of 18, among them, that old favourite, *Sonny Somers*, who won two chases within a fortnight in February 1980. And, oldest of all in recent years, old *Creggmore Boy*, a great favourite of the crowds, and veteran of several Grand Nationals, carried on chasing until he was 22, having won his final race at 17, but been a runner-up in 1961 when he was 21!

While at stud, many horses are active at even greater ages than this. One of the greatest broodmares in the history of racing, *Pocahontas*, whose progeny had untold influence on the course of racing and bloodstock breeding in the nineteenth century, delivered her last foal when she was 25, and after retirement to the Marquis of Exeter's paddocks, died in 1840 at the age of 33. In this century, it is heartening to note that even in 1985 another enormous influence on the stud-book, as well as a great racehorse was grand-sire of a winner. This was the great *Hyperion*, foaled in 1930, a gallant little horse owned by Lord Derby and much loved by the public, who won the 1933 Derby, and who, by the time he died at the age of 30, after a quarter of a century at stud, had sired many Classic winners particularly on the female side, and been responsible for the sires and dams of countless important races not only in Great Britain but in America and all over the world.

Ante post betting   Traditionally, this is betting that takes place before the day of a big race, often several weeks or even months beforehand, as distinguished from the usual betting immediately before any given race. The term has been given several derivations, the most likely being a connection with the 'post betting' that occurred in earlier days. Bets used to be struck on Newmarket Heath, for instance, round the betting posts which can be seen in contemporary illustrations. To bet *ante* post, therefore, was to strike a bet, as today, before the wagering which immediately preceded a race, or match between two horses.

There are many big races, notably those comprising the Spring Double and Autumn Double as well as the Classics: the Grand National and events at Royal Ascot, Goodwood, York, Cheltenham and elsewhere on which bookmakers advertise betting prices long before the event, and which can attract a lot of business. In the case of the Guineas races and Derby (*see CLASSICS*) bets are struck as much as a year or more before the actual race, usually at considerably longer odds than are available nearer the day, and on it. The mechanics of ante post betting are examined in more detail in Chapter Four, but the main advantage from a backer's point of view is the possible securing of a long price about the horse he fancies; bookmakers, meanwhile, can form a betting market well in advance, trim prices accordingly and reduce liability, and, in some cases, use the ante post market themselves in order to offset a possible loss. Despite the fact that many big

---

SPORTING INTELLIGENCE.

MANCHESTER RACES.—Thursday.

Although this was to be looked upon in the light of a by day, the card was a heavy one and there was manifold promise of excellent sport. The day was one of glorious bright sunshine and summer like warmth, instead of the clouds and cold winds to which we have been so long accustomed, and as a consequence the attendance was enormous, much larger than on any previous off day. Some time was cut to waste when the horses were at the post for the first race, the City Welter Plate, in consequence of the temper displayed by Acrobat, who, after a false start, could not be induced to join his opponents until Glover dismounted and led him up. They then left the post in close o··   and Reay, E··· ··v, and · ··ve
· t·   · ·

·un easily,   ··ck, .   —   —   ·
others, and A Maiden Plate was .   ·y a length, after a good race, by the colt by The Palmer, beating the Kingcraft filly and five others. There was some little betting on the Royal Hunt Cup during the day, which we give below.

BETTING ON THE COURSE.
ROYAL HUNT CUP.

12 to 1 agst Sir Joseph (t.)	100 to 6 agst Fiddlestring
100 — 8 —— Avontes (t.)	(taken)
100 — 8 —— Sidonia (t.)	20 — 1 —— Cradle (t.)
100 — 7 —— Lady Ronald	33 — 1 —— Flotsam (t.)
(taken)	33 — 1 —— Priscillian (t.)

ORDER OF RUNNING, THIS DAY.

	H. M.		H. M.
Beaufort Stakes	2 0	Gerard Selling Plate	4 0
Summer Plate	2 30	Optional Sale Plate	4 30
Wilton Welter	3 0	Selling Handicap	5 0
Salford Borough Cup	3 30		

ante post gambles have been successful (see Chapter Three) the continued existence of this form of betting suggests that bookmakers find that it, despite losses, is a worthwhile exercise. That it is long-standing practice is illustrated in the reproduction on page 11 of the prices available on the Royal Hunt Cup at Royal Ascot 1879, and laid on other racecourses in the week before the race.

In the past few years, there has been an extension of ante post betting by the bigger bookmakers. This takes the form of offering prices on the morning of the day on which certain bigger races are to be run. Advertised in the sporting press, and known under various names such as 'early prices', these, like the traditional form of ante post wagering, offer the attraction of possible longer odds than those available immediately before the race or races in question that afternoon. This, particularly on Saturdays, has become a popular and lively feature of the betting scene, with, on occasions, some very successful bets being struck.

Apprentice allowance   In order to compensate for inexperience, apprentice jockeys receive an allowance in terms of weight, according to the total number of winners they have ridden. This weight is subtracted from the weight their horse is set to carry in a race, except in races confined to apprentice riders only. The scale of allowance is as follows: 7 lb until the apprentice has ridden the winner of 10 Flat races under the rules of any recognised Turf authority; thereafter 5 lb until he or she has won 50 such Flat races; thereafter 3 lb up to a limit of 75 winning races. In all cases Apprentice races are excluded from these totals.

Examples:
1. A. Ladd, apprenticed at Newmarket, has a natural weight of 7 st 8 lb. He has ridden 51 winners, but five of them were in races confined to Apprentices, so he is therefore entitled to claim 5 lb allowance. He is down to ride *Cobweb* for his stable in a race. This filly is set to carry 8 st 1 lb in the race. The full 5 lb allowance can therefore be claimed, but A. Ladd will have to carry 2 lb lead in his saddlecloth in order to weigh out at the correct weight of 7 st 10 lb. (Lead weights inserted in strips into the saddlecloth constitute the method of adjusting weight in all races.)
2. Miss Eve Saxon, apprenticed to a Lambourn stable, has a natural weight of 7 st 3 lb. She has ridden nine winners, so therefore is entitled to claim the full 7 lb allowance. She is engaged to ride *Kettledrum*, a colt set to carry only 7 st 10 lb in a handicap race. She can therefore weigh out at 7 st 3 lb, her riding weight, and will carry no lead in the saddlecloth, at the same time reducing the weight allotted to *Kettledrum* by 7 lb.

Similar allowances apply to National Hunt races with a notable proviso that they cannot be claimed in the Grand National, nor in selling races. There are quite complicated rules concerning allowances to other National Hunt riders such as conditional jockeys and amateur riders. *Ruff's Guide to the Turf* gives the full details under Jockey Club Rules.

No apprentice jockeys are allowed under the age of 16, or over 24. In the days when Lester Piggott began his meteoric career there was, fortunately, no such lower limit. Lester was apprenticed to his father, Keith Piggott, who trained at Lambourn, Berkshire. He had his first winner at the age of 12 on *The Chase* at Haydock Park in August 1948. He lost his right to the 7 lb allowance the following May, to the 5 lb allowance in October 1950, and on 26 May 1951, still only 15 years of age, he lost entirely his right to claim when he rode *No Light* into the winner's enclosure at Hurst Park.

The value of a good claiming apprentice particularly in a big handicap cannot be over emphasised, particularly at their natural riding weight. If they are talented, their light weight and ability to make their allowance more than compensate for inexperience can be a winning factor, with the reservation that apprentices do not do well in competition with senior jockeys on courses that require very skilful and experienced jockeyship, notably the Derby course at Epsom, the round course at Ascot, and the equivalent at the main Goodwood meeting. (Apprentices are discussed in more detail in Chapter Ten.)

At the post   Nothing to do with ante *post* betting, not these days anyway. Horses, when they have arrived at the point from which a race is to be started, are said to be 'at the post'.

Autumn Double   Both the Cambridgeshire Handicap (1 mile 1 furlong) and the Cesarewitch (2¼ miles), first run at Newmarket in 1839, take place at an interval of about a fortnight in October. Each race normally attracts outsize fields, in particular the Cambridgeshire; hence the bookmakers offer big prices about some of the runners, and an attempt to nominate the winner of both races, especially in the ante post market which precedes them, is known as the Autumn Double. In other words, the choice for each race is combined in one bet, a double (see Chapter Six for more about doubles in general and how winnings are calculated). The longest priced Autumn Double of recent years, in terms of starting price, was in 1984 when *Tom Sharp* (returned at 40/1) won the Cesarewitch, and *Leysh* (33/1) the Cambridgeshire. A bet of £1 double on them would have returned £1,393 before deduction of betting tax, but even these long odds might have been bettered in the ante post market. The shortest-priced Autumn Double in the same period (once again at starting price) occurred in 1978 when the 9/2 favourite, *Centurion* won the Cesarewitch, and *Baronet* (12/1) won the Cambridgeshire: odds for the double being 70/1 before tax. Again, these prices almost certainly could have been, and undoubtedly were bettered in the ante post market. Between these two extremes can be seen the attraction of the Autumn Double, not only for punters but for bookmakers who take a real beating only when well-backed horses win both races. The heyday of the Autumn Double, when some spectacular gambles were landed, has probably passed. Because there are so many other good races with valuable prize money available, horses are not so often specially prepared for months beforehand with, in particular, the Cambridgeshire in view. But it still does happen, and, as ever (despite high prize money these days) with the traditional objective: a successful gamble as the afternoon sun goes down early and the mists gather on Newmarket Heath. Coupling the winner of the Lincoln Handicap with that of the Grand National is similarly known as the Spring Double.

Bad legs   A more common condition among racehorses than the public generally realise. To understand it, and, indeed, to appreciate the whole process of racing and training horses to race, it is necessary to think of the horses as equine athletes, which indeed they are, and, in this perspective, it can be considered whether Sebastian Coe would shine over 100 metres, would race if he had jarred his legs badly, or would dream of taking part in a contest without first and last using a track suit? To take these points in equine terms, horses also have ideal distances over which they should compete — a crucial factor when it comes to weighing up their chances in a race — they wear blankets and rugs in the paddock before a race, and afterwards, when perspiring, have a 'string vest' thrown over them and blankets again, and they, no less than their human counterparts, pull muscles when racing, strain tendons, and because of leg trouble, either chronic or temporary, may 'break down' altogether and be unable to race.

The horses's forelegs, particularly when jumping fences, and to an extent when running on hard ground, come under great pressure, and it is the forelegs which give trainers the greatest anxiety. Bad legs as a chronic condition occur for a variety of reasons, including heredity. A protective measure, similar to the support stockings worn by human beings with varicose veins, consists of bandages, sometimes semi-permanent, on the forelegs. *Arkle*'s great rival over fences, *Mill House* wore bandages. *Crepello*, the celebrated Guineas and Derby winner of 1957, had suspect tendons and, as described by Dick Francis in *Lester, the Official Biography*, wore strong supportive bandages on his forelegs, 'the sort called Newmarket Boots, which were made of doeskin and sewn on tightly, semi-permanent. They had to be turned round on the legs every day to dislodge any piece of grit which might have slipped inside'. It is noteworthy that trainers are extremely proud (see Chapter Ten) and rightly so, when they have managed a big success with horses who are unsound in their legs. Some examples are the Grand National winners *Aldaniti* (1981, trained by Josh Gifford), the Queen Mother's Whitbread and Grand Military winner *Special Cargo* (Fulke Walwyn), the 1966 Cesarewitch winner *Persian Lancer* (Ryan Price) and that great stayer *Le Moss*, winner of the long-distance 'triple crown' of Ascot Gold Cup, Goodwood Cup and Doncaster Cup two years running 1979-80 (Henry Cecil). Sometimes tendon trouble is treated by blistering, or firing, a medieval and barbaric operation which the Royal College of Veterinary Surgeons, favouring the use of modern drugs and new techniques, is trying to ban. Newmarket possesses a special Bad Legged Horse Gallop on Warren Hill. It is made substantially of peat and special application has to be made for permission to use it. The best guide to whether a horse has suspect legs, wears bandages, or has been blistered or fired is *Timeform*. (See Chapter Five.)

Betting on the rails   In the members enclosure of racecourses, book-makers are not allowed to make a book. However, a high proportion of those who are either members or pay for entrance to that enclosure, frequently go to the racecourse with the prime intention of having a bet. To get over this difficulty, the leading bookmakers have pitches immediately next to the rails separating the members from Tattersalls' Ring; they actually stand in Tattersalls, but display their personal boards (without prices) on the rails, and conduct business over the rails, as well as on the Tattersalls' side. Much of the business is done with credit customers, but some cash is taken, if in big enough amounts, on the Tattersalls' side and big business is done with other bookmakers through their runners. Rails bookmakers have their own association, and they comprise the top end of the racecourse betting market, as well as being vital to the price shifts of that market. But no longer, as used to be the case, do they dictate those movements exclusively. This is because 90 per cent of betting today takes place off the course. Heavy support for a particular 'betting shop horse' will force the price down on the racecourse because the money for it finds its way to the racecourse, and, in particular, the rails, by telephone, and by tic-tac and immediately the shorter price is relayed to the other betting rings on the course. (The betting market on the course is dealt with more fully in Chapter Four.)

Blinkers   A device consisting of a hood which fits over a horse's head, with shields at the eye-holes which restrict the horse's peripheral vision. The purpose is to concentrate the horse's attention ahead by cutting out what might have been seen on either side. The fitting of blinkers for the first time is indicated in the more informative racecards published in the morning papers, and is always worth noting — although, while it sometimes secures a dramatic improvement in a horse's racecourse performance, it should not be regarded as a sovereign specific for poor form. Blinkers are used more frequently these days than they used to be, and have lost their reputation for being the tell-tale sign for a horse of dodgy character. In other words, although there are still unreliable horses who invariably wear blinkers, there are also perfectly genuine animals whose performance is better when wearing them. *Timeform* gives good comments on whether a horse is genuine or not, and the effect of blinkers on performance. A converse hint on a horse's capabilities occurs when, after being tried in blinkers, he or she races next time without them.

Blow up   Nothing to do with 'went like a bomb' which, self-evidently, is something quite different. A horse that has 'blown-up' or which 'blew up in the straight' is one which, without explosion of any kind whatsoever — rather the reverse in fact — suddenly loses its place in a race after going well up to that point. It happens for a variety of reasons, sometimes lack of stamina, or fitness, and is also known as 'stopping to nothing'.

Bumping and boring   Sometimes, in the final stages of a race, a horse may be tiring, and the jockey is unable to prevent him or her veering off a straight line, bumping an opponent, and 'boring' that opponent off its intended course. This may affect the opponent's chances, and in certain instances may cost him the race, in which case there will almost certainly be an objection by the losing rider; equally certain, in any case, is that when bumping and boring occurs there is a strong possibility of a stewards' inquiry during which the evidence of the film from the camera patrol and a video re-run will be examined.

The Calendar   Term for the *Racing Calendar*.

Came again   A phrase used in the form book to indicate a horse that has renewed its effort after dropping back in a race.

Camera patrol   First officially used at Newmarket on 30 June 1960. Cameras originally photographed the closing stages of a race from different angles, including head-on, and later the coverage was extended to provide, by means of a mobile camera, a complete visual record of a race. The prime aim is to provide evidence when an objection is lodged, or there is a stewards' inquiry. With widespread use of closed-circuit television on racecourses, the video re-run reinforces the evidence of the camera patrol. Together, their use has been instrumental, in recent years, in discouraging the skulduggery and malpractice in race-riding that used to occur in days gone by.

Card   Abbreviation for racecard and meaning, usually, a given day's programme at a race meeting. Appears in newspaper headings such as 'Chepstow Card' or 'Card for Uttoxeter'. Used in phrases such as 'The best bet on the card is ...', also 'Going through the card'. This means, specific- ally, selection or association with every winner on the card. From time to time, a newspaper correspondent will 'go through the card', an occurrence to which his paper will justifiably trumpet attention the following day. Sir Gordon Richards, whose total of 4,870 winning rides still stands as a record today, as does his feat of being champion jockey 26 times between 1925 and 1953, almost went through the card on two successive days long before he was knighted. At Chepstow, on 4 October 1933, he rode all six winners, and, the following day, rode the first five winners, then, sadly, in the last race on the card, on *Eagleray*, was beaten into third place by a neck and a head.

Carpet   Anyone bemused by Channel 4's presentation of betting with John McCririck's slow-motion tic-tac and use of strange betting terms may be interested to know that 'carpet', one of his favourites, derives from criminal slang for a three-month 'stretch' in prison. Hence 'carpet' is 3/1 in the betting. The late John O'Neill had a far wider grasp of esoteric betting, however, and his return of the starting prices in the press room of northern racecourses is much missed. Apart from communicating in a marvellous Cockney rhyming slang delivered in a broad Manchester accent, John used to announce the starting prices in the following code (still used today) compounded from rhyming slang, back-slang, bingo, and other sources including the aforesaid criminal usage.

Straight up	Even money	Bundle (of sticks)	6/1
Bits against/on	11/10	Nevis (back-slang)	7/1
Nevis to rouf	7/4	Garden (Garden Gate)	8/1
Bottle (of glue)	2/1	Chinese odds	9/1
Carpet	3/1	Cock and hen (or Cockle)	10/1
Burlington (Bertie)	100/30	Macaroni (rhymes with pony)	25/1
Rouf	4/1	Double carpet	33/1
Jacks (alive)	5/1		

Tic-tac signals also give rise to the following: Wrist 5/4, Half arm 6/4, Shoulder 7/4, Top of the Nut 9/4, and Between the Eyes 5/2.

Cast in his/her box   Horses which have lain down in their stable loose-box, or travelling horsebox, and have difficulty in getting up again off the straw are said to be cast in their box; not a welcome happening on the day of a race. Abbreviated often simply to 'cast', as in 'he was cast this morning'.

Chalk jockey   A phrase used (also 'Chalkie') to describe a rider who is not successful enough, or, in the case of apprentices, who have not yet ridden enough winners to justify having their names painted on one of the jockeys' and riders' boards which fit into the numbers board on the racecourse. Instead, the name is chalked or whitewashed on a blank board.

Chase   Common abbreviation for steeplechase, which term, in turn, is derived from the fact that in Ireland in 1752, Mr Edmund Blake was challenged by Mr O'Callaghan to race their hunters four and a half miles across country from Buttevant church to that at St Leger, the steeple of the latter being the winning post. From that event was evolved eventually National Hunt racing, the cornerstone of which is the steeplechase, but without the steeples. A chase, these days, is a race over fences (as distinct from hurdles) distance from two miles to four miles plus, but most commonly three miles. The fences, constructed of birch, consist of plain fences, open ditches (a ditch 6 ft wide is on the take-off side of the fence), and a water-jump which is spectacular, but which many consider an unnecessarily dangerous obstacle which has cost the lives of chasers in the past, including that of the 1957 Grand National winner *Sundew* when he was racing the following season at Haydock Park. Except for the water-jump (at least 12 ft wide and not more than 3 ft high) all fences must be not less than 4 ft 6 in in height. At Aintree, where the Grand National takes place, the fences are lower on the landing side than on the take-off side. (Haydock Park also has 'drop fences', and horses that do well here are worth noting for Aintree.) The Grand National, however, owes much of its spectacle and reputation to the fact that some of the fences are higher and wider than anywhere else; for example, the famous Becher's Brook (4 ft 10 in high × 3 ft 3 in wide), Valentine's Brook and the Canal Turn (both 5 ft high × 3 ft 3 in), and, highest of all, at 5 ft 2 in (though only 2 ft 9 in wide), The Chair, jumped only on the first circuit, and which looks higher than it is because it stretches across only half instead of the full width of the course. To add to the difficulty there is a 6 ft wide ditch on the take-off side. John Francome, the former champion National Hunt jockey, has rated it the most formidable fence in the world, while Mr Chris Collins (now one of racing's administrators) who, as an amateur rode *Mr Jones* into third place in the 1965 Grand National, saw it thus when he walked the course before the race: 'I looked forward towards a dark green bungalow which rose out of a moat. It got larger and larger as I approached ... I foolishly went up and looked into the ditch. I stood on the guard rail and gazed down into a chasm. I had to remind myself that *Mr Jones* had already jumped it twice ...' (*The Horseman's Year 1966* ed. Dorian Williams). (See also Chapter Nine.)

In general, how stiff an obstacle any given fence on a racecourse is, depends to an extent on how tightly-packed with birch it is, and this varies a good deal, from course to course. The fences at Kempton Park and Newbury, for example, may look fairly innocent to the spectator, but they are stiff fences, and it is no good picking a doubtful jumper on these courses. By contrast, to my eye at least, back at Aintree, The Chair these days seems to be more loosely packed at the top than it used to be. After the field has charged over and partly through the top of it in the National the somewhat tattered remains of The Chair look as if a giant vegetarian rat has been giving the evergreen his close attention.

The headquarters of National Hunt racing in general and chasing in particular is Cheltenham (see Chapter Nine) which features the Gold Cup during its great Festival meeting every March, but the sport flourishes throughout the country.

Under the Rules of Racing horses cannot be put to fences until at least July of the year in which they are four years old. In practice, it is common for chasers not to appear in public until they are five or six, often after they have had a hurdling career.

Classics   As pointed out by Peter Willett in his book *The Classic Racehorse*, '... Classic is not found in the list of Definitions in the British Rules of Racing or in the corresponding French rules, the Code des Courses'. He also draws attention to the anomaly that in the *Pattern Race Book*, published jointly by the racing authorities of Great Britain and France, there is a section giving advance notice of the dates and conditions of 'The Classic Races in England, Ireland and France'.

'Classic' when applied to a race, therefore, is a term consecrated by long usage, and, to quote Peter Willett once again, 'Classic races ... are races of long standing which habitually attract the best horses and are regarded as the criteria of excellence'. More specifically, the Classics are open only to three-year-olds, and are five in number in England:

Course & Distance	Time	Race	Open to	First Run
Newmarket				
Rowley Mile Course	Spring	2000 Guineas	Colts & Fillies	1809
Newmarket				
Rowley Mile Course	Spring	1000 Guineas	Fillies only	1814
Epsom 1½ miles	Summer	Derby	Colts & Fillies	1780
Epsom 1½ miles	Summer	Oaks	Fillies only	1779
Doncaster 1¾ miles	Autumn	St Leger	Colts & Fillies	1776

Before the early years of this century, the Classics now open only to colts and fillies were also open to geldings. They were excluded from the 2000 Guineas from 1904 onwards, and from the Derby and St Leger two years later. At the time of writing it is being suggested that the St Leger be re-opened to geldings because of the waning prestige of this oldest classic (see also Chapter Nine). In fact, the only record of a gelding being placed in the Derby seems to be that of *Curzon*, runner-up to Lord Rosebery's *Sir Visto* in 1895, while *Courlan*, third to HRH The Prince of Wales's *Diamond Jubilee* in 1900 appears to be the only gelding placed in the history of the St Leger.

As far as fillies are concerned, it is rare these days for them to contest either the 2000 Guineas or the Derby, owners and trainers preferring to run them in the equivalent Classics open to fillies only: the 1000 Guineas and Oaks. The last filly to win the 2000 Guineas was *Garden Path* in 1944, although Jack Gerber's *Bebe Grande* was runner-up in 1953 to the northern-trained colt *Nearula* after leading for much of the race. The only other filly this century to win the 2000 Guineas was that outstanding racehorse *Sceptre*, owned and trained by the gambler Bob Sievier, in 1902. She turned out again two days later and won the 1000 Guineas at 2/1 on. In both races she established new course records for time. Her next Classic victory was the Oaks, the relentless Sievier having run her in that race, again, only two days after her previous race, which in this case was the Derby, in which she finished fourth. Finally, she won the St Leger in a canter by an easy three lengths. Thus, this extraordinary filly had not only survived a punishing and callous programme (if it can be called that; she ran, all in all, a dozen races that season, starting with the Lincolnshire Handicap!) but established in the process a Classic record which is unlikely ever to be beaten; *Sceptre* ran in all five Classics, won four of them, and, but for a bruised foot on Derby Day, might well have swept the board.

The last filly to win the Derby was *Fifinella* in 1916, and she also won the Oaks, a double achieved only eight years previously by *Signorinetta*, while more recently, *Nobiliary* was runner-up to *Grundy* in the 1975 Derby.

By contrast, the record of fillies in the St Leger in recent times is much more consistently impressive. In 1985 *Oh So Sharp* won this oldest Classic as well as, previously, the 1000 Guineas and Oaks, a feat in which she was emulating, this century, another great filly of Edwardian times, *Pretty Polly* (1904), *Meld* (1955) and *Sun Chariot* ridden by Gordon Richards in the colours of HM King George VI in 1942 (although the Oaks during the war was run at Newmarket instead of Epsom).

In 1977 there was another Royal success: HM The Queen's filly *Dunfermline* won both the Oaks and St Leger, and in 1983 *Sun Princess* achieved a similar double.

It is important to realise that, originally, there was no set intent to establish a pattern of Classic races. It simply evolved, and had become recognised as a pattern probably about the middle of the 19th century. Classic winners have profoundly influenced the development of the thoroughbred, as well as achieving great prestige because in general they have proved themselves the best of their age and breed. For the public the Classics, and the Derby in particular, exert great fascination, and to the racing enthusiast the names of past winners in the record books are the equivalent of Grace, Ranjitsinhji, Hobbs, Bradman, Larwood, Hutton and so on in *Wisden*.

As a medium for betting, the Classics generally provide excellent opportunities. Well-advertised form mostly works out, except in a poor all-round year; well-backed horses tend to win, and, in strong ante post markets, there are opportunities for long prices, for example:

		1 January 1986	Starting Price
2000 Guineas winner	*Dancing Brave*	12/1	15/8F
1000 Guineas winner	*Midway Lady*	25/1	10/1
Derby winner	*Shahrastani*	25/1	11/2
Oaks winner	*Midway Lady*	10/1	15/8F

As a final footnote, it should be added that the titles 2000 Guineas and 1000 Guineas bear no relation whatsoever to the prize money for those races. Sponsored by General Accident, the value to the winning owners in 1985 amounted to more than £180,000 for the two races together.

Cleverly   A horse which wins more easily than the winning distance suggests is said to have won 'cleverly'. He or she may equally be said to have won 'with something in hand'. It happens often on the Flat where a jockey has let the horse do only enough in order to win. The full amount of distance by which he or she might have won is therefore unknown both to the public, and, more important, to the handicapper who can only guess at the horse's true capability. Such horses are worth noting for the future on this sort of evidence which will be given in the form books and amplified in publications such as *Raceform Notebook*. Another phrase in the same connection is when a winner is noted as 'not extended'.

Colt   Male horse aged between two and five years.

Conditions races   All races other than handicaps. The conditions of a race determine the weight each runner will be set to carry: they may be based on age, sex, value of previous races won, and other factors, with weight allowances being made, for example, for not having won a race at all. The weight an older horse has to concede to a younger one varies throughout the Flat season and National Hunt season, becoming less and less as the season progresses. The precise weights are determined by application of the Weight for Age Scale (q.v.).

Examples:

1.   Newmarket. July Meeting. Princess of Wales's Stakes. Weights: 3-y-o colts and geldings 8 st; fillies 7 st 11 lb; 4-y-o and up, colts and geldings 9 st; fillies 8 st 11 lb; penalties, since 2-y-o, a winner of a Group 2 race 3 lb; of a Group 1 race 5 lb. (*See PATTERN RACING* for explanation of Group 1 and 2)

2.   Epsom. Summer Meeting. 180th Woodcote Stakes (6 furlongs) for two-year-olds, entire colts and fillies. Weights: colts 9 st; fillies 8 st 11 lb; maidens allowed 5 lb; horses which have never run allowed in addition 3 lb.

3.   Market Rasen. August Meeting. Cleethorpes Novices Hurdle for four years old and upwards, which, at the start of the current season, have not won a hurdle. Weights 4-y-o 11 st; 5-y-o and up 11 st 3 lb; fillies and mares allowed 5 lb; penalties for each hurdle won 7 lb.

Thus, as with apprentice jockeys, inexperience is allowed for in horses, and previous success makes further success harder. A higher proportion of favourites and well-backed horses win in conditions races, especially 2-y-o races, than in handicaps; but beware placing too much reliance on a literal interpretation of form shown in a conditions race if a horse subsequently runs in a handicap, because it does not necessarily, for various reasons, translate lb for lb. Equally it is well worth studying the conditions of races and particularly the amount of penalty incurred for previous success which may not be enough to stop further victory.

NB. Beginning in 1987 the Jockey Club introduced a controversial measure to increase from 3 lb to 5 lb the allowance received by fillies from colts in 2-y-o Pattern Races.

Courses   One of the outstanding features of racing in Great Britain is the huge variety of the 59 racecourses, all turf, providing differing tests of ability for horses both on the Flat and over jumps, as well as pleasure in this very variety for racing enthusiasts. Twenty courses stage both Flat racing and jumping; 15 are devoted to the Flat only, while no fewer than 25 cater for jumping only. Newmarket, Flat racing's 'headquarters' both historically and in the number of horses trained there, has two courses adjoining one another, but separate entities as far as racing is concerned: these are the Rowley Mile course where the stands, at the time of writing, were under-going major reconstruction, and the July Course, used during the summer. The standard of racing at Newmarket is always high, as it is throughout the year at Ascot which has the biggest average daily attendance of any racecourse in the country. The downs at Epsom have witnessed the Derby since 1780, but Chester is the oldest known course, racing being recorded there as early as 1540. Fuller details of the principal courses are given in Chapter Nine, while a recommended comprehensive guide to them all, as well as hotel and leisure facilities in the vicinity is (latest edition) *Travelling the Turf* published by Kensington West Productions.

Most of the jumps-only courses are anything but principal racecourses, but that does not make them any the less important in the pattern of variety. Many of them take place on small, friendly country courses, as different in atmosphere from the National Hunt 'Mecca' at Cheltenham (which, like Newmarket, has two courses also) as Royal Ascot is from, say, the little course staging flat racing only on the downs above Bath. They range from Perth and Kelso in Scotland to Bangor-on-Dee in Wales, from Sedgfield in Co Durham to Plumpton in Sussex, from Market Rasen in Lincolnshire to Newton Abbot, Devon and Exeter and others in the West Country.

Some courses are right-handed, some (a slight majority) left-handed, and although many are approximately oval, there is a huge variety of differing shapes: Ascot, triangular; Windsor and Fontwell, figures-of-eight; Chester, circular; Brighton, like a big U with a kink in the lower part; Epsom, fittingly, like a great horseshoe with one straight side; Goodwood, like a bent hairpin, and Salisbury, like a straightened one; Carlisle, pear-shaped, and Hereford, almost square. This is all in great contrast to, say, the United States where, although there is racing on turf, more takes place on dirt, and the tracks are fairly uniform, with a standard distance of $1\frac{1}{4}$ miles. Also unlike the States, where, because of the climate, race-meetings last for weeks rather than days, the majority of meetings in the UK last for only one, two, or three days. The longest continuous racing in Britain, in fact, takes place at Goodwood at the main July/August meeting which lasts for five days.

Dead-heat   This occurs when, even with the aid of the photo-finish, a judge is unable to declare an outright winner of a race. Before the advent of the photo-finish there was frequent uproar when the judge declared a dead-heat when it seemed plain to everyone else that there had been a definite winner. In many cases, the angle of the actual finishing line is very difficult to assess correctly on some racecourses and the uproar was not justified, although in other instances it was. Owners, trainers, to say nothing of an army of outraged punters would have been correct in their assessment that they had been robbed by the judge's eyesight, or lack of it, because in a dead-heat the owners of horses concerned share the prize money and bets on the winners are settled to a reduced stake (for full details see Chapter Six). The first dead-heat decided by photo-finish occurred at Doncaster in 1947, the horses being *Parhelion* and *Salubrious*. Sprint handicaps tend to result in more dead-heats than other events, when several horses may be within inches of winning in what is sometimes called a 'blanket finish' (in other words, when the horses are so close they could all be covered by a blanket).

There have been several multiple dead-heats in the fairly distant past.

The abbreviation used in the form book for dead-heat is 'd-h'.

Declarations   There are two declaration stages before a race: the first four days beforehand, and the second by noon on the day preceding the race. These are known as Four Day Declarations, and Overnight Declarations. Declaration means a declaration to run, but by no means all the entries declared at the four day stage remain in the race at the next stage. This happens for a variety of reasons, among them being that a trainer, having seen the four day declarations (published in the sporting press) decides not to run because of the opposition remaining at that stage. A study of the four day declarations can be rewarding particularly before the busy Bank Holiday programmes, when there may be a dozen or more race-meetings. A horse may be seen to be declared at the four day stage at several meetings, and the trainer's choice at the overnight stage will be for the race in which he considers the horse has the best chance, in the light of the opposition in that race and in the races he has missed. The horse is not, of course, guaranteed to win, but at least the trainer has given a hint worth taking. Declarations, as a system, replaced the unsatisfactory and haphazard publishing of 'probable runners' in that time of great change in Turf administration, the 1960s. The system is administered by the Jockey Club's 'Civil Service', Weatherbys at Wellingborough, and trainers declare runners there by telephone or telex by the appropriate times. But during the 1988-89 jumping season all this will change, except for the administration. The Jockey Club are to introduce a radically different system involving the drastic reduction of the time between entry and race to only five days, and with only one, overnight, declaration. Trainers will make entries via Prestel to Weatherbys' computers.

Distance
1. The distance is a point 240 yards from the winning post. There is no mark on the racecourse to indicate it, but it is frequently referred to in form summaries and the form book e.g., 'Led at the distance, soon went clear'. However, courses *are* marked out along the straight (by the running rails on the far side) with a prominent sign indicating how many furlongs from the winning post. The distance is thus 20 yards before the one-furlong marker is reached.
2. Horses are sometimes judged (rarely on the Flat, but quite often at jumping meetings) to have won 'by a distance'. This, technically, is also 240 yards, but usually means that the winner and runner-up are separated by such a margin that the judge cannot make an accurate estimation by eye.
3. The distance of a race. No race on the Flat can be less than 5 furlongs. There is no limit on how long a Flat race can be, but in practice there are not many races beyond 2 miles. The longest race in the calendar is the Queen Alexandra Stakes at Royal Ascot over 2¾ miles, a race which the immortal *Brown Jack* (see Chapter Eight) made his own by

winning six times between 1929 and 1934. On some racecourses (Chester is a notable example) some races are run over so many furlongs and a stated number of yards over the number of furlongs. It is important to note some of these instances when assessing a horse's chances: for instance 1 mile 3 furlongs 100 yds (a distance raced over at Sandown Park) is nearly half a furlong over 1 mile 3 furlongs and only 120 yards short of 1½ miles.

In National Hunt racing, no chase or hurdle can be less than 2 miles. There used to be 1½-mile hurdles, but these were abolished, to the relief of all concerned, some years ago. The longest jumping race is the Grand National about 4 miles 856 yards.

4. Winning distance. The shortest winning distance is a short-head (in practice, sometimes, not much more than a whisker, judged on the photo-finish film), then a head, then a neck, then half-a-length, and so on. The French also have an intermediate winning distance translated as a 'Short-neck'. Here are the distances with their usual abbreviations:

Short-head	sh	One and a half lengths	1½l
Head	hd	Two lengths	2l
Neck	nk	Two and a half lengths	2½l
Half-a-length	½l	Three lengths	3l
Three-quarters of a length	¾l	Four lengths etc	4l
A length	1l	A distance	Dist.

There is a further abbreviation used in the case of a horse placed third, but so far back as to make accurate estimation of distance an irrelevance. In this case, the horse is judged to be a 'bad third', which appears in the form book, say, where the distance between first and second is three lengths, as '3l, Bad'. This occurs most commonly in chases.

Doll   Hurdles singly used to mark direction in National Hunt racing, usually when part of the course is waterlogged or unusable for any other reason, when that part of the course will be said to be 'dolled off'.

Draw   The draw for which position a horse shall occupy in the stalls at the start of a Flat race is made on the day before the race at the overnight declarations office (*see WEATHERBYS*), and is drawn by lot. There is no draw for places in National Hunt racing. Number one in the draw occupies the extreme left-hand position (in stall number one — the number being indicated over the front of the stall), the horse drawn two goes into stall number two, and so on. On certain courses (see Chapter Nine) a low number in the draw, or high number, over certain distances and sometimes depending on the going may give advantage in running, so it is important to study what effect the draw may have, especially with big fields, and how horses are drawn. The draw is published in the newspapers (and on the racecourse appears both on the racecard and numbers board) but it took a long and hard campaign to secure this advantage to those off the course wanting a bet, as well as to trainers and jockeys wishing to plan in advance how their horse should be run. Until the late 1960s, the draw was not made until shortly before a race, and sometimes (the Lincolnshire Handicap used to be an important case in point with an often enormous field, and the draw crucially affecting a horse's chance) backing a favourite ante post which ultimately received a bad draw was so much money thrown away. That particular extreme situation has not substantially been altered today, but at least the overnight draw gives time for reconsideration, and the benefit in ordinary day-to-day Flat racing is striking as far as off-course punters are concerned, in particular. There is one anomaly to be noted, however. For example, in 1981 *Great Eastern* won the Wokingham Stakes at Royal Ascot, drawn 30 in a field of 29! This has a logical explanation, despite the seeming illogicality. Overnight there were 30 runners, but on the morning of the race one horse was withdrawn, leaving only 29. In cases such as this, the remainder of the field still occupy their original allotted draw positions at the start, and a stall is left unoccupied where the absent horse was drawn.

Drifter   A horse whose price lengthens appreciably, or 'drifts' in the betting before a race, say from 3/1 out to 8/1. It means that the bookmakers expected it to be backed, possibly by stable connections, but there is little money for it, and so, after prudently quoting a shortish price when the market opens, the price is gradually lengthened. Not, usually, a hopeful sign for the punter, although it often happens that a horse from a stable which does not bet in big amounts is 'put in' at a short price when the market opens, drifts, and wins. (See Chapter Four for more on this.) The opposite to a drifter is a 'springer', a horse whose price tumbles dramatically, say from 7/1 or 8/1 or even longer, perhaps to be returned 6/4 favourite. This *is* a hopeful sign for the punter able to watch price movements, if not on the course, on television or in the betting shop. Springers to watch for particularly are those in two-year-old races, especially two-year-old selling races. Springers to treat with caution, however, occur with poor and/or small fields and a consequently weak betting market where quite small amounts of money on a horse can cause dramatic fluctuations in prices. Also, even in a reasonably strong betting market, the fact that a horse's price tumbles does *not* automatically mean that it will win; but, at least it usually means that is fancied by those who know most about its chances, and the money is down.

Dwelt   A horse that does not immediately get away when the stalls doors open is said to have 'dwelt at the start', abbreviated to 'dwlt' in the form book. It also happens in National Hunt racing where there are no starting stalls, but the longer the race the less important this becomes in its effect on the outcome of the race, or the horse's performance in it. Similarly, a horse that is slowly into its stride at the start of a race earns the abbreviation 's.i.s'.

Dying   'He died a furlong out' is not to be taken literally; simply meaning that the horse's effort petered out at that point.

Each-way bet   To bet each way (*not* both ways) is to stake equal amounts for a win and for a place. (See Chapter Six for definitions of *placed* horses according to the number of runners and type of race.) On the racecourse it used to be difficult for the ordinary punter to get a bookmaker to lay an each way bet on the racecourse except in big events such as the Derby and Grand National. It is easier nowadays: some bookmakers will take each way in certain races, and put a notice on their boards 'Each way taken' if they are prepared to do so. Credit bookmakers on and off the course, betting shops, and the Tote, on and off the course, all take each way bets.

E.B.F.   Initials of the European Breeders' Fund.

Entire   A male horse that has not been gelded (castrated). (*See GELDING.*)

Entries   Entries for a race have to be made to Weatherbys several weeks or, in some cases, months before the event. Entries are made by the trainers of the horses, and owners, via the trainers, have to pay a fee for entering a horse in a race. The fees range from the extreme of the Derby at £800, with entries closed over three months beforehand, to the other extreme of, say, a National Hunt race at the sporting little fixture of Cartmel, of £2, closing less than three weeks before the race. In between there is a range of fees at levels far less exalted than that of the Derby, with a huge number of races at between £5 and £10 to enter.

But simple entry is not the end of the story. If, having been entered, the horse in fact runs in the race on the day, there are other fees to be paid. In most instances it consists simply of paying extra money at the declaration stage as for instance in the Jennifer Browning Handicap Stakes over a mile at Ripon on the evening of Derby Day, 1986. It cost £5 to enter this race, and £20 extra 'if declared to run'. If it is decided not to go ahead at the Four Day Declaration the owner, instead (once again, via the trainer) *declares forfeit*; that is he says goodbye to his or her original entry fee. In the case of this particular race there was an original entry of 122, of which 85 paid *forfeit*. This left 37 in at the four day stage, of which 20 were declared overnight. Thus, a further 17 horses withdrawn at that stage would cost the owners £25 each (having entered *and* declared at the four day stage).

Big races, however are usually more complicated than even this. They include a separate forfeit stage, or stages in between.

Thus the Derby: on 4 June, 1986 *The Ever Ready Derby Stakes (Group 1)... 1½ miles ... for three-year-old entire colts and fillies; £800 to enter, £700 unless forfeit declared by 20 May; £500 extra if declared to run ... Closed 26 February.*

The total entry was 261; £800 (entry fee) *forfeit* declared for 207; £1500 (entry fee plus fee for horse left in after 20 May) *forfeit* declared for 36.

On 31 May, therefore, at the four day stage the original enormous entry had been boiled down to only 18 — a mere 6.89% of the original list, with the owners of those 18 paying on behalf of each horse a total of £2000 for the privilege. In the event, there were only 17 actual runners, so one owner paid his full £2000 whack without even the pleasure of seeing his colt take part (*see PRIZE MONEY*).

To take another race: the Grand National shares with the Derby tremendous popularity, and it has not one, but two forfeit stages after the entries have closed, although not costing anything like as much as those at Epsom:

Liverpool, Saturday 5 April, 1986. The Seagram Grand National Steeple Chase (Handicap) ... £50 to enter ... £60 extra unless forfeit declared by 11 February; £60 extra unless forfeit declared by 18 March; £120 extra if declared to run.

Thus, for an owner to run a horse in the Grand National would cost £290.

Acceptors. 'Big Race Acceptors' is a heading sometimes seen in the newspapers. Below it will be a list of horses remaining in a big race after a forfeit or four day declaration stage.

A dramatic change in the entry system is due to take place, as from the 1988-89 jumping season. At the root of the change is a much reduced time of only five days between entry and the actual race, with only one declaration stage, overnight. When the system becomes operational trainers will make entries via Prestel to computers at Weatherbys.

Even money   (*See under ODDS*)

Favourite   The horse or horses at the shortest price in the betting. When there are more than one they become joint favourites. Several methods of betting depend on backing the favourite, either by name or simply nominated as 'favourite'. The horse next in the betting is known as the second favourite, and so on.

Field
1.   In general, this refers to the total number of runners for a particular race. Hence 'The field for this year's Derby will be the smallest since *Nijinsky* beat ten opponents in 1970' does not mean that an unusually cramped alternative to Epsom racecourse has been found.
2.   In betting terms it means the shortest priced horse in any given Field, so, effectively, that is the price of the favourite, as in the bookmakers' shouts of 'Six to four the field ...' (*see ODDS*)
3.   The field book is a bookmaker's record of bets taken on a race, kept by the bookmaker's clerk on specially ruled paper on a large clip-board, or in a bookmaker's central office in the case of ante post betting. The field book records bets taken, prices laid and to whom (either by name or ticket number) and the total liability should any given horse win (called the take out).
4.   Field money is the bookmakers' term for the total amount staked on a race out of which must come take out and profit.

5. Fielding against the favourite means that bookmakers are laying the favourite excessively (in the expectation of it not winning).

Filly   A female horse of under six years of age, when she officially becomes a mare, although beyond four years they are often referred to as mares or racemares. Game fillies and mares exert a powerful influence on the affections of racegoers, more so, perhaps, than colts. I wish I'd been around to see *Sceptre* (*see CLASSICS*) and *Pretty Polly*, beaten only once in this country in 23 races, and that on her final appearance in a career which lasted till she was five. Two-year-old unbeaten performances apart, it ranged in distance from the mile of the 1000 Guineas and Coronation Stakes to the $2\frac{1}{4}$ miles of the Jockey Club Cup at Newmarket, and took in three Classics, the Coronation Cup (twice) the Champion Stakes and much else besides on the way. Even further back, I can only marvel at the achievements of, for example, *Beeswing* (after whom a valuable race is named at Gosforth Park, Newcastle) who, between 1835 and 1842, won 51 of her 64 races including four Doncaster Cups and the Ascot Gold Cup; another stayer *Alice Hawthorn* who won over 50 races in the 1840s; and *Catherina* who won the astonishing total of 79 out of 174 races between 1833 and 1841. There was no cotton wool and whisking quickly off to stud in those days!

Form   The form of any given horse is the sum total of its achievements or otherwise on the racecourse as recorded in the form book (see Chapter Five), or extracted from the form book at length in the sporting press, and in a rather more compressed presentation in other newspapers. A horse which has 'no chance on the book' is one whose form, on close examination, does not give it a winning chance in a future race. Just as music can be seen as merely a series of notes written on paper for a musician to play, so the form book provides only facts. Equally, musicians are capable of varying perform-ances from the same set of notes, and the facts in the form book are similarly open to differing interpretations. One of the simplest methods of assessing form can be used if horse A has run against horse B, and they are due to meet again in a race.

In Race 1 over $1\frac{1}{2}$ m   Horse A, carrying 9 st, has beaten horse B, also
at Epsom.   carrying 9 st, into third place by a total of four
Going soft.   lengths.

They are due to meet again within a fortnight at Newmarket carrying the same weights, but over a distance of $1\frac{1}{4}$ m. The going forecast the day before the race is good, and, considering only the question of weight and distance between the horses at the finish of race 1, it seems that horse A again has the beating of horse B. But the panel of newspaper tips in *The Sporting Life* on the morning of the race reveals a division of opinion. Only four experts think that horse A should, as they write in their appraisal of the race, 'confirm the form' with horse B (and consider that whatever other factors other than simple weight and winning distance may be brought to bear, four lengths at level weights is a lot to make up). The majority of newspaper experts are of the opinion that horse B should 'turn the tables on' or 'reverse the form with' horse A.

In reaching this conclusion, they will have consulted evidence from the form book other than the obvious fact that both horses meet again at precisely the same weight and there was four lengths between them in race 1. They may also have seen race 1 with their own eyes, and have consulted one or other of those indispensable adjuncts to assessment of form, *Timeform* and *Raceform Notebook*, as well as taken in features such as *Seen in Running* in *The Sporting Life Weekender*. These are the facts they have found and to which they have given due consideration:

1. In race 1, horse A was having his third outing of the season, and had already won once. Horse B was having his first outing. The race should therefore have done horse B more good in terms of fitness, and condition and possible improvement than horse A.

2. In previous seasons horse A's winning form was best at 1½ m; horse B's was best at 1¼ m.

3. Horse A is known to perform better on soft going, whereas horse B is known not to perform so well in these conditions, in fact, needs good ground to give of his best.

4. Horse A is known to act well on the gradients and turns at Epsom, but has not shown such good form in past seasons on stiff, galloping courses such as Newmarket. Horse B, on the other hand, has always gone well on such courses, being a big, long-striding animal.

5. The pace in the early stages of race 1 was fairly slow, which should have favoured horse B (by reducing the length of the 'real race' to a distance he is good at) but didn't, because his jockey got into all sorts of trouble in the straight. Having gone for an opening to make a winning effort two furlongs from home, a horse closed the gap which he was going for next to the running rails. The jockey then had to switch horse B round other horses to the outside, and by the time he had got horse B clear and into top gear, it was too late.

All these are an unlikely set of circumstances to meet all together in one race, but they serve as examples which occur individually and need consideration when studying the small print in the form book. Considering the circumstances, in fact, it is surprising that anyone tipped horse A to win, and indeed, the result of race 2 was that Horse B trotted in, beating his former rival by an easy three lengths (but the bookmakers had also read the form book and he was returned even money favourite). The following day in the newspapers it was noted that horse B had 'turned the form upside down'. Who else knew?

When horses have met in a previous race as in the above extremely theoretical example, the relative merits purely in terms of weights and winning distance could not be clearer. But, more frequently, horses have not come into direct opposition. Instead (and here we have to introduce horse C) they have met, in different races, a common opponent. Thus:

Race 1 Ascot over 1½ m. Going good.	Horse A carrying 9 st finished fifth. Horse C finishes third, carrying 9 st also. There are three lengths between them at the finish. (Interpreting this in handicap terms, at 1 lb per length, horse C is a 3 lb better performer on this running than horse A.)
Race 2 Ascot over 1½ m. Going good.	Horse B carrying 9 st beats horse C, also carrying 9 st, into second place by 2 lengths. (Interpreting this in handicap terms, horse B is a 2 lb better horse than horse C on this running.) Therefore, via horse C, horse B is, on form, a 5 lb better prospect than horse A.

In race 3 at Sandown Park over approximately 1½ m, going good, horse A, carrying 8 st 11 lb is due to meet horse B carrying 9 st. On a strict interpretation of the previous form horse B thus has to *give* 3 lb weight to horse A, but is a 5 lb better horse, and should therefore win by 2 lengths, since he has a 'pull in the weights'. This is known as 'taking a line through horse C' but, it must be emphasised, *is* a strict interpretation, the value of which is reinforced by the fact that the distances of all the races is the same approximately (Sandown has a further 118 yards added on to its 1½ m course) and the going is good. But other factors, previously mentioned, such as fitness, pace, incidents in previous running, and race-time should also be considered. In National Hunt racing the form is further complicated by how well or badly a horse jumped in a particular race.

Finally, the word 'form' is often related to a particular race, as in the phrase 'The Coventry Stakes form is working out rather well,' meaning that horses beaten in the Coventry Stakes have been running consistently with the form shown in that race, and several of them, perhaps, have subsequently won. They will then be said to have 'advertised' the Coventry Stakes form. The converse is to 'let the form down'.

Front runner   A horse who likes to go out in front and stay there, or 'cut out the running'. *Timeform* and the form book give plenty of hints on this preference. Conversely, many horses have to be 'covered up' until the last minute because once in front they tend to idle, thinking they have done enough. Again, *Timeform* and the form book give the clues. Tracks on which front running tactics often pay off are Chester and Sandown Park.

Gelding   A colt or male horse which has been gelded (castrated). There are several reasons why it may be thought wise to have a racehorse 'cut' or gelded. Ungelded older horses which remain in racing often become temperamental and difficult to deal with; gelding would have normally made them more amenable, partly through taking their minds off sex, and through the change in temperament caused by a shift on hormonal balance common to all neutered animals, human beings included. Thus a gelded horse is more likely to concentrate on racing, and is certainly far easier to train when older. In National Hunt racing there is a further practical reason for gelding horses, and that is the discomfort, to put it at its mildest, suffered by entire horses in brushing through or over fences made of birch. All but a small minority of chasers are geldings. In Ireland it is customary to geld intended future chasers at a very early age. The last entire (i.e. not gelded) winner of the Grand National was *Battleship* in 1938, ridden by Bruce Hobbs who recently retired from training. The last entire Cheltenham Gold Cup winner was *Fortina* in 1947. He subsequently proved his worth, for good measure, at stud and for a long time his progeny put him among the top half dozen National Hunt sires (and he is grandsire of chasers still racing today).

On the Flat, many races, including the Classics, are not open to geldings, although several races have now been opened to them. These include the semi-classic Eclipse Stakes over 1¼ m at Sandown Park in early July, and the Ascot Gold Cup, the premier race for stayers in the calendar. The logic of opening the Ascot Gold Cup to geldings rested partly, it seems, on the sad decline (see Chapter Eleven) of interest on the part of breeders (with one or two notable exceptions) in out-and-out stayers, although it is arguable that the admission of geldings to the race might reduce the status of Ascot Gold Cup winners. The reason for this is based on the nonsensical assumption that if a valuable (in future stud terms) colt is beaten by a gelding, then devaluation instantly sets in. This, in turn, rests on the fact that a gelding is worthless in stud terms, whereas a colt can win the Derby or Prix de l'Arc de Triomphe and is instantly worth millions of pounds to a stud syndicate; yet a king among horses such as *Arkle*, because he was a gelding was worth no more on the day after he won the Cheltenham Gold Cup than the day before. The snobbery of breeders nonetheless, will not cloud the vision of those racegoers who admire the exploits of geldings without whom National Hunt racing would not tick, and gallant deeds on the Flat such as those of *Teleprompter*, an international flag-bearer for English racing, owned by Lord Derby and trained by Bill Watts, and winner of the Budweiser-Arlington Million in the USA.

A notable escapee from gelding was *March Past*. Ken Cundell, his trainer was going to have him cut, but relented for the sake of the owner, Mrs Trimmer-Thompson, whose first horse this was. *March Past* more than repaid the 'kindness'. He became one of the most successful and prolific sires of recent times, and grandsire of the great *Brigadier Gerard*.

Going The state of the ground for a race meeting. The following official categories appear in the form book and are given in advance forecasts in the newspapers: hard; firm; good to firm; good; good to soft; soft; heavy. In muddy conditions, the form book may also note 'Soft with heavy patches' or will differentiate between the going on different parts of the course as, for example: 'Going: round course, soft. Straight course, good to soft.'

The state of the going is perhaps *the* most important random factor in determining the outcome of a race. Some horses prefer soft going, or go better on it ('likes some cut in the ground' or 'likes some give underfoot'). Others give of their best only when the mud is flying and will be noted in the reference books and elsewhere as a 'confirmed mudlark'. Some horses dislike soft conditions and need good going ('needs the top of the ground') while a few actually prefer firm going ('likes to hear his hooves rattle').

Clerks of the Course, who are responsible for defining the state of the going, come in for occasional heavy wiggings in the press when their assessment does not appear to be all that it might be. Science has come to their aid with an instrument with the rather sinister title of 'Penetrometer'. This, when inserted into the ground at various points of the course, is meant to give quantified readings for the state of the going. However, at the time of writing, its use was only in the experimental stage; meanwhile, prodding with a walking stick remains prevalent among methods used.

A change in the going can occur overnight after a heavy downpour, so, not only is it necessary to note a horse's preference, if any, for a particular kind of going, but an eye should be kept on the weather forecast for a meeting. The going as advertised in all good faith in the newspapers in the morning may be 'good'; but in actual fact rain may have changed it, after the newspapers have been printed, to soft, or worse. This, at one extreme, causes last minute withdrawals of horses whose chances have been knocked out by the rain; conversely, it may transform a near certain loser into a possible winner.

Handicap A handicap is a race in which horses are allotted different weights in order to give each of them, theoretically, an equal chance of winning. Like George Orwell's animals, however, some horses are more equal than others, and the fact that handicap races almost always produce a clear cut winner is a lasting tribute to the fact that horses, while usually producing the form of which the handicapper thinks them capable, do vary slightly (if for no other reason than that, like human beings, they are not always feeling on top of the world). The term derives from 'Hand-in-the-Cap', a method fully explained in Pond's Rules of Racing in the mid 18th century. The basis of handicapping is that horses are 'allowed' weight one to another according to Weight for Age (q.v.) and according to the distance by which one beats the other in a race, with due allowance made for the state of the going and other factors such as the overall pace at which the race was run. In a 5f race one length separating horse A and horse B means a weight difference of 4 lb. Over 1½m plus, as well as in National Hunt races, the usual allowance is 1 lb per length. Thus, over a sprint distance horse A carrying 9 st beats horse B carrying the same weight ('at level weights' in other words); horse B is therefore 4 lb 'inferior' to horse A. In the next race, the handicap reads: horse A 9 st, horse B 8 st 10 lb. In a National Hunt 3 m Chase, horse A carrying 11 st beats horse B carrying 10 st 12 lb by 4 lengths. The handicapper may then adjust the weights for the next time they meet so that horse A carries 11 st 4 lb and horse B carries 10 st 12 lb, thus, in theory, equalising their chances.

Handicapping is carried out by Jockey Club handicappers whose handicap for any particular race is based on central information contained and regularly up-dated in Weatherbys' computer. This provides a handicap 'rating' for every horse in training qualified to run in a handicap (in the case of 2-y-o they are not rated until July of their first season's racing, and no horse can be handicapped until it has run three times). These ratings are the basis on a scale from 0 upwards for the graded handicaps introduced in recent years, which are designed to give fairer opportunities for handicap horses all round. Thus, at its lowest, a handicap race may be restricted to horses rated 0-25, while a better class handicap race may be for the scale 0-50. The ratings are revised every week and a list of horses whose handicap mark has changed appreciably is published in the sporting press. These lists are well worth keeping an eye on. The handicap range in a flat race is from 7 st 7 lb to 9 st 7 lb; in National Hunt races, from 10 st to 12 st (there is also a special scale for the occasional so-called 'high-weight' handicaps). But, despite the restricted range, when the handicapper deals with the entries for a given race, he will allot weights below the permitted bottom weight, because frequently the top weight is withdrawn, and the weights have to be raised accordingly. Thus:

Original handicap:	top weight	horse A	9 st 7 lb
	next in weights	horse B	9 st 1 lb
	two bottom weights	horse C	7 st 7 lb
		horse D	7 st 7 lb

But in actual fact, the handicapper has given C and D a 'real' assessment of 7 st 6 lb and 7 st 2 lb respectively. Before the declaration stage horse A is withdrawn. The weights are raised by 6 lb all round, thus the two bottom weights which were 'out of the handicap' and stood little chance, now have a proper mark and a chance to compete at proper handicap terms:

New handicap, as run:	top weight	horse B	9 st 7 lb
		horse C	7 st 12 lb
		horse D	7 st 8 lb

With multiple entries a trainer can use the raising of weights to his advantage by entering a top weight he doesn't intend to run, after he has had a chance to see how the opposition is handicapped.

Admiral Rous was the first Jockey Club handicapper, and acknowledged to be one of the finest that ever lived. More recently, Dick Whitford was a well known and uncannily accurate 'private' handicapper i.e. he produced his own ratings, and once wrote: 'A good handicap is like a work of art; a painting by Picasso or a symphony by Beethoven. It is not the product of a statistician or an accountant or a computer with its peripheral equipment. A good handicap, in fact, is the creative act of a good handicapper; a balancing of fine judgements; an appraisal of will o'the wisps; an array of intelligent guesses'. And it is thus that 'private' handicaps, including those published in newspapers as 'ratings' as well as publications such as *Raceform Private Handicap*, are devised, showing how the 'private' handicapper differs from the official assessment of a horse's ability and relative chance in a race.

WEIGHTWATCHER

ALL horses entered in handicaps are given a rating based on a scale from 0 (the worst) to 100 (the best) by the Jockey Club's official handicappers. This list shows the horses which have been reassessed by the handicappers by 2lb or more for the week commencing January 23.

For the most part the new ratings below are based on the horse's performance during the period Jan 8-14 but in some instances it can reflect an earlier performance if the horse concerned has not been entered in a handicap in the meantime.

Similarly the old rating referred to is in most cases the figure at which the horse was rated for the previous week, but if the horse had not been entered for a handicap that week it is for the last week it was.

Occasionally a horse running well on a Thursday, Friday or Saturday will be rehandicapped a week early.

HURDLERS			
Horse	Old	New	Diff
Alcazaba	16	13	− 3
All Fair	45	40	− 5
Anita's Apple	13	3	−10
Arabian Sea	28	24	− 4
Ballyannagh	7	1	− 6
Barwar	19	32	+13
Biras Creek	24	28	+ 4
Black River	25	30	+ 5
Black Spout	3	0	− 3
Bold Illusion	40	49	+ 9
Bonanza Boy	58	60	+ 2
Boulevard Roy	9	7	− 2
Braunston Brook	47	42	− 5
Broad Wood	6	14	+ 8
Bronze Effigy	20	39	+19
Cape Town Girl	4	0	− 4
Chatterspark	9	4	− 5
Christo	43	40	− 3
Chrysaor	69	74	+ 5
City Entertainer	36	61	+25
Clara Girl	24	17	− 7
L O Broadway	48	42	− 6
Lockner Lad	37	33	− 4
Loddon Lad	39	47	+ 8
Mischievous Jack	27	29	+ 2
Miss Felham	17	32	+15
Molojec	43	41	− 2
Moorland Lady	5	10	+ 5
More One Way	7	9	+ 2
New Farmer	30	32	+ 2
Night Guest	23	30	+ 7
Northern Interest	18	22	+ 4

CHASERS			
Horse	Old	New	Diff
Admiral's Cup	63	59	− 4
Annette's Delight	50	55	+ 5
Autumn Zulu	31	41	+10
Bally-Go	50	46	− 4
Barryphilips Disco	13	22	+ 9
Beau Ranger	79	77	− 2

Head lad   Not a lad at all, but usually a very mature second in command of a racing stable on whom much responsibility for organisation, feeding the horses, and running the yard devolves. A good head lad can make a stable, and a bad one break it. Some head lads become trainers in their own right. There is also the travelling head lad who is chiefly responsible for accompanying horses on their journeys to and from the stable and race-course.

Hobdayed   An operation for horses which are unsound in wind. *Timeform* will say whether a horse has been hobdayed.

Hot pot   Term from Victorian racing journalism meaning a very hot favourite; still occasionally used today.

Hurdles   Horses beginning their careers on the National Hunt scene usually begin over hurdles, even though the ultimate intention is to put them to fences. (A proportion of chasers, including ex-hunters and point-to-point horses, never jump a hurdle in their lives and, correspondingly, a few hurdlers remain hurdlers for the rest of their racing careers.) No horse can race over hurdles until the July of the year in which he is three years old, but, in practice, the majority of hurdlers of this age, and also many at four years old are bought out of a Flat racing stable in the autumn, or winter following the decision not to run them any longer on the Flat. Ability to stay a long distance on the Flat is not a prerequisite of making a successful hurdler where the minimum distance is two miles, and some races even longer, up to three miles.

The three-year-old may start in races, once called juvenile hurdles and confined to that age group, or in novice hurdles for which the qualification is never having won a hurdle by the start of the current season. The Rules lay down the specification for hurdles: that they must be not less than 3 ft 6 in in height from the bottom bar to the top bar; they consist of bars of wood, such as willow or oak interspersed with birch, broom or gorse, and driven in sections across the hurdles course (which is separate from the steeplechase course) at an angle sloped from the take off side. The top bar of a hurdle these days is padded so that horses do not rap themselves badly when striking the hurdle; this has reduced the clatter which used to be heard like successive rounds of rapid riflefire round the racecourse during a hurdle race. But there is still plenty of noise, as well as danger in the often furious pace. One danger occurs when a hurdle has been nearly kicked flat, but not quite, and it swings back. Falls in a hurdle race, though less frequent than in a chase, can be more dangerous with a tighter bunched field and at a faster pace. The Rules of Racing also lay down that there must be at least eight flights of hurdles in a two mile race, with an additional flight for every complete quarter of a mile beyond that distance.

In a hurdle race, a horse's speed is of more importance than impeccable jumping ability. That is not to say that hurdlers do not have to be able to jump, obviously they do, but a jumping error can be made in hurdling and got away with; over fences the same error would mean a fall at the bigger and wider obstacles.

Famous hurdle races include the Champion Hurdle and Triumph Hurdle (for four-year-olds) at the Cheltenham Festival, the Tote Gold Trophy (Handicap) at Newbury, and the Imperial Cup at Sandown, while there are many more recently established valuable sponsored prizes for hurdlers, including the Ladbroke Christmas Hurdle at Kempton Park on Boxing Day, the Food Brokers and Primula 'Fighting Fifth' Hurdle at Newcastle in November and the Glenlivet Hurdle (for four-year-olds) and Sandeman Aintree Hurdle both at the Grand National meeting in early April.

Hurdlers as well as chasers in the past have become public favourites and they include: *Sir Ken*, three times winner of the Champion Hurdle (1952-54), ridden by Tim Molony; the well loved *Persian War*, game little winner of the same race three times (1968-70) and runner-up in 1971 in the colours of Mr Henry Alper, which intentionally resembled those of West Ham United FC;

and the dual Champion Hurdle winner *National Spirit* (after winning in 1947 and 1948, he fell at the last flight, leaving *Hatton's Grace* clear for the first of his three victories — achieved between the age of nine years old and 11 years old). More recent public favourites in the Champion Hurdle have been *Night Nurse*, winner 1976 and 1977, third the following year; *Monksfield*, winner 1978 and 1979, runner-up in 1977 and 1980; *Sea Pigeon*, winner 1980 and 1981 (when he was 11 years old) and runner-up the two previous years; and, not least, *Dawn Run*, the mare that captured the affections of the Cheltenham crowd.

In the frame   This term means that a horse has won or been placed, in other words, had its number hoisted in the winning frame on the racecourse numbers board.

Jockey Club   Not a Jockeys' Trade Union organisation, but the oldest Turf Authority in the world, which had its origins at the Star and Garter, Pall Mall, in 1751, was incorporated in 1970 by Royal Charter, and is the governing body of horseracing in Britain, both on the Flat and over jumps. Formerly, jumping meetings were administered by the National Hunt Committee, but in 1968 this body was amalgamated with the Jockey Club. Under the provisions of the Royal Charter, the Jockey Club has complete jurisdiction over and is responsible for the administration, organisation and control of all horseracing, race meetings, and racehorse training in the United Kingdom (except Northern Ireland, which is under the control of the Irish Turf Club).

As recently as a quarter of a century ago, the Jockey Club was widely seen and greatly criticised as a stuffy, self-electing, self-perpetuating *cabal* in the petrified hands of racing peers, a majority of whom jealously guarded their privileges and perquisites, and who, oblivious to the existence of anyone outside the Jockey Club rooms with the interests of racing at heart, were adamant in their refusal to acknowledge the need for progress. This view undoubtedly had a kernel of truth, although it took no account of the membership of, for example, Lord Howard de Walden, a racing peer of enlightened and forward looking opinions; nor that of the late Tom Blackwell, similarly disposed, and with an energetic business background. Since that time, however, the Jockey Club has made efforts to reform its outlook and to broaden the basis of its membership to include a wider variety of individuals with deep knowledge and experience of the racing industry, as well as, in some cases, proven ability as administrators outside it. There are today about a hundred members of the Jockey Club, and ten honorary members. This is about the same number as the Jockey Club and National Hunt Committee *in toto* listed in *Ruff's Guide* for 1963; but the composition of the Jockey Club in the same publication 22 years later appears significantly different. There are now the distinguished retired trainers Arthur Budgett and Sir Noel Murless. There is, too, Helen Johnson-Houghton, a *de facto* trainer before women were officially permitted to train.

She is one of six women members of the Jockey Club. (Women were first admitted in 1977.) Among those successful both in racing and outside it are Louis Freedman (senior steward in 1986), Sir Freddie Laker, Sir Michael Sobell, Lord Weinstock and a dozen others: Robert Sangster, whose fortune came from football pools, and who is one of the biggest owners and dealers in bloodstock in the country, is a member; John Hislop and Peter Willett both of journalistic backgrounds, have distinguished reputations in the breeding world and have been elected; so too, the most recent election from Fleet Street, Peter O'Sullevan, while owners from overseas prominent in British racing include the following honorary members: Prince Khalid bin Abdullah, Raymond Guest, Captain Marcos Lemos, Paul Mellon, and HH Aga Khan. Until his death in 1986, Sir Gordon Richards, that great former champion jockey as well as trainer, was an honorary member. There are many who considered that his sterling attributes, not least his exemplary contribution to the conduct of racing, would have been better recognised by election to full membership. He was the first, and, so far, the only former professional jockey to have been a member of the Jockey Club.

There are seven stewards of the Jockey Club. These are headed by the senior steward and deputy senior steward (each elected for a three year term — formerly only one year, which gave little time for them to make their influence felt) and include the chairman of the Jockey Club's four standing committees: administration and finance, discipline, licensing, and race planning. Committee meetings apart, the Stewards hold bi-monthly meetings, the first of which is also attended by the chairman of the Horse-racing Advisory Council and by the other two Jockey Club appointees to the Horserace Betting Levy Board. Under the terms of the Royal Charter, four statutory general meetings of the Jockey Club are held each year, at which members discuss and vote on matters raised by the stewards. There are also additional general meetings.

The Jockey Club has its premises at the Jockey Club Rooms in the High Street, Newmarket where it owns enormous tracts of land including the Heath where the racing takes place, as well as training gallops, and other freehold property in the town. There are also large modern offices in Portman Square, London. The day-to-day administration of racing is in the hands of Messrs Weatherbys who have furnished this service since 1770 (and on a contractual basis since 1970).

Joint This is the name given to the bookmaker's temporary 'establish-ment' on the racecourse consisting of board on which odds are chalked, and, increasingly so today, indicated in marker ink; metal collapsible tripod on which the board is mounted and which supports the satchel into which banknotes go (and from which lucky punters are paid out) as well as a tin tray which holds coinage, chalk and sponge. An integral feature of the joint consists of the wooden steps from which the bookmaker shouts the odds and distributes his tickets, and which, before racing, can be seen piled in Tattersalls and other betting rings like so many boxes in an abandoned fish market. Also on the steps (which are, in fact, open sided boxes) is the bookmaker's clerk who enters in the field book every bet as it is laid, and with lightning mental arithmetic notes in other details such as how much the firm stands to lose if the bet is a winning one. Near the joint there may also be a third member of the team, the bookie's runner, who reads the tic-tac and is then despatched to lay off bets, usually, on the rails. The late Victor Chandler (father of the present bookmaker of the same name) used to have a runner called Leslie, and few meetings went by without the very distinctive gravelly voice of Victor being heard among the hubbub of '*Take* six to four' appealing for 'Lesleeeee ...' who had gone missing for a moment. The location for the joint is known as a pitch and these are allocated in strict order by a special committee.

Levy Board   The commonly used abbreviation for the Horserace Betting Levy Board. This statutory body was established in 1961, the same year in which betting shops were made legal. The prime object of the Levy Board was and is to siphon back some of the money that annually goes into betting in order to apply it in various directions for the good of racing. The operation has expanded greatly in the scope of the racing activities and interests it funds; but, taking inflation into consideration, the sad fact is that the levy (through no fault of the board itself, be it added) is collecting no more money in real terms than it was 20 years ago, and probably marginally less. The 24th annual report of the Levy Board estimated the yield from the 23rd levy scheme (1984-85) at £20 million which, together with the Tote's contribution of £677,000, and interest payments, provided the board with a total income of £20,800,000. This can be compared with the figures for 1964-65, when the total levy yielded £3,152,000 (of which the Tote was bearing a significantly higher proportion, quite unrelated to the relative turnover — on which the levy is based — between Tote and bookmakers).

The income is, nonetheless, spread among a wide variety of uses for the benefit of racing and breeding; it is simply a pity that there is not more to go round. The uses to which Levy Board money is put include prize money, technical services on racecourses, security, racecourse improvements, veterinary research, horse and pony societies, point-to-points, apprentice training, and farriery. Racecourse Technical Services (which operate, for example, the photo-finish, camera patrol, electric timing on certain courses, public address and racecourse commentary, starting stalls and closed circuit television) and United Racecourses (Epsom, Kempton Park, and Sandown Park) are wholly owned subsidiaries of the board which also finances Racecourse Security Services, responsible for the entire range of activities aimed at preventing horses being got at, by doping or other means.

The Levy Board came into being in the 1960s, a time when a force ten gale rather than just a wind of change was blowing through racing. Among measures and ideas which date from that time and now taken for granted are overnight declarations, starting stalls, the overnight draw, the patrol camera, trainers' licences for women, the growth of commercial sponsorship (started in the late 1950s) which gave a new impetus to National Hunt racing, as well as growing participation in overseas races and the promotion of the idea that racing in the UK on the highest level should be interlocked with that in Ireland and France. Chairman of the Levy Board at this time was the late Lord Wigg. The present Chairman is another long time racing enthusiast, the former Director General of the BBC, Sir Ian Trethowan. The remainder of the board consist of two members appointed by the Home Secretary, the Chairman of the Horserace Totalisator Board and the Chairman of the Bookmakers' Committee.

Maiden   Nothing to do with the sex of a horse — a maiden is a horse, either colt, filly, or gelding which has not won a race. A maiden hurdler is one who has not won a hurdle race. Occasionally races are framed for maidens at closing, i.e. on the date that entries for the race are closed. More usually this form of maiden race is restricted on the entry form to horses that have not won by a certain date, commonly a week or so before the closing date. Should an entry win a race between the stipulated date and the actual race itself, a penalty in terms of weight will be incurred, as in, for example:

June. Brighton. Lewes Stakes 1¼ miles. £2000 added to stakes for three-year-olds and upwards which, before 21 May have not won; weight 3-y-o colts and geldings 8 st 8 lb, fillies 8 st 5 lb; 4-y-o and up, colts and geldings 9 st 8 lb, fillies 9 st 5 lb; penalties, after 20 May, a winner 6 lb; of two races, or of one value £2,000 (or more) 9 lb. Closed 4 June.

This kind of maiden race is worth looking at, and, in the case of a winner carrying a penalty, to see in the form how easily the horse won. Sometimes this may show that it could win again despite the penalty. Far more common than the above are races for maidens at starting: horses that, up to the day of the race, have not won. These are normally run at weight-for-age with allowance for fillies against colts and geldings. There is sometimes a weight allowance for horses who have never run before. Maiden races may be confined to two-year-olds, or three-year-olds (these are the most usual categories) but also, as seen above, to three-year-olds and older. Maiden races confined to 2-y-o and 3-y-o can provide good betting opportunities, but the market is the best guide, except in instances where a horse is an unknown quantity not only to the public, but to owner, trainer and jockey as well, and wins at a long price.

Mare   Female horse of more than five years old. If she has been retired to the paddocks for breeding purposes she becomes a brood mare. It is fairly usual these days (compare, for example *Beeswing*, or even *Sceptre* and *Pretty Polly* under *FILLY*) not to give fillies a long racing career. In most well bred cases, provided they have won a race of some sort, if possible, they will be retired before they are four years old to be mated with a stallion standing at stud. In the bloodstock industry, fees are charged for a stallion's services, usually on a no-foal-no-fee basis, and the foal is the property of the owner of the mare. Rich owner-breeders such as Jim Joel with their own mares to breed from, are themselves, sad to say, a fast diminishing breed and, in 1986, Mr Joel, at 92, decided to sell his collection of brood mares; a very sad occasion.

Monkey   Betting term for £500. Hence the bookmaker's shout of, for example: 'I'll take two monkeys'. (Meaning he will take £1000 to return £500 plus stake back, less tax, if the favourite at 2/1 on wins) (*See ODDS*). A strange shout, to be sure, to the uninitiated, but nothing to do with 'I don't give two monkey's'.

Morning glory   A horse which shiningly produces marvellous work in his home gallops of a morning, but utterly fails to reproduce the same sort of performance on the racecourse.

Names   Rule 40 of the Rules of Racing requires some explanation. It states: 'No owners shall make use of an assumed name for the purpose of entering or running horses'. The penalty, should a horse be so run, is disqualification. The reason behind the rule is the prevention of the use of a *nom-de-course* in order to disguise the true identity of an owner. This used to be quite common practice. Thus, *Ruff's Guide* gives the winner of the 1000 Guineas in 1854 as 'Mr Howard's *Virago*'. This conceals the identity of Henry Padwick, a notorious and rapacious moneylender of the time. The owner of the 1879 Derby winner, *Sir Bevys* is recorded as one Mr Acton. This, in fact, was Leopold de Rothschild, who took his 'name' from the place near London where he had a stud, and which, in its present suburban incar-nation, hardly leaps to the mind as a place where a racing stud might be found. And several Classic winners, including *Lemburg*, *Bayardo*, and *Gay Crusader*, the Triple Crown winner of 1917 (who was sired by *Bayardo*) are down in the ownership of a certain 'Mr Fairie'. This was the *nom-de-course* of Mr A.W. Cox, a taciturn Australian who had made an enormous fortune in the Broken Hill silver mines. Sir George Chetwynd, meanwhile, whose malpractice on the Turf led to one of the greatest of all Victorian racing scandals, was 'Mr Mortimer' in his early days. In more recent times, that great and immensely likeable owner-breeder, Sir Victor Sassoon, used a *nom-de-course* (though in racing in India, China and Hong Kong, not in the UK). It was formed from his initials so he became 'Mr Eves'. Hence he called his stud the Eve Stud, similarly his villa in the Bahamas and the reason why Lestor Piggott's stables at Newmarket are called 'Eve Lodge' is that the name is a tribute to the warm friendship between the former champion jockey and his family and Sir Victor and Lady Sassoon.

Not only do owners these days have to identify themselves accurately, but horses also must be named before they can race. The 1797 Derby winner is still only vaguely recorded as the 'Duke of Bedford's brown colt by *Fidget* out of sister to *Pharamond*'. There were several other early Classic winners who were unnamed at the time they won. *Bay Middleton,* who became a pervasive influence in the stud book through his progeny, had been named by the time he won the 1836 Derby, but not when he took the 2000 Guineas earlier in the season. The rules now forbid this practice, although when a horse first goes to a stable yard, he or she may not have a name, and will simply be known, at first, as 'the *Kris* colt', say, or 'the *Moorestyle* filly', after their sires.

The art of naming racehorses, however, appears to be in decline these days. Names used to be an apt play on those of their sire and dam. *Whistler,* foaled in 1950, for example, was well named, in view of the lawsuits the artist of the same name was involved in. He (the colt that is) was by Panorama out of Farthing Damages, and a glance at the dam's side of his pedigree shows that he was by no means the first in his family to have a witty name:

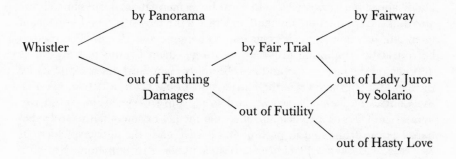

by Panorama

Whistler

out of Farthing
Damages

by Fair Trial

out of Futility

by Fairway

out of Lady Juror
by Solario

out of Hasty Love

From there it is a long way to the current runners *Weloveyouwednesday, Itsgottabealright, Who's Zoomin Who, Mrs Muck* and *Hellcatmudwrestler,* all of which names seem charmlessly unrelated to pedigree however much they mean to the owners, and more than that, cause pangs of sympathy on behalf of the shattered dignity of the poor creatures who are forced to bear them. Nine out of ten marks, however, to the owner (or whoever first named the horse) of *Aah Jim Boy* which brings an appropriate 'Treasure Island' and Robert Newton memory out of the pedigree: by Riboboy out of Parrot Fashion, who was by Pieces of Eight.

It is, moreover, still possible to get a clue as to pedigree from the name which can help in assessing the possible best distance of the horse, as, for example, with the progeny of the sprinting sire *Mummy's Pet.* Current instances are *Mummy's Fancy, Mummy's Favourite, Mummy's Secret, Butler's Pet* and *Pearl Pet.* Against this, the difficulty without knowledge of Arabic, of making such an assessment with an increasing percentage of names (however apt to the owners — from *Abou-Aziz* (by Auction Ring out of Ellida) to *Zaytoon* (by Formidable out of Lady Constance) — is one which seems likely to be with us for some time. This is a reminder of a jumper of a few years ago who was named *Abdul the Bul Bul*— by Gigantic out of Turkish Tourist. Also in 1869 a horse called *Neurasthenipponskalesterizo* ran in a steeplechase at St Albans. This would have been disallowed by Weatherbys' computer these days. Horses (presumably the computer is unable to cope with them) of more than 18 characters in the name are barred. So, too, is the use again of the names of winners of the most famous races.

National Hunt   This embraces all steeplechases and all hurdling, and is descriptive of courses which exclusively stage these events, or the winter activity of certain courses devoted to Flat racing during the summer. There used to be a separate governing body called the National Hunt Committee (*see JOCKEY CLUB*). Previously it was the Grand National Hunt Committee, which gave rise to the name of the Grand National Steeplechase.

Non-trier   A horse which does not give its best running. This used to happen a great deal, and there are innumerable instances of horses being 'pulled' by their jockeys, often in order to attempt to bamboozle the handicapper, get a lower weight than the horse merited on its true capabilities, and thus have something 'in hand' in a race if the ploy succeeded — which it often did. It is now a much exaggerated phenomenon. Horses often used to be run at the beginning of the season to get them fit; this was known as 'training on the racecourse' and has effectively been fined out of existence by the stewards. In the days of the barrier start in big fields, a famous Clerk of the Course (Malcolm Hancock) used to tell the jockeys to line up in two lines: 'Non-triers at the back', he once told me. The camera patrol and video have been instrumental in putting an effective end to non-triers, which, in any case, was often a figment of a beaten punter's imagination. 'Not off a yard,' 'Not wanted today' would be the comments to rationalise any failure on the part of the judgement of the punter; that, at least, still happens today. A genuine example of non-trying that happened decades ago is illustrated in another story told to me, this time by the late Jack Topham, senior race reader and the power in the field behind *Raceform* for many years. He told me of a race at Windsor, the figure-of-eight course by the Thames (the strong Yorkshire accent of this big man has to be imagined): 'I was at Windsor one day when a jockey — you'll know who I mean, he's training now and he won an Imperial Cup — well at the bottom turn he was third and by the time they'd got to the junction he was nowhere. I said to him afterwards: "You'd have been quicker coming up by river!" There's one that wasn't wanted. All together, now, with the Salvation Army Psalter ...'

Numbers board   A mine of information for those who bother to read it on the racecourse. Essentially a metal frame about 20 ft high usually situated opposite the stand on the course beyond the far running rails and worked by a system of pulleys and counter weights. It gives the name of each jockey taking part in the race (*see CHALK JOCKEY*). The numbers carried on the saddlecloth of each horse, corresponding to the numbers on the racecard (and in the morning papers) appear on the left of the name of the jockey who is riding the horse, once again black on white except in the case of claiming apprentices whose numbers appear as follows: 7 lb allowance — red number on white; 4 lb allowance (steeplechases and hurdle races, and National Hunt

Flat races) *or* 5 lb allowance (flat races) black number on orange; 3 lb allowance — white number on blue. On the right of the jockey's name appears the draw for places at the start. Underneath the jockey's names are separate boards which give the state of the going, details of overweight, and colour changes, as for example when an owner is running more than one horse and the jockeys are distinguishable by different coloured caps. All this information is taken down as the race starts. After the race, the numbers of the winner and placed horses go up in a small, separate frame to one side of the main board; in the case of a photo-finish the letter P appears 'in the frame'. When the jockeys have been weighed in after the race and found to be carrying the correct weight corresponding to the one they weighed out with before the race, the 'all right' signal is displayed on the numbers board. This is done by hoisting a blue flag, or showing a blue light. Bookmakers pay out winning bets when the 'all right' signal is shown. If there is an objection or/and stewards inquiry, a red flag is hoisted, or red light shown. When the inquiry is completed, and placings are unaltered, the red flag or light is replaced with a white flag or light. Inquiry completed and placings altered are indicated by replacement with a green flag or light, and the hoisting of the correct placings in the frame. All this is backed up by the public address system. If there has been an inquiry, bookmakers pay out winning bets when the result is made known.

Nursery handicap   A handicap confined to two-year-olds only. It used to be the rule that no nursery could be run before September, but now they are commonly run in August, and some even in July. (See Chapter Twelve for more on nurseries as a betting medium, and analysis of favourites and top-weights.)

Odds   Prices at which a bookmaker lays odds. Prices are odds against, even money, or odds on:

Even money is when an equal amount is laid by a bookmaker to the amount put on by a backer. 'Evens this favourite,' 'Even money the field' are the shouts in the ring. In other words, for every £1 staked £1 is returned.

Odds against are when the bookmaker offers more money than the amount staked, fractional though it may be.

Odds on is the term used when bookmakers offer less money against the amount staked, also frequently in fractions. Thus a successful bet at odds of 2/1 against (two to one against) wins *twice* the amount staked. At odds of 2/1 on (two to one on) it will win only *half* the amount staked. So, for every £1 wagered at 2/1 against, £2 is returned plus stake back but less tax and for every £1 wagered at 2/1 on, 50p is returned plus stake back, less tax. Similarly, a successful bet at 6/4 against (six-to-four) wins *1½ times* the amount staked and at 6/4 on yields *four-sixths (i.e. 2/3rds)* only. So, for every £1 wagered at 6/4 against, £1.50 is returned plus stake back, less tax and for every £1 wagered at 6/4 on only 66p is returned plus stake back, less tax. Or, in a more usual racecourse version of such bets, £4 on at 6/4 against would return £6, while £6 on at 6/4 on would yield £4, again less tax. In shouting the odds on the racecourse when *laying* odds bookmakers can be heard as follows: 'Two to one the field,' 'I'll go two's this favourite', all meaning 2/1 against. But 'I'll *take* two to one,' '*Take* six to four,' 'Seven to four on this favourite,' all mean that the prices quoted are odds on, and that the bookmakers are *taking* odds. These shouts are sometimes complicated by shouts of 'I'll take two hundred to one,' or 'Two hundred to one this favourite' (or name of a horse). These shouts do not mean over cramped or over generous odds, that is 200/1 on and 200/1 against (although the latter can be a genuine quotation, sometimes, on Derby Day). The meaning is £200 to £100 on or against. Similarly 'Five hundred to one you don't name it'.

Bar one. In the fruity hubbub of Tattersalls' Ring before a race can often be heard 'Five to one bar one,' or 'Four's Bar,' yielding the impression that bar one and/or bar are ever present runners in every race, an impression the pre-race presentation on television does little to dispel, although they do quite frequently say something on the lines of 'Ten to one bar these four,' having listed the prices of the first four horses in the betting market. The shouts can be interpreted as follows: 'Five to one bar one' = five to one against, or better, all the rest of the field *except* the favourite. 'Four's bar' = four to one, or better, all the rest of the field except the horses already quoted, including the favourite, at odds of less than 4/1 against.

Longer odds, shorter odds. 10/1 is longer or a longer price than, say, 5/1 (and much longer, say, than even money, or an odds on price) Conversely, an odds on 'chance', (as the phrase goes), is said to be shorter in the betting, or in the market, than a horse quoted at odds against. 'Henry Cecil's Derby candidate is bound to start at a short price this afternoon' means that the horse trained by Henry Cecil which is a Derby entry is bound to start at about even money, or odds on, though it might be quoted in the market (at least to begin with) at slightly ('a shade of') odds against. On the other hand, 'long odds can still be had about this quietly fancied Grand National candidate,' refers to prices usually in excess of 10/1.

When a horse's price contracts in the market it is said to shorten or come in. When the odds on offer become larger, it is said to lengthen or go out, and if it goes out appreciably, say, from odds on to 2/1 against, or from 4/1 to 10/1 it will be said to have 'taken a walk in the market' (*See DRIFTER*), or 'Gone badly in the market'. Short odds are said to be 'cramped'; long odds, if 20/1 or above, give rise to saying that the horses to which the prices refer are not only 'outsiders' at 'any price you like' but 'rags' or 'out with the washing'.

Fractions. There is a very ancient racing chestnut about the bookmaker teaching his child to count. The lesson goes. 'Evens, 11 to 10, six to five, five to four, 11 to eight ...' and so on. At least this superannuated joke possesses the merit of illustrating some of the bizarre fractions used in the Ring which have more logic in them than might appear at first acquaintance. Below is a full list of the odds in smaller fractions, which will be more readily understood when it is realised that they are based on the English currency in use before decimalisation in 1971. To convey why the fractions are as they are, totally unchanged since before that date, it is unnecessary to explain the details of the old currency (of which no one under 21 can have much more than a vague recollection), except to say that, essentially, as far as betting was concerned there were eight half-crowns (8 x 2 shillings and sixpence) to the pound, or sovereign as it used to be even earlier in the century. Also, but of minor significance, there were 10 florins (or two shilling pieces, which survive, some of them as the 10p piece) to the pound. There were also 10 shilling notes (half-sovereign coins earlier) worth half the value of a pound. The abbreviation for pence was 'd'.

The frequent occurrence of 4s and 8s in the list may therefore be seen in this light.

Present Odds	Actual Fraction	Amount won in pre-decimalisation currency to the given stake: £1	£10	10 shillings (£½)
Evens				
11/10	One and 1/10th	£1 and 1 Florin	£11	11 shillings
6/5	One and 1/5th	£1 and 2 Florins	£12	12 shillings
5/4	One and a quarter	£1 and 2 Half Crowns	£12.10s	12s 6d
11/8	One and 3/8ths	£1 and 3 Half Crowns	£13.15s	13s 9d
6/4	One and a half	£1 and 4 Half Crowns or 10 Shillings	£15	15s
13/8	One and 5/8ths	£1 and 5 Half Crowns	£16.5s	16s 3d
7/4	One and three quarters	£1 and 6 Half Crowns	£17.10s	17s 6d
15/8	One and 7/8ths	£1 and 7 Half Crowns	£18.15s	18s 9d
2/1				

The list then goes on: 9/4, 5/2, 11/4, 3/1, 100/30, 7/2, 4/1 and up to 9/1 in halves and whole numbers; thereafter up to 12/1 in single whole numbers, then up to 20/1 two 'points' at a time.

The settling of bets at these odds in the old currency (except for small bets under 10 shillings) can therefore be seen to have been a good deal easier than it is today, if a comparison is made between the table above and the late 20th century ready reckoner published below. However, decimalisation has made some bets, notably multiple bets, easier to calculate. The one figure that stands out from the table as seemingly anomalous is 100/30. Why, suddenly, a 100 to 30? This may be understood by translating it back to 100 shillings to 30 shillings, in other words, £5 to a £1.10s stake. That stake, in its day was £5 to £1.5. £1.5 of a pound today, however, is £1.50 and, somehow, the ready reckoner gives the return to that sum as £5.00½, which can be taken as at least one rather minor benefit of decimalisation, perhaps.

Settling apart, the change to new pence has had only one effect on the odds, and that is the sweeping away of the old and now nostalgic sounding figures of 100/8, 100/7, and 100/6. Off the course these have been rounded to 12/1, 14/1 and 16/1, which are obviously easier to settle in new currency, though the old odds are still available, if requested, with many Tattersalls bookmakers.

Odds Ready Reckoner   Winnings shown include return of stake, but no tax deducted.

S.P.	10p	20p	25p	50p	£1.00	£5.00
1/3	13½	26½	33½	67	1.33½	6.67
2/5	14	28	35	70	1.40	7.00
4/9	14½	29	36	72½	1.44½	7.22
1/2	15	30	37½	75	1.50	7.50
4/7	16	31½	39	79	1.57½	7.86
8/13	16½	32½	40½	81	1.61½	8.08
4/6	17	33½	42	83½	1.67	8.33
8/11	17½	35	43½	86½	1.73	8.64
4/5	18	36	45	90	1.80	9.00
5/6	18½	37	46	92	1.83½	9.17
10/11	19	38½	48	95½	1.91	9.54½
Evens	20	40	50	1.00	2.00	10.00
11/10	21	42	52½	1.05	2.10	10.50
6/5	22	44	55	1.10	2.20	11.00
5/4	22½	45	56½	1.12½	2.25	11.25
11/8	24	47½	59½	1.19	2.37½	11.87½
6/4	25	50	62½	1.25	2.50	12.50
13/8	26½	52½	66	1.31½	2.62½	13.12½
7/4	27½	55	69	1.37½	2.75	13.75
15/8	29	57½	72	1.44	2.87½	14.37½
2/1	30	60	75	1.50	3.00	15.00
9/4	32½	65	81½	1.62½	3.25	16.25
5/2	35	70	87½	1.75	3.50	17.50
11/4	37½	75	94	1.87½	3.75	18.75
3/1	40	80	1.00	2.00	4.00	20.00
10/3	43½	87	1.08½	2.17	4.33½	21.67
7/2	45	90	1.12½	2.25	4.50	22.50
4/1	50	1.00	1.25	2.50	5.00	25.00
9/2	55	1.10	1.37½	2.75	5.50	27.50
5/1	60	1.20	1.50	3.00	6.00	30.00
11/2	65	1.30	1.62½	3.25	6.50	32.50
6/1	70	1.40	1.75	3.50	7.00	35.00
13/2	75	1.50	1.87½	3.75	7.50	37.50
7/1	80	1.60	2.00	4.00	8.00	40.00
15/2	85	1.70	2.12½	4.25	8.50	42.50
8/1	90	1.80	2.25	4.50	9.00	45.00
17/2	95	1.90	2.37½	4.75	9.50	47.50
9/1	1.00	2.00	2.50	5.00	10.00	50.00
10/1	1.10	2.20	2.75	5.50	11.00	55.00
11/1	1.20	2.40	3.00	6.00	12.00	60.00
12/1	1.30	2.60	3.25	6.50	13.00	65.00
14/1	1.50	3.00	3.75	7.50	15.00	75.00
16/1	1.70	3.40	4.25	8.50	17.00	85.00
20/1	2.10	4.20	5.25	10.50	21.00	105.00
25/1	2.60	5.20	6.50	13.00	26.00	130.00
33/1	3.40	6.80	8.50	17.00	34.00	170.00

Off   The off is the start of the race, officially timed, as in betting shop commentaries: 'They're off Warwick. Off Brighton. Off at all meetings'. Off-course bookmakers will not take bets after this time. However, on the course it is often possible to have a bet in the very early stages of longer races, particularly steeplechases. (See Chapter Seven.)

On   Betting term meaning that a bet or side bet has been struck: '60 to 40 the favourite falls'. 'You're on'. Or 'What did you back?' 'I couldn't get on'.

Overweight   When a jockey cannot, physically, get down to the weight due to be carried the difference between that weight and what the weighing room scales show is called 'overweight'. It is yet another piece of information given on the numbers board, e.g. when a horse in a handicap is weighted at 7 st 13 lb, and the jockey cannot turn the scales, with the saddle and saddlecloth included, at less than 8 st 2 lb, he has to declare 3 lb overweight.

Pattern Races   The most important flat races in Europe have been formed into a coherent 'pattern' throughout the season to give suitably spaced opportunities for the best horses according to age, sex and racing distance. These Pattern Races are divided into Groups One to Three depending on the amount of prize money. The next best races are called Listed Races.

Penalty   The term given to the extra weight added to a horse's original weight in a race as a consequence of having won in between being entered for that race and actually running in it. Various examples of penalties, often 7 lb, are given in the conditions of races elsewhere in this alphabet. It is worth studying the conditions of a race to see what the penalty values are: some are simply 'straight' penalties for winning any race, some are 'graded' penalties according to the value of race won. The better the class of race, the better the penalised winner. Penalised horses, especially if they have won easily, are often worth following up for another win.

Photo-finish   A camera is installed in line with the winning post which photographs the finish of a race, and, in the instance (very frequent on the Flat) of several horses being closely involved at the finishing line, the judge (*see RACECOURSE OFFICIALS*) calls for a photograph to decide the winner and/or other placings (*see DEAD HEAT*). The photograph shows the horses, a scribed-in finishing line, and a mirror image of the horses (to circumvent parallax error). The photo-finish, operated by Racecourse Technical Services, was first used at Epsom in April, 1947, when *Parhelion* was judged to have beaten *Salubrious* in the Great Metropolitan Handicap. In the early days of the photo-finish, the professional backer, Alex Bird was wildly successful in beating the bookmakers in the market which was formed as soon as a photograph was announced. This was during the days when the film took rather longer than it does today to be processed (*see also NUMBERS BOARD*). Alex Bird used to stand in exact line with the finish, close one eye, and not move his head as the horses passed the post. The bookmakers (on certain courses, e.g. Cheltenham, and also at Ascot and on the Rowley Mile at Newmarket where the horses often race wide apart, it is quite difficult to judge a finish correctly from a distant angle) frequently selected the wrong horse to make favourite in a photo-finish, laying odds against the other(s). Alex Bird, who tells his full story in *The Life and Secrets of A Professional Punter*, took a fortune out of the ring by using his technique.

Pitch   The precise place in the betting ring allotted to bookmakers by the Committee of Bookmakers known as the Pitch Committee. The best pitches on a racecourse are in the front rank of Tattersalls' Ring and diminish in desirability the further back they are towards the racecourse running rails — rather like the graduation from orchestra stalls to pit, and based on the fact that the front row are likely to attract more customers because they are situated nearest the stands. There is no shortage of applicants for pitches, which are allocated in strict order of seniority of appearance in the ring and length of service; but a well established firm cannot count on automatic allocation should the incumbent bookmaker retire or die, and whoever takes the firm over has not served his time actually standing up in the ring. A case in point occurred when, a few years ago, Victor Chandler, a great personality in Tattersalls, died. His son, 'young Victor' had not done his time by then out of the office and so the Chandler pitch in Tattersalls was not renewed. 'Young Victor,' however, bets on the rails these days, as did his father at certain meetings. In Tattersalls today there are several firms, not necessarily under the name of the original bookmaker, representing past generations of bookmakers, among them Jack Levy who carried on from his father Morry Levy, another great bookmaking name.

Place   A horse that wins, is second, third, or even, quite frequently these days, finishes fourth in a race. These are placings according to which the prize money for the race is awarded, and they differ, particularly in the case of fourth placed horses, from the placings a bookmaker or the tote will pay out on for a place. As far as betting is concerned, in small fields of five to seven runners commonly only the first two are 'placed', and in most of the remainder of races places are paid on the first, second and third, with the exception of certain big handicaps and the Derby where a fourth place usually qualifies for pay-out. (For details see Chapter Six.)

Pony   Term commonly used to mean, not a small version of the horse, but the sum of £25 staked. Similar to Monkey in ring usage, as in the shout 'I'll lay four ponies'. Very strange!

Pressure   A horse which, off the bit, has to be driven to keep his place in a race or to make further effort is said to have come 'under pressure'.

Prize money   This is made up of the sum total of the fees paid in entries, forfeits and declaration by the owners, and a sum added by the racecourse executive and/or, increasingly these days, commercial or other sponsors. National Hunt racing, in particular, in recent years has greatly benefited from commercial sponsorship. Once the Grand National used to be the only big prize worth going for. Today there are many substantial prizes over the jumps, although none that can match the hundreds of thousands of pounds for races such as the Derby on the Flat. The prize money, not all that long ago, was simply divided up between the winning owner and those who had taken second and third places with their horses. A percentage of this, by unwritten agreement, went to trainer and jockey, but that, except for a cup or plate in addition, was that. Today, in *Ruff's Guide* there is an entire page in the Rules of Racing devoted to the distribution of prize money, with percentages calculated to two places of a decimal affecting not only owners, jockeys and trainers but stables (i.e. lads and lasses) the apprentice training scheme, jockeys' valets, and Jockeys Association Pension Fund. There are, however, no breeders' bonuses, as paid overseas, notably in France.

Racecourse officials   All are licensed annually by the stewards of the Jockey Club.

The Clerk of the Course makes or breaks a racecourse. It is through his enterprise in attracting sponsorship, ingenuity in framing races that will attract fields to bring in the crowds, and ideally the stars of the equine world that will really pack the stands out on which the success of a racecourse depends. But apart from running the course in a strategic sense, he is also responsible for all the routine and smaller details from checking out the racecard to the printers to seeing the racecourse stables are properly disinfected. A busy man, and not only on race-days.

The Clerk of the Scales is responsible for weighing jockeys and their equipment according to the rules, as well as promulgating information on the numbers board and furnishing the starter with a list of runners.

The Starter is responsible for starting the race from starting stalls (on the Flat only). He is responsible for 'calling the roll' of jockeys at the start, seeing the horses are either loaded into the stalls, or lined up properly for the start. When all is ready he will mount his rostrum and the field will come 'under starter's orders' after which even if a horse fails to start he is deemed a runner, or withdrawn (*see effect on bets under WITHDRAWALS*). If there is a false start, through malfunction of starting stall or any other reason, the field may be recalled by a flag operated down the course by a starter's assistant. When the field has arrived at the start, they are said to be 'at the post'.

Stewards. Three stewards for each race meeting are appointed by the racecourse executive and approved by the stewards of the Jockey Club. The stewards are in overall control of a race meeting, including disciplinary matters when they may order stewards' enquiries or hear evidence on objections. They may impose fines or suspensions, or if they feel that it is warranted, refer a matter to the stewards of the Jockey Club. If they consider a jockey has made a frivolous objection they may fine him. The stewards are also responsible for deciding, in bad weather, to abandon a race meeting, and during frosty weather in winter they will hold inspections of the course the previous day, or earlier, as well as on the morning of racing to decide whether or not it is possible to race.

Racing Calendar   Name of the weekly publication which appears with the authority of the Jockey Club giving entries in full for future races, weights allocated in handicaps, as well as other information such as details of the official findings of inquiries, fines imposed, list of unpaid forfeits and other notices of Jockey Club decisions and business. It costs too much for the everyday, ordinary racegoer, but is widely studied by professionals, in particular, trainers, who find in it the first news of how their horses have been treated in handicaps, for example. Published by Weatherbys.

Racing Information Bureau   The Racing Information Bureau, founded in 1964, is the press and public relations organisation operating on behalf of all the racecourses in Britain and the Horserace Betting Levy Board. It also acts as a sales promotion agency for the racecourses, specialising in helping clubs and affinity groups of all kinds to organise a day at the races for their members.

The Bureau maintains a small central office of Ascot and operates through four regional officers, each of whom look after about 15 racecourses. Both the regional PROs and the Central Office work closely with the growing number of sponsors of the sport, assisting them to maximise the return on their investment in racing, and to achieve the commercial objectives of the sponsorship.

Through a computerised mailing list, the RIB prepares and despatches more than 500 press stories each year, providing racing 'copy' to the hundreds of smaller provincial newspapers which do not employ their own racing journalist. The RIB also founded and administers the Racegoers Club, established in 1968 with the dual objective of stimulating interest in racing among its members and increasing racecourse attendances.

Racing plates   Light weight horseshoes fitted for racing, unlike the heavier shoes horses wear for work on the gallops.

Rails
1. The white posts and rails which mark out a racecourse on either side, and known in full as running rails. When it is reported that '... his jockey found an opening on the rails ...' it does not mean that quite literally but that during the running of a race, a gap has opened alongside horse A running next to the rails, and the jockey on horse B,

just behind, has seized the opportunity and taken his horse through it, passing between horse A and the rails.

2. Rails which separate different betting rings (*see BETTING ON THE RAILS*).

Ringer   Name given to an older horse illegally running in a race in the name of a younger one. Because of more mature development, a four-year-old, for example, early in the season, has a tremendous pull in the weights if he can masquerade in a race confined to three-year-olds. The object of ringing is to hoodwink authority and land a gamble. Two of the best known cases which did not succeed are those of *Running Rein*, a four-year-old who finished first in the 1844 Derby, and *Francasal* who was involved in a celebrated attempted coup in 1953 at Bath (see Chapter Three).

Starting price   Often abbreviated to SP. Starting prices are the odds which appear in the newspaper results columns, are heard on television and radio, and form the basis for the pay out in betting shops and by credit bookmakers. It is determined on the racecourse by a representative of *The Sporting Life* and one from the Press Association who, before each race, note the varying prices on the rails and in Tattersalls, and after consultation at the 'off', reach a consensus on what they consider the fairest majority version of how each horse is quoted when the race is started. The problem is the very fact that a 'market' means varying prices and, although a favourite may be quoted by most bookmakers at 11/8, others will be marking at 6/4, and yet again, others at 5/4. At longer prices there may be even greater variations, so, understandably, since the difference between, say, 4/1 and 5/1 could make a great difference in the amount paid in the SP offices and betting shops, not every bookmaker agrees that the SP returned is the correct one. The job, however, is tackled with a first intention of fairness by the journalists concerned who bring great integrity, as well as a deep understanding of the betting market to their task, which also requires the skill and shrewdness to size up quick betting moves and their significance. Doug Newton is the *Sporting Life's* senior man, with more than 30 years experience, day in, day out, in the ring — but still smiling. Of the arguments that occur from time to time with bookmakers who may disagree with a particular SP return, he says: 'An argument or two is inevitable occasionally. If we didn't get arguments I'd know we weren't doing our job properly,' and adds, 'We're like football referees, really, we have to be impartial — and sometimes we're just as popular!' Before Doug Newton took over, Geoffrey Hamlyn was chief man for the *Life* for many years, and today is a member of Tattersalls' Committee on Betting (see Chapter Two). Most punters may imagine that the prices that are returned within a few seconds of a race result somehow occur by spontaneous combustion or are concocted and transmitted directly from the bookmakers at the course without intervening arbiters. The men who are the lynchpins in this vital service deserve greater credit. *The Sporting Life* and Press Association hold the copyright on starting prices, which is sold to the Extel (Exchange Telegraph) — and now to the Satellite Information Services — who in turn provide the service to newspapers, television, betting shops and credit bookmakers. Before the Press Association took over, *The Sporting Chronicle* representative (for many years the late Bob Watson) partnered the man from *The Sporting Life.*

Tic-tac   The system of tic-tac on a racecourse represents what flags were to Nelson, and what satellite communications are to the Fleet today. Betting moves, money put on, who has put it on, are all signalled by the white gloved representatives of bookmaker firms, and read by their own tic-tac men. Tic-tac is one of the strange and abiding features of the English and Scottish racecourse scene, lending a tremendous air of secrecy and big money changing hands, and all beyond the range of the average racegoer who, even if he could read tic-tac sign language, with the waving arms, and lightning Swedish drill bends, it would be of no use, because like Fleet signalling again, the signs are not transmitted in 'plain language', they are further encoded by reference to what is known as the twist card. Thus on the racecard the numbers of horses in an eight horse race run in sequence from one to eight. But on the twist card, which again differs from firm to firm of tic-tacs, they are jumbled so that one may be seven, seven may be six, and so on.

There are two main firms operating on southern racecourses, one being that of Mickey Stuart (late Hokey — because the original firm made the East End ice cream called Hokey Pokey), the other run by Billie Brown and called Fingers (named after the late Micky Fingers). In the Midlands, the Lloyd family run the tic-tac, and there are other firms in the north. To make things more complicated, the actual tic-tac sign language varies from region to region. Bookmakers subscribe to the tic-tac services, and, in the past, they were much used by big backers to place commissions.

The Tote   The usual abbreviation for the Horserace Totalisator Board — chairman Lord Wyatt. It provides the alternative means of betting to the bookmakers, and was instituted by Act of Parliament in 1928. One of its stated aims at the time was to generate money to support racing, and this it does today via the Levy.

Following the establishment of the on-course Tote in 1928 an off-course subsidiary, Tote Investors Ltd, was set up for the purpose of accepting off-course Tote credit bets which were transmitted to the racecourse pools. At this time bookmakers operated on all racecourses and could also accept credit bets by telephone off the racecourse. But off-course cash betting remained illegal by Tote or bookmaker. The law was frequently broken, however, by the bookmakers, who operated a network of illegal betting through factory and street runners. This structure continued from 1929 until 1960 and during this period the Tote was able to make contributions to racing of nearly £9 million, while the bookmakers gave virtually nothing.

In 1960 the Betting and Gaming Act legalised off-course cash betting, but the opportunity to establish an off-course Tote monopoly was missed. Bookmakers were given licences to bet by local magistrates. A year later a new organisation was established by statute, the Horserace Betting Levy Board, empowered to levy money from both bookmakers and Tote for the benefit of racing.

Betting shops spread throughout the country and reached a peak of 15,780 in 1968. The Tote was unable to take part in this off-course betting boom. Although allowed to run betting shops like the bookmakers, they were not allowed to offer starting price betting. And this is what the public were used to, for they had traded illegally at starting prices for many years. The proliferation of starting price betting shops had an adverse effect on the Tote's financial position and in 1972, in order to restore their competitive position, the Tote was empowered by Act of Parliament to accept bets at starting price as well as Tote odds.

Today the Tote in Britain is organised into three distinct sections. First there is pool betting on the racecourse — their original function. The Tote operates at every racecourse in Britain throughout the year six days a week. Computerised win, place and dual forecast pools are run at all meetings.

The second section is Tote Credit, formerly known as Tote Investors. It is probably the largest credit business in Britain with over 30 regional offices plus at least one office on every racecourse. Tote Credit offers its customers credit facilities at Tote odds and starting price. All Tote bets accepted on the racecourse are placed in the pool but not all off-course bets are passed into the pool with the exception of jackpot and placepot. This is because, being in direct competition with the bookmakers, the Tote must offer the facilities of betting right up to the off of each race. Some critical bets are placed in the pool if they are received in time, and the rest are settled at the price returned by the Tote on course.

The third division is called Tote Bookmakers and it is responsible for 119 betting shops off-course and a further 22 on-course offices. Like Tote Credit they accept bets at Tote odds (except on-course) and starting price, but in cash not credit. They have the largest turnover of the three divisions. Some bookmakers also offer their customers the facility to bet at Tote odds for which they pay a copyright fee.

Turn of foot   A commonly used expression meaning a horse's capability for speed and/or acceleration.

Weatherbys   This is, in effect, the Jockey Club's civil service, dating from the time in 1770 that James Weatherby, a solicitor practising in Northumberland, was invited by the Jockey Club to move to Newmarket and become Keeper of the Match Book, Stake Holder, and Secretary to the Jockey Club. Today Weatherbys on behalf of the Jockey Club, continue to supply the complex administration required for racing in the United Kingdom. This they do from their headquarters in Wellingborough, Northamptonshire and from their offices in Portman Square, London, which are shared by the Jockey Club.

At Wellingborough some 60 of the total of 180 staff are directly engaged on racing administration using automated office systems based upon the latest computer technology. Amongst a multiplicity of tasks they maintain all of racing's records, grant names for horses, approve 'colours', issue passports for horses, take all entries, declarations and cancellations. The last two operations are centred on the Odecs department where the unpopular balloting out and eliminations take place, races are divided, weights raised and the draw made for starting stalls. Following the actual races the official returns arrive at Wellingborough for recording and from which a financial account is produced for each race and the monies collected and distributed under the Rules of Racing.

As part of racing administration the *Racing Calendar* and the programme books are produced and published at Wellingborough using computer editing and typesetting routines.

The Weatherbys staff at Portman Square provide the secretariat for the stewards of the Jockey Club, advising them on a wide range of matters and implementing their decisions. This office is the centre for liason with other national and international bodies involved in racing. Other essential activities which are administered at Portman Square include the formulation and interpretation of the Rules of Racing together with work on behalf of the Jockey Club Disciplinary Committee, the granting of licences and permits to owners, trainers and jockeys, the control of point-to-point racing, and last but not least, the important and complex task of race planning.

Weatherbys' proprietorship of the *General Stud Book* started in 1791 when another James Weatherby, cousin of the above, published the first volume. Volume 40 was published containing some 3,000 pages in two volumes. Administration is based at Wellingborough and at Naas, Ireland, where Irish horses are registered.

Now an intergral part of the controls of the *Stud Book*, the bloodtyping scheme promoted by Weatherbys in conjunction with the Equine Research Station at Newmarket has developed to handle 7,000 specimens annually. With the opening of the laboratory at the Irish Equine Centre in late 1985, the facility is now available to handle the entire thoroughbred crop of the two countries each year. The importance and the complexity of safeguarding international standards of registration and control for thoroughbred breeding is reflected each year when Weatherbys organise and host the International *Stud Book* Conference.

In 1983, following four years of development, Weatherbys introduced the world's first computer system for the automated production of pedigrees for the sales catalogues of Tattersalls and Goffs. Major breeders and bloodstock agents are now able to interrogate the computer at Wellingborough for pedigree and statistical information.

Wellingborough's computer systems provide essential statistics for racing and breeding, the most prominent example of these is the *Statistical Record* which is published four times a year by Weatherbys. This publication was joined in 1984 by *The Stallion Book* a new annual which presents extensive details on stallions. Similar technology is used to provide racecard services to many racecourses and data and editorial services for other organisations at home and abroad. Notable among these is a system developed in 1983 for Raceform Ltd to produce their weekly *Raceform* and *Chaseform* publications.

Weight for age This is the scale, originally devised by Admiral Rous, which lays down how horses of differing ages improve month by month throughout a season, the differences being expressed in terms of weight. The weight for age scale provides the basis for the weights carried by horses in conditions races, as well as a ground rock for handicappers.

Weight for Age Table

Allowance assessed in lbs, which 3-y-o will receive from 4-y-o, and 2-y-o will receive from 3-y-o

		APRIL		MAY		JUNE		JULY		AUG		SEPT		OCT		NOV
		Mar & 1-15	16-30	1-15	16-31	1-15	16-30	1-15	16-31	1-15	16-31	1-15	16-30	1-15	16-31	
5 furlongs	2	32	31	29	27	26	25	25	23	21	20	19	18	17	16	15
	3	13	12	11	10	9	8	7	6	5	4	3	2	1	–	–
6 furlongs	2	–	–	30	29	29	28	27	26	26	24	22	21	21	20	18
	3	15	14	13	12	11	10	9	8	7	6	5	4	3	2	1
7 furlongs	2	–	–	–	–	–	–	–	–	–	–	24	23	23	22	21
	3	16	15	14	13	12	11	10	9	8	7	6	5	4	3	2
1 Mile	2	–	–	–	–	–	–	–	–	–	–	27	27	26	25	24
	3	18	17	16	15	14	13	12	11	10	9	8	7	6	5	4
9 furlongs	3	18	17	16	15	14	13	12	11	10	9	8	7	6	5	4
1¼ miles	3	19	18	17	16	15	14	13	12	11	10	9	8	7	6	5
11 furlongs	3	20	19	18	17	16	15	14	13	12	11	10	9	8	7	6
1½ miles	3	20	19	18	17	16	15	14	13	12	11	10	9	8	7	6
13 furlongs	3	21	20	19	18	17	16	15	14	12	12	11	10	9	8	7
1¾ miles	3	21	20	19	18	17	16	15	14	13	12	11	10	9	8	7
15 furlongs	3	22	21	20	19	18	17	16	15	14	13	12	11	10	9	8
2 miles	3	22	21	20	19	18	17	16	15	14	13	12	11	10	9	8
2¼ miles	3	23	22	21	20	19	18	17	16	15	14	13	12	11	10	9
2½ miles	3	25	24	23	22	21	20	19	18	17	16	15	14	13	12	11

CHAPTER TWO

How It All Began: A Brief Chronology of the History of the Turf and Betting.

Racing has always been, and will always be, a gambling speculation.

Admiral Rous

It is generally accepted that there was racing of a kind in England at the time of the Romans, but the first documented evidence dates from the 16th century. Racing is recorded at York as far back as 1530; Chester had the first racecourse as such in 1540; Queen Elizabeth I visited Salisbury for the races; and a racecourse appeared on a map of Doncaster in 1595.

James I noted Newmarket as an ideal place for sport and Charles I spent much time there, but not until the Restoration (1660), and Charles II, did Newmarket begin to flourish and become the centre for organised racing, among other sports. The King, an outstanding horseman, founder of the Newmarket Town Plate which is still run today, assisted in framing conditions for races which were run over long distances with heats and a final all on the same day. Betting was heavy among courtiers and royal guests, as well as among attendant grooms, footmen and other servants as 'debt of honour transactions' with no cash changing hands until settlement afterwards, and certainly no bookmakers who did not appear for another 150 years. Old Rowley was the name of Charles's much loved hack; the king, in turn, was so nicknamed, and hence the title for the Rowley Mile racecourse at Newmarket.

Tregonwell Frampton (1641-1727), who became known as the 'Father of the Turf', was another influential figure of the time, an arbiter, like Charles II, in racing disputes, and, as Keeper of the Running Horses to Queen Anne (who founded Ascot racecourse in 1711), an early, if not the earliest 'trainer'.

However, the foundation of racing as we know it stems from the importation of stallions from the Near East in the late 17th and early 18th centuries, most significantly the so-called Byerley Turk (1689), the Darley Arabian (c1704) and the Godolphin Arabian (1730). They founded sire lines through, respectively, *King Herod* (usually abbreviated to *Herod*), *Eclipse* and *Matchem* to which all thoroughbreds of the world today trace their ancestry, *Eclipse* having by far the greatest influence. Following this, and up to the first quarter of the 19th century, there was 'a period of intensive evolution ... which resulted in the emergence of the thoroughbred as he is known today ... (when) ... the average height of the racehorse increased by about a hand

and a half, or six inches, and there were corresponding increases in overall size and physical scope, strength, length of stride and speed.' (Peter Willett *Introduction to the Thoroughbred.*)

1715   *Flying Childers* foaled — the first great racehorse, sired by the Darley Arabian, capable of speeds not much less than those of today, subject of much legend and hearsay, and still commemorated on pub signs.

1750s   The Jockey Club was founded in 1751 by racing enthusiasts. The term 'Jockey' included them, and did not then possess only today's narrower and more specialised meaning. The Star and Garter in Pall Mall, London, was one of the original meeting places. Later in the century, at Newmarket, their social headquarters were the Red Lion and the Coffee Room, leased in 1771 for a 50-year period. The Rules of the Jockey Club which began to evolve originally applied only to racing at Newmarket, but, in time, the jurisdiction and authority of the club grew and were accepted elsewhere, so that it became the sole turf authority in the land.

John Pond's *Sporting Kalendar* was first published in 1751, containing regulations which helped to form the Rules of Racing. 1752 saw the earliest recorded steeplechase in Ireland.

In 1758 the Jockey Club passed its first resolution requiring all riders to weigh in after a race; those who did not declare overweight beforehand were disqualified. By 1759 they had opened races to public participation, but betting remained a matter between private individuals.

1760s   Racing colours were first registered at Newmarket in 1762. Richard Tattersall began to organise bloodstock sales in London at Hyde Park Corner. He was an experienced dealer specialising in 'thro-bred' horses; that is, those tracing pedigree from the three best known imported Arab stallions. Tattersall also used the Turf Tavern close by for his business. This was frequented by racing men who did not wish only to inspect the horses for sale but also wanted to bet. Thus, the Turf Tavern became the first centre of off-course betting. This was all conducted, still, 'on the nod'. Meanwhile, at the races themselves, and on Newmarket Heath in particular, betting was conducted round the betting posts in a jostle of men on horseback, and a throng of gambling 'legs', touts, grooms, nobility and nonentities, and tradesmen from the town. This was also all 'on the nod', while some of those who had struck a bet, galloped off after the horses taking part and had a better view than from the rudimentary building which then served as 'grandstand'.

In 1768 Sir Charles Bunbury was elected steward of the Jockey Club. Eventually he became, in effect, perpetual president, and was for more than 40 years the first of the three so-called 'Dictators of the Turf.' Bunbury's influence was far reaching, and felt almost immediately on his taking office. Previously, horses which raced were mostly four years old or upwards, carrying 10 stone and more in punishing heats, commonly of four miles or so. Bunbury was instrumental in introducing racing for younger horses, in age groups, with less weight on their backs, and over not such extreme distances. He can thus be said to have recognised the possibility of developing speed in the thoroughbred at the expense of stamina.

Eclipse was the horse of the decade, and, in respect of his subsequent influence at stud, the stallion of every other decade since. Not raced until he was five, *Eclipse* was unbeaten in 18 races giving rise to the much repeated utterance of '*Eclipse* first, and the rest nowhere', although this originated in a remark of O'Kelly, his owner, when he bet that he could place the runners in a heat in correct order. Since *Eclipse* won the heat, and the rest were all more than a distance behind (i.e. nowhere) O'Kelly, former sedan chairman who had made a fortune out of betting, had wagered correctly.

1770s   Run simply as 'a sweepstakes', the race which two years later became the St Leger, took place in 1776 at Doncaster. This was the first Classic, although the term was not in use until the following century. The fact of the race being for three-year-olds is further testimony to Bunbury's ideas; but the distance was two miles and remained so until 1812.

Highflyer was foaled in 1774. Bred by Bunbury, and a descendant through *Herod* of the Byerley Turk, sold to Lord Bolingbroke, and later bought by Richard Tattersall, *Highflyer* was unbeaten in a dozen races, and when retired to stud (Fee 50 guineas) his progeny made him the greatest sire of his time and earned a fortune for Tattersall, which he acknowledged in an affectionate epitaph when *Highflyer* died. The Highflyer sales are still held by Tattersalls today.

A second Classic was inaugurated in 1779, the Oaks (then the Oakes Stakes) run at Epsom for fillies only, and won by Lord Derby's *Bridget*. The following year Sir Charles Bunbury's *Diomed* won the first running of the Derby, for colts and fillies, and, like the Oaks, over a mile and a half at Epsom. Tattersall's London premises at 'The Corner', as it was known by now, were much expanded. Two rooms were set aside, eventually, for the sole use of members of the Jockey Club, an astute move which ensured a seal of approval for Tattersall from the men who controlled racing. Equally important for backers, Tattersall also established his subscription rooms. This, apart from ensuring that those who seriously wanted to have a wager on, or lay a bet against a horse, could do so with other 'Members of Tattersalls' knowing that settlement would be prompt, and that bets could be struck up to tens of thousands of pounds. The subscription rooms became known simply as 'The Room'. From this stage it was only a step to the origin of the term which still exists on every racecourse two centuries later: Tattersalls' Ring. This evolved because those in 'The Room' who wanted to bet gathered round a large, six-sided, hollow-centred table and quoted prices to one another, argued about them, and struck bets accordingly, and in the way that commodity dealers might arrange a market. Tattersall, anticipating the force of Admiral Rous's later remark (quoted at the head of this chapter) to the effect that racing and gambling were inseparable, undoubtedly realised that by attracting the betting element to 'The Corner', he was sure to promote his bloodstock sales more effectively.

1780s In 1786 the Derby was won by *Sir Thomas* owned by the Prince of Wales, later King George IV, who kept fairly fast company at Newmarket, and was infatuated with the sporting life there. But a scandal early in the following decade involving his horse *Escape* and his jockey Sam Chifney caused the Prince to sell his racing interests and quit Newmarket, never to return.

1790s A handicap involving 14 runners had already been run at Newmarket in 1785, but it was not until 1791, with the Oatlands Handicap at Ascot, that 'the full fascination of racegoers eager to bet on a public cavalry charge became evident', as Dick Whitford, one of the best ever private handicap experts, once wrote in *The Sporting Life*. The Oatlands Handicap drew an estimated crowd of 40,000, who were said to have gambled nearly one million pounds on the race: an event of primal significance for racing, and the forerunner of today's big handicaps such as The Wokingham, Stewards' Cup, and Cambridgeshire. Richard Tattersall died in 1795, but the firm founded by him continued to flourish and dominate the bloodstock sales market.

1800-1825 The early years of the 19th century saw the foundation of the remaining Classic races, and in 1807 the first running of the Ascot Gold Cup, which came to be the outstanding race for stayers. The year after the Battle of Waterloo (1815) a horse-drawn trailer was first used to convey a horse to the races. Before horse-boxes, horses walked to the races, a factor which must have contributed to the toughness of the breed in those days.

As often seems to occur after a war, there was a betting boom after Waterloo. One of its features was the appearance of the list houses, an early form of betting shop. Lists of runners and prices based on those quoted at 'The Corner' began to appear in all sorts of places, shops, clubs, even private houses. They opened up betting opportunities to a wider public than hitherto — but still on credit. New subscription rooms had also been opened at 'The Corner', and with them came a new and less rough and ready betting man to replace the old-style leg. One of these was Richard Crockford who already had much experience of London gambling hells. He was said to have fake teeth and eyes that were 'coffin-cold', but it is to this man, one of the first bookmakers in the proper sense of the word, that we owe today the existence of the Yankee, the Patent and other multiple bets. Crockford was the first to see the immense mathematical probability of profit for a layer in such bets, and he invented the double, treble, and four timer even though these terms had yet to be coined. At the betting posts at Newmarket he stood up and laid these bets by the score, so appealing were they to the big-profit-for-small-outlay mentality. As he took the wagers, he could calculate in a twinkling his liabilities, even though he laid half a dozen bets in as many seconds, and knew that after the last race he would be a richer man than ever. When he died, in 1844, he had built a Newmarket house, gaming rooms in the High Street, and owned a farm and training stables out of the profits.

In 1821, Sir Charles Bunbury died, having wrought changes in racing which set the pattern that would inevitably evolve towards the one we know today. So the scene was set for the next 'Dictator of the Turf', Lord George Bentinck, son of the Duke of Portland, through which connection the Jockey Club was to acquire its wealth, thousands of acres, and further influence at Newmarket. Alan Ross (in *The Turf*) wrote: 'Bentinck was an unscrupulous gambler on a vast scale, an arrogant and successful owner who won seven Classics ... an MP who led the Protectionist Party, and an outstanding turf reformer, especially in his concern for ordinary racegoers and his war on crooks. He invented the flag start, developed Goodwood as a racecourse, and died on the verge of a great political career.' Among his other reforms were the practice of parading runners in the paddock before a race, and numbering them.

1826-1850   The first St Albans Steeplechase took place in 1830, organised by Thomas Coleman. This led to a proliferation of steeplechasing, and Coleman is regarded as the 'father' of the sport in the form we know it today. He had been a stableman, a trainer, and later hotelier. He bought the lease of the old Chequers Hotel in St Albans, rebuilt it, renamed it the Turf Hotel, and it quickly became the equivalent of Tattersalls rooms for chasing. It continued to attract year after year for a decade, bringing great trade to the town, and spectators from all over the country to see riders such as the redoubtable Captain Becher, and horses such as *Moonraker* and *Grimaldi*. By the time the popularity of the St Albans Steeplechase had begun to wane, the sport was well established with a fixture list for just the month of March, 1838, containing 26 meetings at places as far apart as Ashby-de-la-Zouch and Abergavenny, and Cheltenham (racing had begun at Prestbury Park in 1831) to Chatham Garrison.

At Liverpool, meanwhile, steeplechasing had begun, and the race now known as the Grand National was first run at Aintree in 1839. (It did not take this title until 1847, its first name being 'The Grand Liverpool Steeplechase'. The present title stems from the Grand National Steeplechase Committee which was formed to run the race and which eventually evolved into the National Hunt Committee, chasing's equivalent of the Jockey Club until the two bodies were amalgamated in 1968.) A report of the first running of this unique and world famous event as it became reveals that, as a crowd puller, it started much as it continued: 'as early as nine o'clock the road leading to Aintree was crowded with pie-men, chimney sweeps, cigar sellers, thimble riggers and all the small fry of gaming-table keepers ... Not a vehicle of any description that could by any means be made to go was left in the town, not a coach or cab was to be had for love or money ... the grandstand had not accommodation for more than three-quarters of the people who presented themselves.' There was heavy betting among the 40,000 or so estimated to have turned up; the original ante post favourite, *The Nun* at 8/1 was displaced in the market by *Lottery* at 5/1, who, as the sporting sheets of the time would have had it 'duly obliged' ridden by Jem Mason, and beating 16 opponents over the punishing cross-country course.

In 1831, on the Flat, the Jockey Club refused to resolve any further disputes arising at meetings where its rules were not in force. In 1842, it took a further major step, and divorced itself entirely from settling betting disputes. Both these measures came into force under Bentinck. In practical terms, it meant henceforth a more rarefied role for the Jockey Club, as well as the permanent connection between Tattersalls and betting disputes. A later Richard Tattersall, who now ran the firm, was invited by the Jockey Club to oversee a committee which they would license for the purpose of arbitration of betting disputes. This was the origin of Tattersalls' Committee and the rules it evolved, reproduced in an appendix to this book, still govern betting just as Tattersalls' Committee still settles major betting disputes to this day. In a striking echo of previous usage, just as The Room ruled earlier betting, so today when anyone is summoned to Tattersalls' Committee to answer a case of offence against betting rules, they are said to have been 'In the Rooms'. In 1846 Bentinck sold his racing interests for £10,000 and retired from the turf to pursue his political career, but died only two years later. Admiral Rous succeeded him as the third and last 'Dictator of the Turf.'

One further event during this period has to be noted, which had the most far-reaching significance for horserace betting. A man called William Davies appeared on the scene and became known as 'Leviathan' Davies, such were the size of the bets he laid and paid. His significance was that he took and handed out cash, being the first bookmaker to do so. Davies started his cash revolution in the 1840s but its effect was in the following decade and after. Meanwhile, the list houses continued to flourish, in barber's shops, and stalls selling snuff, in warehouses, and back streets. Some were reputable, others not; some paid out, and others greeted the hopes of winning clients with the shutters up and evidence of a moonlight flit. So much so that a House of Commons Select Committee began to sit in 1844 and its findings were to have a great effect after 1850.

By 1850, in fact, racing was in a form which would be recognisable to a racegoer today. In only a century, the Jockey Club, with its 'Dictators of the Turf' had quite revolutionised the sport from a rough and ready affair, into one which could be seen as a basis for the highly organised industry-cum-sport of the late 20th century. From 1850, too, the various changes on the turf were refinements of what had gone before, and the chronology from this point to the present day therefore takes a more abbreviated form:

1850   'Leviathan' Davies loses £50,000 on *Voltigeur's* Derby.

1853   *West Australian* is the first winner of Triple Crown. New Betting and Gaming Act makes cash betting off-course illegal. It is another century before it is made legal; in between the two dates there is much hounding of small bookmakers and backers who offend the new law.

1855   The Jockey Club appoints Admiral Rous (the third 'Dictator of the Turf') as their official handicapper, a man of great probity and shrewdness in assessing horses' abilities. He invents the weight for age scale which is with only minor adjustments, still in use today. George Fordham, known as 'The Terror' or 'The Kid' (because he kidded other jockeys into losing races) was the jockey of this and the next decade.

1859   Jockey Club forbids racing of yearlings.

1865   *Gladiateur* becomes the first foreign-bred colt to win the Derby and was known in France as 'the Avenger of Waterloo'.

1870   The Jockey Club rules that no meeting should start before the week including 25 March or continue beyond the week including 15 November.

1875   Sandown Park, first enclosed racecourse in England, is opened.

1877   Admiral Rous dies.
        Draw for places at the start is made subject of a Jockey Club rule for the first time. The Jockey Club also declares that it will not recognise any meeting not under its rules.

1879   Jockeys have to be licensed.
        Photography reveals the true action of a horse when galloping, thus proving past painters mistaken in their portrayals.
        Fred Archer at the height of his prowess as champion jockey, and the first widely known and popular jockey, whom the public would back irrespective of what he was riding.

1886   Archer commits suicide, and the entire racing world is stunned at the tragedy and loss. He was 29.

1895   The present day seat for flat racing is introduced with American jockeys coming to England and riding 'monkey-on-a-stick winners'.

1897   First Derby recorded on film.
        Starting gate introduced.
        Edwardian turf era at its height with 'plungers' winning and

losing thousands in a single race, led by HRH The Prince of Wales.

1900   The Prince of Wales's horses win both the Derby and Grand National.

1902   *Sceptre* runs in every Classic and wins all but the Derby.

1903   Doping banned by the Jockey Club. *Hackler's Pride* wins the Cambridgeshire, backed down from 33/1 to favouritism, and takes a reputed quarter of a million pounds out of the ring for the Druid's Lodge syndicate.

1910   The Jockey Club decrees that no race on the Flat should be shorter than 5f. National Hunt headquarters established at Cheltenham.

1920s   Number cloths carried for the first time.
         1924 sees the first running of the Cheltenham Gold Cup.
         Steve Donoghue is the reigning champion jockey on the Flat and Fred Rees over the jumps.
         Protective headgear made compulsory under National Hunt rules.
         Sporting press agree that only one amalgamated version of the starting price will be published as a basis for settling bets throughout the country.
         New type of starting gate introduced at Lingfield.

1930s   Dead-heats no longer run off.
         The great era of Gordon Richards begins — he was champion nine times in the century, continued his domination for nearly a quarter of a century.

1940s   Racing suspended for two seasons because of the War.
         Photo-finish is introduced.
         Americans pioneer air travel for horses.
         Post-war times bring tremendous crowds to racecourses and a great boom in betting. At the same time the French, notably Marcel Boussac, the textile millionaire, have great success in the Classics and other important races in England.
         In 1947 the first evening meeting is held at Hamilton Park.

1950s   First running of the race now known as The King George VI and Queen Elizabeth Stakes.
         Electrical timing introduced at Newmarket.
         In the later years of the decade the first sponsored National Hunt

races take place, beginning a great trend and improvement of prize money for the winter game.
Sir Gordon Richards retires, the season after winning the Derby in Coronation Year on Sir Victor Sassoon's *Pinza*.
Lester Piggott wins the Derby for the first time on *Never Say Die*.
Doug Smith is champion jockey five times.
Betting shops legalised.

1960s   The Patrol Camera comes into use as well as overnight declarations.
Lester Piggott is champion jockey.
Starting stalls are introduced at Newmarket in July 1965.
Jockey Club is forced to grant trainers' licences to women.
James Callaghan re-introduces betting tax.

1970s   Jockey Club permits races for women riders.
Computer-assisted handicapping introduced, and graded handicaps on the Flat.
More and more sponsorship of racing, and many more horses competing internationally from the UK.

1980s   Lester Piggott retires from the Flat as does John Francome, champion jockey over the jumps.
Sunday racing under discussion.
Proposals for an all-weather racetrack.

CHAPTER THREE
Frauds, Coups, Plungers, Ringers and Tipsters

'... *It is thought that Gates, Drake and the rest of them took something like £2,000,000 out of the ring between 1897 and 1901. Most of their horses were ridden by the brothers Lester and Johnny Reiff. In their knickerbockers and Eton collars they looked as innocent as choirboys, but the fact of the matter was that either of them would stop any horse if it suited the gang who employed them.*'

(*Headquarters* Richard Onslow)

Because of the inter-dependence of betting and racing, and in the consequent pursuit of money through horses via the need to outwit the bookmakers, secrecy, deception, and outright villainy have frequently played their part in Turf history; as well as the winning and losing in a single race more money in individual bets than most people see in an entire lifetime. The following stories are a random selection of such manipulations, successful and otherwise, which, despite the immense cleaning up of racing during the past few decades, are still evident — and not only in racing novels.

Running Rein's Derby

First past the post in the 1844 Derby was *Running Rein*. After a long investigation, however, Lord George Bentinck was instrumental in proving that *Running Rein* was really *Maccabeus*, aged 4-y-o. When a 2-y-o, *Maccabeus* had been secretly exchanged for the real *Running Rein*, at the time a yearling. This was the first notable exposure of a 'ringer'. The men responsible fled to France and the race was awarded to *Orlando*, the original runner-up.

A more recent celebrated ringer was *Francasal* who was the centre of a long-running press sensation after winning the Spa Selling Plate at 10/1 at Bath in July, 1953. Bets of several thousand pounds at SP had been placed all over the country on *Francasal* who would almost certainly have started favourite had the money been laid off on the course. But this was impossible because just before the race all telephone communication between Bath racecourse and the outside world went dead. A gang with lorry and ladders had cut the wires. This proved the undoing of the men who had engineered an audacious plot to take a £60,000 reward at a false SP. Four were jailed after an Old Bailey trial lasting nearly two months, during which *Francasal* was established to have been in reality an older horse called *Santa Amaro*. Nonetheless, *Francasal* came out of it best in the end as he now has a race at Bath named after him.

Even more recently, *Flockton Grey*, supposedly a 2-y-o, won the Knighton Maiden Auction Stakes at Leicester by a suspiciously easy 20 lengths in

March, 1982, also at 10/1, and, after lengthy inquiries, he was proved to be a 3-y-o called *Good Hand.* Here again, there had been organised backing at SP. At the trial which followed, three men were convicted of conspiracy to defraud, while *Flockton Grey*'s trainer was declared a disqualified person by the Jockey Club.

The Trodmore Hunt

A quite inspired and astonishing plot to take both the sporting press and the bookmakers for a ride occurred on August 1, 1898. The editor of *The Sportsman* was asked to print the card for the Trodmore Hunt race meeting on that day, and the runners and riders duly appeared in the paper. Bets were placed with several bookmakers in the London area, and on the next day the results were also printed in *The Sportsman.* Some bookmakers paid out on these printed returns, but others said they would wait for *The Sporting Life* to publish the results. It so happened that when *The Sporting Life* did publish, they made the SP of one winner 5/2, whereas *The Sportsman* had returned it at 5/1. As a result there was an inquiry and it was found that no such place as Trodmore existed, let alone a Trodmore Hunt, complete with race meeting. Thus an ingenious coup was foiled, but the extremely practical jokers were never traced.

The Hermits of Salisbury Plain

Around the turn of the century, the biggest ring of professional backers were the so-called 'Hermits of Salisbury Plain' and in only ten years were said to have taken at least half a million pounds out of the ring. A single famous coup, when *Hackler's Pride* won the 1903 Cambridgeshire (ridden as a 6 st 10 lb apprentice by Jack Jarvis), netted them £250,000. Scores of other coups were launched from their training headquarters, the remote Druid's Lodge, where secrecy was paramount, no touts were ever seen, all stable lads' mail was opened, and where all that could be heard from the gallops of a horse's chance was the silence of Stonehenge itself.

Charlie Hannam was another great backer of the time and later and was known as 'Old England' because of the then influx of corrupt American gamblers. Once asked how much betting money had gone through his hands, he said, 'I couldn't tell you. Perhaps 25 or 30 millions.' 'Boyo' Beattie was a stable commissioner who not only won substantially for those he put on for, but profited enormously himself and managed to hold on to the money. He kept £30,000 for himself when *Verdict* had a lucky neck win in the 1923 Cambridgeshire, and when he died he left £180,000. The Marquis of Hastings was £120,000 out of pocket when *Hermit* won the 1867 Derby (he had backed the runner-up, beaten by a neck), but another great plunger, Captain Machell, was very much in pocket, as he was when his horse *Disturbance* won the Grand National six years later. His first bet on the horse alone had been £200 on at 500/1. The bookmaker William Chandler, turned backer, is said to have cleared £120,000 from fellow layers when *Ocean Swell* won the wartime substitute Derby at Newmarket in 1944.

The American Dopers

The quotation at the head of the chapter is taken from Richard Onslow's description of the effect of American gamblers on the English Turf at the turn of the century. Gates and Drake were heavy gamblers. They employed a trainer called Enoch Wishard, also American, whose speciality was the use of dope. Their technique was 'to buy a moderate horse that was fully exposed, run it way above its class, fill it with dope, and back it off the board'. The coups that resulted eventually grew into a public scandal, but it was not until 1903, and following demonstrations by the trainer, the Hon George Lambton, that the Jockey Club made doping an offence, which led eventually to the stringent security and other precautions which exist today.

'I Gotta Horse'

This was the racecourse cry of the flamboyant, be-feathered tipster of the 1930s and immediate post-war era called Ras Prince Monolulu. He, and other tipsters of the time, added greatly to the colour of the racecourse scene. One used to dress as a jockey; another, calling herself Mae Marsh, claimed to be the only woman tipster on the course: 'Only this mornin', ladies and gents, 'is Majesty comes up and says "'Ello Mae, wot are you tippin' for the big 'un today?" I says, "Your 'orse, your Majesty," and 'e says, "Quite right. That's the one. No danger." *And* it went in, didn't it, could 'ave won pullin' a cart, *and* at twenty to one ... them's the kind of prices you can expect from old Mae ...' Sadly, the only tipsters left today seem to be the furtive figures peddling dubious brown envelopes in the racecourse car parks. Only once in my life have I ever fallen for the brown envelope trick when years ago at Market Rasen I paid ten bob to a rather anxious looking lad by the gate. On opening the brown envelope I found, rather surprisingly, there was not a blank slip, but the names of four horses. All of them were trained by Lionel Elwell and all of them, even more surprisingly, won. But now the bad news. I backed only two of them, *D'Artagnan* and *Matkah*. Somewhere there's a moral in all this.

CHAPTER FOUR
The Structure of Racing

The history and chronology of the previous chapters brings us to the point where we can look in more detail at various components of today's racing scene, beginning with a difficult question:

Why racing?
Racing began as a sport, and, to an extent, remains so today, particularly in the mud, bravery, and heroics of the National Hunt field. Human beings in the 20th century differ little from the Romans or the Iceni in that they enjoy watching and taking part in activities which involve winners and losers. Many horses, however, dislike losing intensely, and if equines ruled the world would entirely abolish the idea of losing as a philosophical concept. Since they are unable to achieve this, they do the next best thing (again, most of them) and try as hard as possible to ensure they are winners, not losers, against the opposition provided for them by human beings. To go further, since it is possible to win money both by owning a successful horse and by betting on that horse without the cost of actually owning it, here are two even more powerful *raisons d'etre* for racing.

Racing, however, is not competition in its simplest sense. Because human beings are in charge of the horses (although to the disinterested observer of owners, trainers and riders it might frequently seem *vice-versa*), their natures dictate a certain complication of the competition. Racing concerns thoroughbred horses, so the pedigrees of most of them, be it the winner of the Derby, or be it a horse claimed out of a selling race at Plumpton, can be traced right back, and the character and racing ability of their ancestors known in minute detail. It is thus possible, in theory at least, by genetic engineering to breed faster and faster horses, or horses that can stay longer and longer distances at speed. The former, sadly, has become more and more fashionable and prevalent in the past half-century at the expense of the latter — see comparative lists of sires of sprinters and stayers in Chapter Eleven. The motives impelling the breeder of horses are many and varied, ranging from the simple human vanity of wishing to improve on nature, through the desire to achieve a mating that will produce a future Derby winner, to the not uncommon urge to make a lot of money.

This brings us back to money. Racing journalists, and, possibly more important, the sports editors behind the scenes who pull the wires, seem obsessed both in print and on television with the financial angle far more than they ever used to be. On television in 1986, at the York Ebor meeting, far too much gee-whizz was given to the fact that the trainer Michael Stoute had 'gone through the one million pound barrier' in terms of prize money won for his owners, while the betting reporter was almost apoplectic announcing the news of a £35,000-£5,000 bet on the eventual winner of the Tote Ebor Handicap. A day or two later, *The Sporting Life* led on a story with the heading 'Mi££ion-pound Walter!' — all about Walter Swinburn's prospects of becoming the first jockey of the season to have had winning rides worth more than a million pounds in first prize money.

All this is explicable in a sport which, more than ever today, is an industry as well: an industry concerned not only with leisure pursuits but one which also makes a valuable contribution to British exports on the bloodstock side. As will be evident from the preceding paragraph, racing statistics these days are written in millions rather than thousands of pounds, which may account for the journalistic emphasis. But, as with other industries, inflation is the main factor in pumping up the figures on the balance sheet. Prices paid at the bloodstock sales may seem astonomical (although, at the time of writing, apparently past their peak) and prize money may appear more than handsome, yet a comparison between 1985 figures and those of 20 years ago is illuminating, and leads to the conclusion that prize money, in particular, when viewed in real monetary terms has, in fact, declined in value.

	1965	1985
First 10 owners	Won 192 races between them worth a total of £695,757 Average prize per race: £3,623	Won 444 races between them worth a total of £3,622,259 Average prize per race: £8,158
Derby Stakes	Unsponsored. Worth £65,301 to M. Jean Ternynck, owner of *Sea Bird II*	Sponsored by Ever Ready. Worth £204,160 to Lord Howard de Walden, owner of *Slip Anchor*

One final explanation to the question Why racing? The boy Bitzer in Dickens' *Hard Times* responded to Mr Gradgrind's school room demand for the definition of a horse: 'Quadruped. Graminivorous. Forty teeth, namely twenty-four grinders, four eye-teeth, and twelve incisive. Sheds coat in the spring; in marshy countries, sheds hoofs, too. Hoof hard, but requiring to be shod with iron. Age known by marks in mouth.' In betting shops up and down the country there are less articulate Bitzers who would define a horse as a fragment of print in a newspaper. Fortunately, between these extremes of incomprehension there are many thousands of people who actually love horses and find that a sufficient reason to follow racing or be involved in it. They range from the lonely figures who gather at the fences out in the country on a cold afternoon at Fontwell Park, to trainers such as the late Captain Ryan Price who used to keep his retired horses (he called them 'My Pensioners') in a paddock and feed them every day.

Owners

Racing cannot exist without horses, so equally it would not take place
without owners. Racehorse owners today provide more of a mirror to the
times and society in general than they used to. Even after the Industrial
Revolution the ownership of horses and the sport of racing was over-
whelmingly the preserve of a landowning aristocracy who bred, for the most
part, their own horses. The echoes of the Industrial Revolution did not make
themselves heard in racing until long after it had happened. In the first 50
years of the Derby, 1780-1829, the race was won on only 13 occasions by a
mere esquire. By the later years of the 19th century, owners included rich
industrialists and bankers, from the admirable Baron Meyer de Rothschild
among the latter, to the egregious Scottish ironmaster, James Merry, among
the first named. The Rothschild horses *Favonius* and *Hannah* won all but one
of the Classics in 1871, while three years later Merry's horses won three out
of five. Royal interest in racing was rekindled towards the end of the century
by the Prince of Wales, later King Edward VII. He owned three Derby
winners, *Minoru*, after he was crowned, and before that *Persimmon*, and
Diamond Jubilee who won the Derby in 1900, the same year in which the
Prince's horse *Archer* won the Grand National. The first half of this century
saw the zenith of great owner-breeders such as the Joel brothers, the Aga
Khan, Lord Derby, Lord Rosebery and Sir Victor Sassoon.

The scene today is barely recognisable when compared with those earlier
days, so drastically has a hurricane of social change, and squalls of taxation
blown through the parks and paddocks, particularly in the past two decades.
True, HM The Queen more than maintains royal interest, and HM The
Queen Mother, too, in the National Hunt field. Grandson of the old Aga, the
present Aga Khan has become a formidable force in racing in recent years,
just as his grandfather was. In the 1986 King George VI and Queen
Elizabeth Stakes it was interesting to see that his three runners carried three
sets of colours: the chocolate and green hoops registered first by his
grandfather, the green with a red sash of his father the Aly Khan, and his
own green with red epaulettes.

The present era in racing is dominated, as far as owners are concerned, by
the Arab influence. In 1985, 168 horses owned by Khaled Abdulla,
Sheikh Mohammed and the other Maktoum brothers won 275 races in the UK
This is roughly 10 per cent of all the races run on the Flat. Of the top ten
owners (judged in prize money terms) the name of Lord Howard de Walden,
mainly through the success of his Derby winner *Slip Anchor*, was the solitary
English link with a more distant racing past, and that of the Aga Khan with
its rather more recent history. It is rather appropriate that there is this growing
Arab influence as, after all, without the original Arab stallions, racing
would not exist in its present form. Also, since it was the internal combustion engine which ousted the horse as a means of transport, it is a fitting
irony that oil profits are now responsible for helping to keep at least one
branch of horse activity in business. More seriously, the Arab involvement has
given a much needed lift to British racing and aid on the breeding front.

The Arabs apart, the feature of recent years and a true mirror of social change has been the widening of the bounds of ownership. Until the late 1960s, only private individuals could own racehorses. Since then the Jockey Club has progressively altered its rules, so that now a horse may be owned jointly (by up to 12 people), or by a club, or a commercial company. The Jockey Club Rules in *Ruff's Guide* relating to ownership in 1964 took up no more than two lines in a simple definition. Twenty years later they covered nearly three pages. In this exercise in democratisation, many members of the public who would not otherwise be able to afford it are now able to have an interest in the buying and running of a horse. Sometimes, individuals may get together and independently go into ownership; or they may answer one of the frequent advertisements in the sporting press offering a share in a horse, or they may join an organisation such as Full Circle in the north which offers opportunities for participating in ownership. Ownership seems to appeal particularly, for some reason, to the rag trade and to engineering firms and since they are now allowed to advertise via a horse's name, there are now horses promoting the merits of every product imaginable from blouses and brassieres, to computers and machine tools. Clubs are also able to own horses, and among these must be mentioned the Atrabates Cricket Club who own a splendid mare of the same name. *Atrabates* was unbeaten in four hurdle races in 1985-86, and not only that, she made the Club pretty prosperous, winning £21,000 in prize money. The Racehorse Owners Association, which was formed in 1945, looks after the interests of owners. It has about 3,700 members who own between 60 and 70 per cent of the horses in training.

Trainers and Jockeys
(See Chapter Ten)

Bookmakers
These can be divided into:
1. Those who make a book on the racecourse
2. Those who operate betting shops off-course (which includes, for simplicity's sake, those operating betting shops on racecourses, as well)
3. Those who operate a telephone credit service (where an account may be based on pure credit, or cash deposits in advance) or a postal betting service

A number of big firm bookmakers combine two or even all three activities. Some of 2. and 3. will settle bets at Tote prices, if the backer specifies these odds. For this the Tote is paid a copyright fee, otherwise the settlement is at starting price (see Chapter One) or at a 'board' price taken in a betting shop, or equivalent price based on the latest 'show' of betting over the telephone.

On the racecourse, bets are settled at the prices quoted, or if agreed with the backer, SP. Some bookmakers put up signs on their joints that they will settle at SP if required. However they settle, their activities, on-course and off-course, are governed by what goes on in the market on the racecourse. A betting market is formed immediately before each race. The prices fluctuate according to the total of money known to be on a particular horse in the ring as a whole, amounts of significance being signalled by tic-tac from rails to Tattersalls and back, and to the silver ring and bookmakers 'outside' i.e. on the course itself (or, for example, at Epsom on Derby Day in the great melée on the Downs). The amount a price will contract or go out in the market varies, also, according to whether the market is a weak or strong one (see below).

The prices originally on offer in the early stages of any betting market are not, however, based on money bet, but (usually) on how the bigger Tattersalls boards operators think the market ought to go. The earliest prices chalked up are very often shorter than they realistically should be. In the days up to and beyond the great post-war betting boom the true market price was dictated by on-course money, largely by big backers (whether professionals, commission agents betting on behalf of others, including trainers and owners, and trainers and owners themselves). The huge growth of off-course betting since the 1960s has changed all that. Seldom do trainers walk up to the rails, get a price about their horse, and affect the market accordingly. Most money is wagered off the course, and is transmitted, or news of it is transmitted by telephone to the tic-tacs acting for the big bookmakers. The entire market reacts accordingly within a few seconds. The money which causes this is called 'office money' and in the case of big amounts placed off-course which crucially affect the market, the horses are known in the ring as 'betting shop horses'. Going back briefly to the very opening of the market some Tattersalls and other bookmakers in other rings and 'outside' subscribe to a marked card known usually as the 'house card' which gives an opinion on how the day's racing might turn out. This used to be operated by 'Jack the Judge' who charged a fee for the service, and his successor still operates. Basing their prices on the 'house card' and/or their own judgement, the Tattersalls boards bookmakers form the early market.

As the market gets under way, and money starts to reinforce the bookmakers' original opinions of the prices, or causes them to alter prices on the general principle of supply and demand, a punter can learn a great deal from following the market, that is, seeing how the odds are altering. The market can give strong hints on what to back, and, even more important, what not to back. On the racecourse, this involves having a look at successive stages in the 10 minutes or so immediately before a race at how the prices are going. In the betting shop, with the aid of successive prices marked on the board or shown on video, following the market is rather easier, and watching the television makes it equally simple. This is how the television showed the betting on the 1986 King George VI and Queen Elizabeth Stakes:

Shahrastani	Evens	6/5	11/10	
Dancing Brave	11/8	6/4		
Shardari	7/1	9/1	10/1	12/1

Petoski	14/1	12/1	14/1	
Triptych	16/1	20/1	25/1	28/1
Dihistan	66/1	100/1		
Supreme Leader	100/1	200/1		
Boldden	500/1	750/1	1000/1	
Vouchsafe	500/1	750/1	1000/1	

Thus all the market moves can readily be seen on television, and, depending on the channel, backed up with information on why the prices are going the way they are. In betting shops with television or video a similar advantage is enjoyed by the punters. (Television in the shops has probably not made an immense amount of difference in turnover, but has certainly livened up the scene into something resembling a racing, rather than a pure gambling activity. Shouts of 'Come on Patsy, boy,' greet the televised finishes, as Pat Eddery, all unaware, many miles beyond the cathode ray tube, drives one home.) On the racecourse, following the market is rather harder work, because the bookmakers sponge or erase the prices successively as the odds change; but, in general, the punter who can take the trouble should reap the reward.

Weak Markets/Strong Markets. Royal Ascot provides one of the strongest betting markets of the year on the Flat, and The Cheltenham Festival does so in National Hunt racing. The weakest markets are at small, under-patronised courses where the racing is poor. Here, a few hundred pounds can cause prices to tumble several points where in a strong market the same amount multiplied several times over would cause no price change. At Royal Ascot it is traditionally thought that big handicaps such as the Royal Hunt Cup and Wokingham Stakes provide the strongest betting activity. This used to be so, but is no longer the case. There was far more big money going on *Double Schwarz* in the 1986 King's Stand than went on *Perfect Timing*, or any horse for the Wokingham on the same day, as the returns show:

3.45—WOKINGHAM STAKES (HANDICAP) of £30,440; 1st £19,586, 2nd £5,888, 3rd £2,844, 4th £1,322. Rated 0-75. Six furlongs.

STARTING PRICES

10 **Perfect Timing:** Opened 12-1, touched 14-1. Bets of £10,000-£700 each-way, £10,000-£700 twice and £17,000-£500 each way.

12 **Boot Polish:** Opened 12-1, touched 14-1 and 11-1. Bets of £10,000-£700, £5,000-£350 each-way tiwce, £6,000-£500 each way and £10,000-£450.

13 **Philip:** Opened 14-1, touched 12-1. Office bets of £10,000-£700 three times and £5,000-£350 . three times.

13 **Rotherford Greys:** Opened 12-1, touched 14-1. Bets of £30,000-£2,500, £10,000-£700 each-way, £10,000-£800 twice and £5,000-£400 each-way.

 Al Trul: Ope---d 12-1, t- ~d
 ' R~t-   ~~n ~

4.20—KING'S STAND STAKES (Group 1) of £82,380. 1st £48,828, 2nd £18,347, 3rd £8,873.70, 4th £3,930.90. Five furlongs.

LAST TYCOON, b c Try My Best - Mill Princess by Mill Reef (R C Strauss) 3-8-9...C Asmussen   1 (14)
~OUP'~ SCHWA~~ `~ h D~~

STARTING PRICES

9-4 **Double Schwartz:**Opened 3-1, touched 2-1. Bets of £6,000-£2,000, £3,000-£1,000 three times, £11,000-£4,000 twice, £5,500-£2,000, £2,750-£1,000 six times, £12,500-£5,000, £10,000-£4,000 three times, £5,000-£2,000 three times, £2,500-£1,000 four times, £4,500-£2,000, £2,250-£1,000 including office money.

100-30 **Gwydion (USA):**Opened 9-4, touched 7-2. Bets of £3,500-£1,0~~ ~3,333-£1 ~~~ twice

The strongest market in recent times was for the 1986 King George VI and Queen Elizabeth Stakes, as recorded the following Monday by Doug Newton, *The Sporting Life*'s senior man in the ring. This was his story:

'The King George VI and Queen Elizabeth Diamond Stakes, billed in the run-up as "the race of the century", may or may not prove to justify that hyperbole, but as far as the Ascot course betting was concerned it became a prime candidate. Old timers recall the forties and early fifties as betting bonanza years but never, in my 30 years experience or more of returning starting prices, has such a barrage of money circulated at the racecourse for two leading contestants.

The return match between Dancing Brave and Shahrastani caught the betting world's imagination, and in recorded single stakes alone — which ranged from a comparatively modest £400 up to the £11,000-£10,000 laid against Shahrastani — the Derby winner attracted nearly £120,000 and Dancing Brave around £80,000.

And this from only the leading rails and boards bookmakers.

The Tote

The workings of the Tote are outlined in Chapter One. Their latest figures show that their pre-tax profits in 1985-86 totalled £3,205,000 — only £29,000 less than the previous year despite the quite exceptional loss of 129 days racing due to the harsh winter, during which overheads connected with the tote facilities on racecourses continued without any income being received.

The Tote's contribution to racing topped the £2 million mark for the first time. The figure includes payments to racecourses of £1.072m, levy payments of £680,000 and race sponsorship of £252,000. In addition the Tote contributed £383,000 to joint building projects at Fontwell Park, Chester, Liverpool, Stratford and Taunton.

The introduction of a new computerised pool betting system at the major racecourses, which is capable of handling up to 500 ticket issuing machines, has helped the turnover of the Board's Racecourse Totalisator Division to increase by 18% to £27.4m. Considerable improvements have also been carried out to the on-course facilities of Tote Credit, and the popularity of the modernised offices has been reflected in increased credit turnover on the racecourse of over 12% despite the loss of racing.

Tote odds are now available not only at the Tote's own shops, but at over 2,700 shops owned by bookmakers holding the Tote Authority, including three of the four biggest bookmakers.

The bets possible with the Tote are as shown in their publicity — win, place, dual forecast and placepot pools at all meetings and the Tote jackpot at major fixtures as indicated in our racecards.

Minimum stake for single bets in the club, grandstand and paddock enclosures is £2; £1 each way and £1 dual forecast combinations accepted. Minimum stake for all Tote bets in the silver ring, cheap and course enclosures is £1. Jackpot and placepot unit stake is 50p but the minimum investment is £1. Perms from 10p upwards in multiples of 5p for a minimum total stake of £5.

The win pool operates on all races; dual forecast on all races with three or more runners; place pool on all races with five or more runners. Place dividends are paid on 1, 2, 3 and 4 in handicaps of 16 runners or more; 1, 2, 3 in all races of eight runners or more; 1, 2, in races of five, six and seven runners.

In the dual forecast you win if your selections are first and second in either order. If there is no correct forecast the dividend is declared on the winner and second with any other. Stakes are refunded in the win, place and forecast pools if your selection is withdrawn without coming under starter's orders.

The Tote jackpot and placepot always operate on the first six races. If not won outright the pool is carried forward. If there is a part winner, the balance of the pool is carried forward. In the jackpot and placepot non-runners are put on the SP favourite. If there is more than one you are on the favourite with the lowest racecard number.

All Tote dividends include stake and are declared after 4% on-course tax has been deducted.

Ante post betting

This has already been explained in Chapter One, but one word of warning should be given. This concerns the number of horses frequently offered in the earlier stages of betting on big handicaps. The example below analyses the price shifts in the ante post market for the 1986 Goodwood Stewards' Cup. Apart from the 24 eventual runners shown, there were no fewer than 36 other entries given a price at some time during the period under review.

Prices taken from William Hill's ante post lists advertised in *The Sporting Life* from 8 July to the day of the race. Coral's, Mecca, Ladbroke's and other bookmakers showed similar variations, although some prices varied a point or two from Hill's list.

Wokingham place	Horse	Finished	8/7	12/7	19/7	24/7	28/7	a.m. 29/7	SP
	Green Ruby	Won	20/1	20/1	16/1	16/1	25/1	20/1	20/1
	Young Jason	2nd	10/1*	12/1	14/1	14/1	16/1	12/1	10/1
3	Perfect Timing	3rd	25/1	25/1	16/1	14/1	14/1	11/1	8/1 JF
10	Prince Sky	4th	12/1	12/1	9/1	8/1	7/1	8/1	8/1 JF
4	Our Jock	5th	14/1	14/1	11/1	10/1	10/1	11/1	11/1
5	Gold Prospect	6th	25/1	25/1	25/1	25/1	25/1	25/1	20/1
	Measuring†	7th	—	—	—	—	33/1	28/1	16/1
unpl.	Padre Pio	8th	25/1	25/1	25/1	25/1	28/1	22/1	18/1
	Manton Dan	9th	25/1	25/1	33/1	33/1	20/1	25/1	18/1
15	Al Trui	10th	14/1	14/1	14/1	14/1	14/1	16/1	14/1
	Laurie Lorman	11th	—	33/1	33/1	33/1	25/1	22/1	33/1
	Bertie Wooster	12th	33/1	20/1	16/1	16/1	18/1	12/1	9/1
	Ameghino	13th	25/1	25/1	20/1	20/1	14/1	11/1	11/1
	Durham Place	14th	25/1	25/1	25/1	25/1	28/1	25/1	25/1
	Sew High	Also ran	—	—	20/1	14/1	16/1	16/1	12/1
	Glen Kella Manx	Also ran	25/1	33/1	20/1	16/1	16/1	16/1	16/1
	Throne of Glory	Also ran	—	—	—	—	25/1	22/1	22/1
	Ra Ra Girl	Also ran	—	—	—	25/1	40/1	40/1	40/1
	Sudden Impact	Also ran	—	—	33/1	33/1	40/1	40/1	40/1
	Quarryville	Also ran	—	—	—	—	50/1	33/1	50/1
	Soon To Be	Also ran	—	—	—	—	66/1	50/1	66/1
	Derry River	Also ran	—	—	—	—	100/1	100/1	66/1
	Shades of Blue	Also ran	—	—	—	—	200/1	100/1	100/1
9	Hi-Tech Girl	Last	33/1	—	—	—	40/1	33/1	25/1

Race sponsored by the William Hill Organisation who gave £25,000 towards the prize money.

*Young Jason, beaten by only a neck into second place, was reported before the earliest price shown to have been backed by the stable at 33/1 to win a substantial sum.

†Measuring, unquoted until the day before the race probably owes his SP of 16/1 to a good Timeform Rating.

Much has been written about the Jockey Club elsewhere in this book, including Chapter One where the Levy Board is dealt with, and racecourses mentioned with additional detail in Chapter Nine. So we now have all the main components of Turf activity in the UK today. How they all interconnect is shown below in the graphic reproduced from *The Times*.

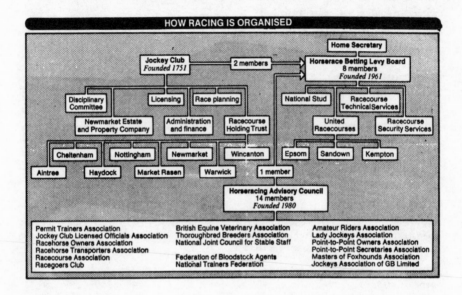

CHAPTER FIVE
Form at the Fingertips: How to Find Winners

Time spent in Reconnaissance is never wasted.

(Military adage)

There is no doubt that the public has never been better informed about racing, with an extraordinary number of daily, weekly, monthly and annual publications to choose from. The influence in bringing this about are first the advent, then increasingly widespread use of the computer to process data and statistics and make them readily available; second, television has meant that there is excellent live coverage not only of racing, but the preliminaries, including last minute hints and betting, as well as, more recently, programmes such as Jim McGrath's on TV-am. To serve a more demanding armchair punter, therefore, newspapers have sharpened up their presentation of racecards. Thirdly, of course, under pressure to recognise the needs of the popular racegoer and stay-at-home backer (both of whom contribute to racing, albeit indirectly, through the levy) the Jockey Club has brought in several reforms in the past two decades, including the overnight draw. The introduction, in the 1960s, of a four day and overnight declaration system, while not specifically designed to ease the clairvoyant requirements of off-course enthusiasts, does so nonetheless; so, altogether, the daily newspaper's presentation of the card is now improved out of all recognition. Only a matter of 30 years ago, this is what a typical racecard as published by *The Times* looked like:

```
3.15.—The CHAMPION HURDLE CHALLENGE CUP.
              with £3,000 added (2m.).
200 Plainsman (Mr. Joseph Bennett) Maund,
                             6-12-0 J. Lindley
030 Quita Que (Mrs. L. Brand) Ireland,
                             8-12-0 Mr. J. R. Cox
111 Caesar's Helm (Mr. A. C. Bryce-Smith) Ireland,
                             6-12-0 C. Finnegan
213 Solatium (Mr. C. G. Crawley) Crawley,
                             7-12-0 M. McCourt
213 Flame Royal (Mr. L. H. Dowling, sen.) A. Thomas,
                             7-12-0 T. Molony
210 Ivy Green (Mr. J. G. Duggan) Ireland,
                             7-12-0 W. J. Brennan
444 Peggy Jones (Gp.-Capt. H. I. Hanmer) S. Palmer,
                             7-12-0 D. Leslie
303 Strait-Jacket (Mr. D. Hickey) Ireland,
                             8-12-0 A. Brabazon
312 Merry Deal (Mr. Arthur Jones) A. Jones,
                             7-12-0 G. Underwood
111 Clair Soleil (Mr. G. C. Judd) Price, 8-12-0 F. Winter
330 Curling Iron (Mr. E. G. Ketteringham) Goodwill,
                             6-12-0 J. Fitzgerald
111 Stroller (Mr. H. Lane) Ireland, 9-12-0  —
110 Straight Lad (Miss D. Paget) H. Nicholson,
                             7-12-0 D. V. Dick
000 Francette (Mr. E. Morris) H. T. Cross,
                             7-12-0 H. T. Cross
100 Winning Hit (Mrs. H. J. Rice-Stringer)
                      Rice-Stringer, 6-12-0 A. Dennis
012 Nanjula (Mr. O. G. M. Williams) O. Williams,
                             7-12-0 P. Morrissey
121 Rosati (Mrs. T. Hanbury) Walwyn, 5-11-12 J. Gilbert
    Tout ou Rien (Comte de Monteynard) France,
                             5-11-12 R. Emery
   15 to 8 Clair Soleil, 9 to 2 Rosati, 7 to 1 Flame
Royal, 8 to 1 Quita Que, 10 to 1 Tout ou Rien,
100 to 7 Peggy Jones, 100 to 6 Straight Lad and Strait-
Jacket, 20 to 1 Ivy Green, 33 to 1 Merry Deal,
50 to 1 others
```

Racecards, too, have taken a similar turn for the better. The present day card from Sandown Park can be favourably compared, with its form summary, betting forecast, and other details with the two earlier cards, both of them historic in that they show the details as presented on the cards of the time for one of *Arkle*'s Gold Cup successes at Cheltenham, and *Pinza*'s memorable victory in Coronation Year. As far as the cards are concerned, not much more than some rudimentary form figures embellish the usual details of breeding and owners' colours, the Derby card being the more primitive. Marks across the horses' numbers can be seen as well as figures also written in. These were the days long before declarations and an overnight draw. The practice then, on the racecourse was to mark off the actual runners from the 'probables' which had been printed (some non-runners can be seen) and to take the draw off the numbers board. An addition to the programme, unusual for those days, was the printing of jockeys' names.

3.30—THE 174th DERBY STAKES (RENEWAL) of 100 sov. each, 50 sov. forfeit if declared by the Tuesday in the week before running, or 10 sov. only if declared by the first Tuesday in July, 1952, with 4250 sov. added (including a trophy value 250 sov.), *for entire colts and fillies foaled in* 1950 ; colts, 9st, fillies, 8st 9lb ; the second to receive 10% and the third 5% of the whole stakes ; one mile and a half (446 entries, 50 sov. forfeit declared for 271, and 10 sov. for 141).—Closed November 6th, 1951.
Declaration of forfeit to Messrs Weatherby and Sons only.

VALUES : WINNER £19,118 10s.: SECOND £2,261 : THIRD £1,130 10s.

	Owner and Name		st	lb	Trainer	Jockey
1	The Queen ....|9....AUREOLE		9	0	C. Boyd-Rochfort	W. H. Carr
	Ch c *Hyperion—Angelola*					
	Purple, Gold braid, Scarlet sleeves, Black Velvet cap with Gold fringe					
2	Ld Antrim ....(l...CITY SCANDAL		9	0	H. Smyth	A. P. Taylor
	B c *Rockefella—Milady Rose*					
	Blue, Gold facings & cuffs, Black cap					
3	M. Marcel Boussac ....|0.....PHAREL		9	0	C. Semblat (France)	J. Doyasbere
	B c *Djebel—Pharelle* (foaled in France)					
	Orange, Grey cap					

	Owner and Name		st	lb	Trainer	Jockey
16	Mr L. Lipton ....6....PRINCE CHARLEMAGNE		9	0	T. Carey	L. Piggott
	Ch c *Prince Chevalier—Swift Gold*					
	Flame, Silver sleeves & stripe, Flame cap					
17	Mr J. McGrath .2|.............NOVARULLAH		9	0	W. Stephenson	C. Spares
	B c *Nasrullah—Nova Puppis*					
	Green, Red seams & cap					
18	Ld Milford ......25.........EMPIRE HONEY		9	0	J. Jarvis	W. Rickaby
	B c *Honeyway—Brave Empress*					
	Black. White sash & sleeves, Gold cap					
19	Mr J. Olding ....13...........VICTORY ROLL		9	0	H. Persse	
	B c *Nasrullah—Chinese Puzzle*					
	Yellow, Black hooped sleeves, Black cap					
20	The late Mr James V. Rank ....CRITICISM		9	0	J. Dines	T. Masterson
	Ch c *Orthodox—Superior*					
	Black, Grey sleeves, Green & Red quartered cap					
21	Mr J. G. Morrison...23.........FELLERMELAD		9	0	N. Cannon	A. Breasley
	Br c *Scottish Union—Jollification*					
	Dark Green, White cap					
22	Mr Chas. H. Rodwell ..18........PETER-SO-GAY		9	0	T. Griffiths	P. Evans
	B or br c *Blue Peter—Soga*					
	Scarlet, White " V," Yellow cap					
23	Sir Victor Sassoon ......5..................PINZA		9	0	N. Bertie	Gordon Richards
	B c *Chanteur II.—Pasqua*					
	Peacock Blue, Old Gold hoops & sleeves					
24	Prince Said Toussoun ..15.........PINK HORSE		9	0	J. Cunnington (France)	W. R. Johnstone
	B c *Admiral Drake—Khora* (foaled in France)					
	Red & White stripes. Red cap					

THE 40ᵀᴴ YEAR OF THE CHELTENHAM GOLD CUP

with £11,000 added (to include a Cup value £300, and also £5,000 given by the Horserace
Betting Levy Board); a Sweepstakes of £15 each, £15 extra unless forfeit be declared by
Tuesday, February 23rd, £15 in addition if declared to run by Monday, March 8th, and £15
in addition unless such declaration be cancelled by Wednesday, March 10th; the second
to receive 20% and the third 10% of the whole stakes; a steeplechase for five-yrs-old and
upwards; five-yrs-old 11st 5℔, six and aged 12st; three miles, two furlongs and about
76 yards (13 entries, viz. 4 at £60, 2 at £45, 4 at £30 and 3 at £15).—Closed January 27th, 1965.

VALUE TO THE WINNER £7,986 10s.; TO THE SECOND £2,239;

TO THE THIRD £1,089 10s.

Rider/Form		Trainer	Age	st	℔	Owner
..................**2** 411	MILL HOUSE .... *b g King Hal—Nas Na Riogh* F. Walwyn		8	12	0	**Mr W. H. Gollings** Black, white slvs and cross-belts, scarlet cap
..................**4** 033/	CADUVAL .... *br g Lacaduv—La Francaise* G. Balding		10	12	0	**Mrs A. R. B. Owen** Green and white stripes, white slvs
..................**5** —	STONEY CROSSING .... *br g North Riding— Sunlit Stream* W. Roycroft		7	12	0	**Mr W. Roycroft** Green, gold "V" back and front, gold stripe on sleeves, gold cap
..................**6** 131	ARKLE .... *b g Archive—Bright Cherry* T. W. Dreaper in Ireland		8	12	0	**Anne Duchess of Westminster** Yellow, narrow black belt and cap with gold tassel

4 DECLARED RUNNERS

By comparison, here and on page 80, is how the modern card appears:

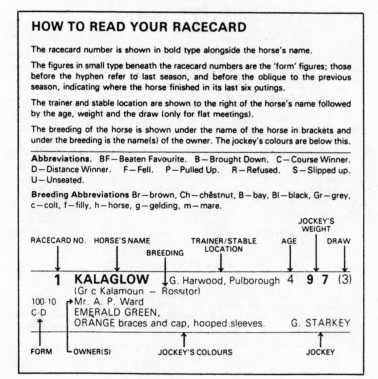

Third Race   3.15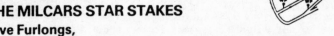

THE MILCARS STAR STAKES

**Five Furlongs,
for Two Yrs Old**

£5000 ADDED TO STAKES

Distributed in accordance with Rule 194 (iii) (a) (includes a fourth prize) for two yrs old only. £10 to enter,
£40 extra if declared to run. Weights: Colts and geldings 8st 11lb; fillies 8st 8lb. Penalties, a winner of a
race value £1500 4lb. Of a race value £3000 7lb.
MILCARS LIMITED have generously sponsored this race, including a trophy value £250, at the option of
the winner. 50 entries, 43 at £10 and 7 at £50. Closed 2nd July 1986. **Owners Prize Money: Winner
£2849; Second £932; Third £441; Fourth £195. (Penalty Value £3707)**   **A SS**

Form		Trainer	st	lb	Draw

1 QUEL ESPRIT   M. McCormack, Wantage   **9 4** (2)
(B c What A Guest – Les Sylphides (FR))
111302   Mr. Ian D. Myers
D BF   WHITE, RED chevron,
RED and WHITE striped sleeves,
RED cap.   S. CAUTHEN

Has won four races already this season at Doncaster, Newmarket, Salisbury
and York. Ran third to Chime Time (winner again this week) at Haydock in June
and was second in Ireland at The Curragh behind Dominion Royale this month.
Has done most of his winning on good ground and should find this stiff track in
his favour.

---

5 BORN TO RACE (USA)   **8 11** (3)
L. Piggott, Newmarket
(Ch c Dr Blum (USA) – Babes Sis (USA))
012   Mr. K. H. Fischer
LIGHT BLUE and WHITE check,
WHITE sleeves and cap.   R. COCHRANE

Comes from a winning American family. Won his maiden at Yarmouth in June
and finished second of six later in the month behind Glow Again at Doncaster.
The stable is enjoying a good first season.

---

6 RIOT BRIGADE   **8 11** (4)
C. E. Brittain, Newmarket
(Ch c Try My Best (USA) – Lady R B (USA))
003   Mr. Philip Noble,
Mr. J. S. Threadwell
YELLOW, DARK GREEN chevron,
DARK GREEN and
YELLOW quartered cap.

Finished third to Le Favori at Newmarket on Saturday over six furlongs. Started
at 10-1 and ran on well in the closing stages to be beaten a neck and a length.
May not be good enough in this company.

---

7 GARNET   R. Boss, Newmarket   **8 8** (1)
(B f Thatch (USA) – Jawhara)
01   Mr. A. Foustok
D   EMERALD GREEN and RED check,
EMERALD GREEN sleeves.   PAT EDDERY

With no disrespect to winning form at Edinburgh, it would be unusual if this
filly who scored there earlier this month, were to prove good enough. However,
the victory north of the Border was readily achieved, although the
quality of opposition hard to gauge would probably prefer more give in the
ground.

Seemingly light years away, but in reality, not much more than a century ago, this is how *The Times* was presenting details of future racing on a day in June 1879. The Royal Hunt Cup was, in fact, won by Captain Machell's *The Mandarin* carrying 8 st 4 lb at 33/1, ridden by Charlie Wood and was not quoted in any of *The Times* ante post lists. He beat *Sir Joseph* by a length and provided yet another gambling success for his owner who very much liked to win this big Ascot race.

Wednesday is perhaps the most pleasant day of the races, as the contest for the Hunt Cup with its large field streaming up the straight mile is one of the prettiest sights of the meeting. The Cup is a piece of plate value 300 sovs., added to a handicap sweepstakes, and there are 66 entries, out of which a field of 20 runners may come to the post. Isonomy is top weight with 9st., but he has too much weight to carry and will probably be reserved for other races at the meeting. Belphœb 8st. 9lb., is a good mare over the course, but both she and Rylstone, 8st. 5lb., may be withdrawn in favour of Lady Ronald, 7st. 2lb., who is well handicapped if she can only stay the course. Placida, 8st. 6lb., is fairly treated if in her best form, as she has considerably less to carry than the ordinary weight-for-age impost ; but she seems to have gone off since she was a three-year-old. Mandarin, 8st. 4lb. ; Master Kildare, 8st. 3lb. ; Spendthrift, 7st. 5lb. ; and Leghorn, 6st. 1lb., are trained by Cannon, and whichever is the selected one of the stable is sure to be heavily backed at the post and will probably run well. The same may be said of Bonnie Scotland and La Merveille, each 7st. 10lb.; Visconti, 7st. 9lb. ; Morier, 7st. ; Bute, 6st. 5lb., who ran very fast in the Two Thousand Guineas, and Chocolate, 5st. 12lb., all trained by Peck. Avontes, 8st. 3lb., and Broad Corrie, 6st. 5lb., are in Taylor's stable, and of these the first-named on his running last autumn ought to have a great chance, while it must not be forgotten that he finished fourth last year   Sir Joseph, 8st 11b.. is

How far the presentation of racing information has progressed in daily papers (*The Sporting Life* and *Racing Post* included, but dealt with later) can be judged by the racecard from *The Times* printed overleaf.

SP Forecasts in Daily Papers
Too much reliance should not be placed on the betting forecasts given in the daily papers outside the specialist racing bracket. Most of them rely on the Press Association SP Forecast circulated to all newspapers on the afternoon before racing is due to take place. This forecast can be, at times, extremely erratic.

Preparing a betting forecast is or should be an extremely skilled task, and very often a thankless one. The best betting forecasts used to appear in the midday edition of the *London Evening Standard*, compiled with immense enthusiasm and verve by Les Murray, who used to tip under the name of

Guide to our in-line racecard

103 (12)   0-0432 TIMESFORM (CD,BF) (Mrs J Ryley) B Hall 9-10-0 .... B West (4)   88 7-2

Racecard number. Draw in brackets. Six-figure form (F-fell. P-pulled up. U-unseated rider. B-brought down. S-slipped up. R-refused). Horse's name (B-blinkers. V-visor. H-hood. E-Eyeshield. C-course winner. D-distance winner. CD-course and distance winner. BF-beaten favourite in latest race). Owner in brackets. Trainer. Age and weight. Rider plus any allowance. The Times Private Handicapper's rating. Approximate starting price.

2.15 KING GEORGE VI RANK CHASE (Grade I: £31,696: 3m) (10 runners)   C 4

401	214-F03	BEAU RANGER (White Bros (Taunton) Ltd) Miss J Thorne 8-11-10 S Smith Eccles	76 33-1
402	11F0-11	BOLANDS CROSS (C,D) (Ali Abu Khamsin) N Gaselee 7-11-10 .... P Scudamore	87 5-1
403	0/12110-	COMBS DITCH (B,D) (R Tory) D Elsworth 10-11-10 .... C Brown or S Sherwood	96 11-2
404	PP-2212	CYBRANDIAN (D) (I Bray) M H Easterby 8-11-10 .... —	84 12-1
405	320-141	DESERT ORCHID (R Burridge) D Elsworth 7-11-10 .... C Brown or S Sherwood	80 10-1
406	3F0-141	DOOR LATCH (D) (H Joel) J Gifford 8-11-10 .... R Rowe	86 12-1
407	U43-111	FORGIVE'N FORGET (D) (T Kilroe & Sons Ltd) Jimmy Fitzgerald 9-11 ... M Dwyer	● 99 F2-1
411	F1-F134	VON TRAPPE (CD) (P Scammell) Mrs J Pitman 9-11-10 .... B de Haan	80 20-1
412	122-332	WAYWARD LAD (CD,BF) (Mrs S Thewlis) Mrs M Dickinson 11-11-10 .. G Bradley	97 4-1
413	1032-21	WESTERN SUNSET (S Sainsbury) T Forster 10-11-10 .... H Davies	86 16-1

1985: WAYWARD LAD 10-11-10 G Bradley (12-1) Mrs M Dickinson 5 ran

FORM BEAU RANGER (11-3) 3rd, failed to quicken, beaten 3¼l to I Haventalight (10-11) at Cheltenham (3m 1f, £7700, good, Dec 5, 6 ran.) BOLANDS CROSS (11-1) won well 15l from Clara Mountain (10-7) with VON TRAPPE (11-10) 4th beaten over 40l at Lingfield (3m, £10298, soft, Dec 6, 5 ran). COMBS DITCH yet to race this season has twice finished second in this contest. Last outing hampered by a loose horse, earlier (11-8) won 2l from DOOR LATCH (11-8) with FORGIVE'N FORGET (11-10) 4th beaten 7½l at Haydock (3m, £11163, soft, Jan 18, 7 ran). CYBRANDIAN (11-2) beaten 10l by FORGIVE'N FORGET (11-2) at Haydock (3m, £7418, good to soft, Dec 10). DESERT ORCHID (11-5) returned to form winning well by 12l from Charcoal Wally (11-5) at Ascot (2m, £6801, good, Dec 13, 8 ran). DOOR LATCH (11-1) won easily 15l from Sign Again (10-3) at Ascot (3m, £13789, good, Dec 13, 12 ran). FORGIVE'N FORGET last year in the Cheltenham Gold Cup (12-0) 3rd beaten 3½l by Dawn Run (11-9) with WAYWARD LAD (12-0) 2nd beaten 1l (3m 2f, £54900, good, Mar 13, 11 ran). WESTERN SUNSET (11-1) won 5l from Half Free (11-9) with VON TRAPPE (11-1) 3rd beaten 8l at Huntingdon (2m 5f, £5640, good to soft, Nov 25, 3 ran). WAYWARD LAD has won this race three times. Latest (12-0) 2nd beaten 1½l by Burnt Oak (10-2) at Doncaster (3m 2f, £5208, good, Dec 13, 5 ran). Earlier this year (11-10) 3rd beaten 5½l to FORGIVE'N FORGET (11-10) with CYBRANDIAN (11-2) 2nd beaten ½l at Wetherby (3m, £9408, soft, Nov 1, 6 ran).
Selection: WAYWARD LAD

The Falcon (as well as being known as The Mole because his nose was always in the form book). His SP forecasts were unrivalled, and widely used on the racecourse as a reliable guide. Now there is no midday edition, there is no equivalent in the popular press.

Facts to remember when looking at an SP Forecast are that it cannot accurately gauge the amount of money that may go on a favourite, or a well-backed horse, or the extent to which bookmakers will eventually push prices of outsiders out in order to attract some money with which to pay out on a 'good thing'. Therefore backers of favourites often complain when they find they have supported a horse at, say, 2/1 on when the papers judged it to be a 6/4 chance. Conversely, backers of outsiders, expecting 12/1, are frequently pleasantly surprised by a return of 25/1 or 33/1. Particularly difficult to forecast are the prices of maiden two-year-old races containing a lot of previously unraced runners. The forecast may be based on 'whispers' from Newmarket, or other advance information, or the fact that a particular stable does well with its two-year-olds first time out; but when the winner, forecast at 20/1 others, is returned at 11/4 fav, who can blame the SP forecast compiler in all honesty? A final point on SP forecasts: they can be notoriously misleading if the market turns out to be a weak one, with small amounts of money causing wide fluctuations in prices.

Newspaper Tips

These are a vexed question. The point to remember here is that the racing journalist is obliged to give a selection for every race in every card on a given day. That may amount to 30 selections on a Saturday, or about 100 on a Bank Holiday Monday. Whether or not he may think that there are no more than two good bets on an average card, or, more frequently, none at all, he still has to go into print. The remarkable fact, bearing this in mind, is how consistent the newspaper experts are, and confirming this, the results of a survey of all national newspaper tips on six Saturdays in June/July 1986 are published below:

Newspaper and Correspondent	Total winners given	Percentage of successful selections
1. *The Times* 'Mandarin' (Michael Phillips)	54	30.34%
2. *Daily Mirror* 'Newsboy'	47	26.4%
3. *Daily Mail*	46	25.8%
4. *Daily Telegraph* 'Hotspur' (Peter Scott)	45	25.28%
5. *Guardian*	43	24.15%
6. *Morning Advertiser*	41	23.03%
7. *Today*	38	21.35%
8. *Star*	38	21.35%
9. *Sun*	42	23.59%
10. *Daily Express* (Bendex)	35	19.66%

Saturdays were chosen because tipping for five meetings stretches, to put it at its politest, even the best of racing journalists. A total of 28 race meetings were involved, and 178 races, which seemed a fair sample (about 6% of all Flat races). Michael Phillips was an outright winner here, beating all the specialist racing paper tipsters, from which his nearest rival was Diomed (Adrian Cook) of the *Racing Post* with 49 winners. His individual best day (11 winners from 33 races) also beat all popular press correspondents' totals, and was bettered only by *The Sporting Life*'s Man on the Spot who, the following week, tipped 12 from the same number of races at five meetings. Inevitably, at the time of the year the survey was taken, with form reasonably settled and going either good or good to firm, a fair number of favourites, some of them short priced, were tipped. The public have a hankering for longer priced success, and were not disappointed by a 14/1 winner each from Augur of the *Sporting Life*, and the *Sun*; 9/1 winners each from Hotspur of the *Daily Telegraph*, and the *Star*; an 8/1 winner from Bendex of the *Daily Express*, and several 7/1 winners.

This brings us to the vexed question of *The Sporting Life Naps Table*. The nap selection of a correspondent is, or should be, the horse that correspondent considers has the best chance of all the runners on that day (correspondingly, his next best — sometimes abbreviated simply to n.b. — is the runner with second best chance of the day, in his opinion). *The Sporting Life* award a Challenge Cup and there is also a cash prize at the end of each racing season for the racing correspondent who finishes top of their naps table, the position being decided on profit to £1 level stake per nap selection. For the 1986 Flat season there were 35 contenders for the title, including all 12 London based dailies, 11 dailies published outside London all over the country and including Wales and Scotland, five Sundays, one *Racing Post* expert, and five *Sporting Life* correspondents, plus Dick Hunter from the *Weekender*.

At the time this book went to press, Richard Baerlein of the *Guardian* was battling it out at the top with the *Sunday Mirror*. Baerlein at this point had napped 40 winners out of 117 best of the day selections, with a level stakes profit of £61.76. The *Sunday Mirror* had chosen 45 winners out of 112 nap selections, with a profit of £57. Some way behind these two trailed the rest, headed by Crusader of the *East Anglian Daily Times* in third place with a very respectable figure of 41 winners out of 116, but a profit of only £25.85 which suggests a policy of safety in short priced naps. Richard Baerlein went to the top of the table when *Patriarch* won the Royal Hunt Cup at Royal Ascot in June at 20/1. Previously the *Sunday Mirror* had been top with £46.89 profit, and Baerlein second with £38.82. One other correspondent, Scotia of the *Scottish Daily Express*, napped *Patriarch*, and thereby leapt from 21st place in the table to eighth, turning a loss of £8.33 overnight into a profit of £11.67. But the interesting fact about the Royal Hunt Cup is that no fewer than 14 of the contestants in the naps table chose to nominate a horse in the race. Not only that, eight different choices from the 32 runners were given as their idea of the best bet of the day, with only Richard Baerlein and Scotia of the *Scottish Daily Express* scoring a bullseye. Two days later, in another big handicap at Royal Ascot, the Wokingham Stakes, a different eight contenders for the Naps Championship went for a big win, choosing four separate runners in the 27 horse race; none of them was successful.

A similar picture was presented in the next big handicap of the season, the William Hill Stewards' Cup at Goodwood the following month. Of the correspondents on London based papers alone six out of 12 napped a runner, two others made a Stewards' Cup runner their next best, leaving only Peter Scott (Hotspur of the *Daily Telegraph*) and Bendex of the *Daily Express* not attempting a nap in the race. The conclusion is fairly obvious and should be noted by those who tend to follow racing correspondents' nap selections. The naps table does, in fact, exercise a kind of tyranny. It is a £1,000 carrot, and a scourge at the same time. Were it not for the naps table, it is doubtful whether there would be such a high proportion of naps in these big handicaps, offering as they do the temptation of going for a big priced winner rather than a safer, shorter priced horse on the same card (it is interesting that on the day *Patriarch* was successful for Richard Baerlein and Scotia, the *Sunday Mirror* also napped a winner: but it started at 9/4 joint favourite).

Having said this, I do not wish to imply that correspondents are impelled by this motive alone. In big handicaps they are often convinced that their nap choice really is the best thing of the day. *Patriarch*, for example (although possibly looking at the race with hindsight) was an excellent choice, with all the right credentials for the Royal Hunt Cup (see Chapter Nine), while a similarly qualified horse, which was napped by Richard Baerlein in the Stewards' Cup at Goodwood narrowly failed to take him even further ahead. However, whatever loopholes there might appear to be in the handicap, the idea that there can possibly be a choice of eight 'best bets of the day' in a race of 32 runners rather stretches the imagination.

Let the final words on the wisdom or otherwise of following nap selections rest with my late friend Quinnie Gilbey, and taken from his zestful autobiography *Fun Was My Living*. First, on a lighter note, on the final day of the Flat season one year, Quinnie was quite some way adrift in the naps table, and with, seemingly, no chance. His selection for the last big race of the season, the Manchester November Handicap, was a 10/1 chance, but even that, were it to win, would have left him still some way short of the top. Having phoned his selection, he than ran into Peter O'Sullevan in the Midland Hotel. Peter had news of a horse trained by Ryan Price called *Chief Barker*: 'How about that for a good outsider?' he said to Quinnie, who dashed to the telephone, cancelled his original 'copy' and selected the horse. Next day it won at 33/1. Quinnie zoomed to the top of the table with a profit of £27.13.0 (£27.65) having napped 75 winners and 109 losers getting up 'on the post' to beat his nearest competitor. More seriously, Quinnie wrote: 'A journalist's position in the naps table is largely a matter of luck, and is in no way a criterion of his merits as a writer or as a judge of racing ... it is illogical that journalists should set such store by their position in the competitions run by *The Sporting Life* and *Sporting Chronicle*, but worry they do, and so much so that these competitions were responsible for the early death of one of my colleagues and have taken years off the lives of several others ...'

Coverage

The tabloid revolution in Fleet Street, as well as the demise of the early editions of London evening papers, has had its effect in depriving racing followers of coverage of the sport, that is to say reports of the previous day's racing, future news and plans, and in-depth analysis of the day's racing (but see under *TELEVISION*), as against racecards which these days contain far more information than they used to. The notable (broadsheet) exceptions are *The Times* and *Daily Telegraph*. The *Daily Telegraph* has long given serious coverage, but *The Times* is now an excellent racing paper with an entire page of lengthy reports on most days, and (worth noting) frequent mention of trainers' future plans. The *Guardian* does not give such extensive coverage but has the advantage of both Richard Baerlein and Chris Hawkins.

Writers

The best three writers on racing in the daily and Sunday press are, alphabetically, Richard Baerlein, John Oaksey and Brough Scott. All of them work for the more expensive papers and have space accordingly. In the popular papers, Jack Millan and David Phillips bring great distinction to the difficult art of compressing wisdom into tabloid form (although, of the tabloids the *Daily Mail*, Millan's paper, gives the best coverage in terms of column inches).

Richard Baerlein worked first on the *Sporting Chronicle* before the war, then afterwards for 10 years on the *Evening Standard*. He has been racing correspondent of *The Observer* for more than 23 years, and of *The Guardian* for nearly 20. Experience built over these years, and an unrivalled grasp of the betting scene help to make his column indispensable, particularly in the assessment of big handicaps and other big races. Not a man for 'perhaps,' 'seems to have a chance' or 'on the other hand', his direct style is unique, and a great pleasure to read.

John Oaksey — as John Lawrence he had a great reputation as an amateur rider under National Hunt rules before he joined the *Daily Telegraph* 30 years ago, and *Horse and Hound* a little later. As Marlborough in the *Daily Telegraph*, Audax in *Horse and Hound*, and under his own name in the *Sunday Telegraph* the racing scene is enriched by the elegance with which he describes it. No one has a more apt turn of phrase; for example, when once describing the real distance of a short-head victory as he wrote 'no more than the thickness of the paper on a bookmaker's cigar.' The late Clive Graham, when he was the distinguished Scout of the *Daily Express* once said to me about John with no malice, but maybe a little envy: 'I suppose he must run out of words one day.' So far there is no sign of it.

Like John Lawrence, Brough Scott also graduated into journalism from National Hunt riding as an amateur. Brough ghosted a 'Lester Piggott' column for the *Evening Standard* and is now at the top of his profession, with a great gift for transmitting the racing experience to paper, as well as presenting it on television. *The Sunday Times* does not give racing the coverage it deserves, but Brough Scott is always worth reading.

Sunday papers
Racing, except from the *Sunday Telegraph*, *Sunday Express* and *Mail on Sunday* gets a poor deal these days. For a long time it has been fighting a losing battle with soccer in the winter, and cricket and athletics in the summer, depending on the obsession of various sports editors with those activities. In particular, the amount of space grudgingly allowed to reports in popular Sunday papers of racing on Saturdays shows neither recognition of the immense popularity of the sport, nor the fact that most important racing takes place on that day. Possibly, in this area, television is to blame, the wrong assumption being that if racing enthusiasts did not go racing they will have seen the action live the previous afternoon on television, and if they did go to the races they will have seen both the real thing and a re-run on Saturday evening. The notion that anyone might not have seen television is beyond the wit of any popular newspaper today. Among the popular Sundays, however, the day is saved for racing by Tom Forrest in the *Sunday Express* (he used to be backed up by Dick Francis). Over the years, he has maintained a consistent high standard of informed comment. In the *Mail on Sunday* Ivor Herbert brings an ex-trainer's eye, and a sharp pen to bear on the racing scene in some excellent features.

Sporting Dailies
The Sporting Life, which long ago incorporated the popular Victorian racing

paper *Bell's Life of London*, has established itself over the years as the paper which everyone professionally connected with racing, trainers, jockeys, bookmakers, the rest of the racing press, as well as anyone else seriously interested in racing, must buy. *The Life* provided, and continues to provide a paper almost entirely devoted to racing, with detailed cards for every meeting, full form summaries, entries for future big races, four day declarations, special reports from Newmarket and much else besides. Opposition consisted of the early editions of the London evening papers, and the *Sporting Chronicle*, which had a circulation mainly in the north of England, and which was a product of the great Thomson presses at Withy Grove, Manchester but gradually (and sadly) the opposition has folded. One by one the London evenings went, leaving finally only the *Standard* which, in turn, gave up its midday edition. Then the *Sporting Chronicle* ceased publication, leaving *The Sporting Life* alone in the field — not the best of situations for a newspaper; monopolies may be fine in theory, but not healthy in practice. However, in 1986 the *Racing Post* appeared, providing a rival once again for *The Sporting Life* which is livelier, more innovative and more worthwhile than it has ever been. It is required reading for anyone going racing or viewing the racing from home and telephoning a bet or using the betting shop. This is how the racecard is presented in *The Life*:

3.10 **Holsten Pils St Leger Stakes (Group 1)** 🅲4 1¾m 127yds
£120,000 added to stakes; distributed in accordance with Rule 194 (ii) (a) (Includes a fourth prize); for three yrs old, entire colts and fillies. Holsten Pils St Leger Course; £720 to enter, £630 ex unless forfeit dec by Aug 26, £450 ex if dec to run; weights: colts 9st; fillies 8st 11lb. HOLSTEN DISTRIBUTORS (UK) LTD. are most generously sponsoring this race. The added money to include a Wedgwood Dinner Service value £6,000 for the winning owner. HOLSTEN will also present a trophy value £500 to the winning trainer. The rider of the winner will receive an embroidered jockey's cap value £250. THERE WILL BE A PARADE FOR THIS RACE. (Total ent 68, 46 pay £720, 12 pay £1,350)—Closed July 9.

Penalty value: £110,592; 2nd £41,283.60, 3rd £19,741.80, 4th £8,502.60

1 1-11010	**ALLEZ MILORD(USA)** --btn fav- (Jerome Brody)............................ G Harwood	9	0	...............G Starkey 4
2 -1321	**CELESTIAL STORM(USA)** (Richard L Duchossois)........................ L M Cumani	9	0	...............S Cauthen 5
3 0-44100	**FAMILY FRIEND** (Sir Michael Sobell) W R Hern	9	0	...............W Carson 9
5 111113	**MOON MADNESS** (Lavinia Duchess of Norfolk) .... J L Dunlop	9	0	.... Pat Eddery 6
6 310311	**NISNAS** (Fahd Salman)............... P F I Cole	9	0	...................T Quinn 2
7 122102	**ROSEDALE(USA)** (N B Hunt)....... J L Dunlop	9	0	.............B Thomson 8
8 230320	**SIRK** (Cheveley Park Stud)......... C E Brittain	9	0	...............M Roberts 3
9 0-32312	**SWINK(USA)** (N B Hunt) J E Pease, in France	9	0	.............C Asmussen 1
10 111-231	**UNTOLD** (Sheikh Mohammed) ... M R Stoute	8	11	..........W R Swinburn 7

Nine runners

FORECAST: 7-2 Untold, 4 Moon Madness, 9-2 Celestial Storm, 5 Allez Milord, Nisnas, 7 Swink, 20 Sirk, 50 Family Friend, 66 Rosedale.

Last Year.—OH SO SHARP, 8-11, S Cauthen 11/8 on (H Cecil) 6 ran.

1 ALLEZ MILORD(USA) *yellow, red sash, black and white hooped sleeves, red cap*
2 CELESTIAL STORM(USA) *royal blue, yellow sash, yellow cap, blue spots*
3 FAMILY FRIEND *pale blue, yellow and white check cap*
5 MOON MADNESS *sky blue, gold quartered cap*
6 NISNAS *dark green*
7 ROSEDALE(USA) *light and dark green check, light green sleeves, green cap*
8 SIRK *red, white sash, Royal blue cap*
9 SWINK(USA) *light and dark green check, light green sleeves, white cap*
10 UNTOLD *maroon, white sleeves, maroon cap, white star*

Form is fully given, and reports fully back up the statistical account giving all the details of running, betting and results.

THE figures before the horse's name indicate its placings on this season's outings, the most recent being on the right. Where a hyphen appears, form figures to the left of it are figures from last season. Where a diagonal stroke appears, form figures on the left are from previous seasons.

Figures in brackets after the name indicate the horse's age and weight in stones and pounds that it is set to carry. The weight only is given where a race is for horses all of the same age.

For two-year-olds only, the foaling date and, where available or applicable, the purchase price, are shown in parentheses immediately following the name.

The letters that come next indicate the horse's colour and sex (example: "b c" — bay colt) and the names that follow are those of its sire, dam and grandsire. Next in black type is the horse's winning record — year, distance, state of the going and course. The total win prize money is then given, with this season's winnings in parentheses for all except two-year olds.

For the horse's most recent outings the nature of the information given is largely self-evident.

The monetary figure is the value of the race to the winner. The letters "bl" after the jockey's name indicate that the horse wore blinkers, visor or a hood. A figure with an asterisk (e.g. 5*), after the name indicates that the jockey was a claiming rider, and the figure denotes how many pounds he claimed. In all cases the weight the horse is shown as having carried is the actual weight carried after deduction of any allowance.

-/, 3 ᵛ,   ⸗ Cay(USA) (9-ᴸ, ⸗/; ᵛ , ⸗. 1½l, 2l, ½l, 2l, ½l. 1m 41.21s (a 2.71s). (Following a stewards' inquiry, Bold Arrangement was relegated to fourth position and second place awarded to Nomrood). SR: 73/68/62/ 60/54/52.

11-11 DANCING BRAVE(USA) (9-0) b c
Lyphard(USA) — Navajo Princess by Drone. 1985, 1m firm (Newmarket), 1m good to firm (Sandown); 1986, 1m good (Newmarket), 1m soft (Newmarket). £129,312 (£122,545).

May 3, Newmarket, 1m (3-y-o), good, £107,145: (Group 1) 1 DANCING BRAVE(USA) (9-0 , G Starkey , 3), held up, progress over 3f out, led over 1f out, quickened clear, impressive (15 to 8 fav op 2 to 1 tchd 85 to 40); 2 Green Desert(USA) (9-0 , 9); 3 Huntingdale (9-0 ., 12); 4 SHARROOD(USA) (9-0 , W Carson , 1), ran on from 3f out, stayed on final furlong (14 to 1 tchd 16 to 1); 15 Ran. 3l, 1½l, hd, 1½l, ½l, sht hd. 1m 40s (a 1.1s). SR: 47/38/ 33/32/27/25.

April 17, Newmarket, 1m (3-y-o), soft, £15,400: (Group 3) 1 DANCING BRAVE(U-SA) (8-7, G Starkey, 6), well placed, led over 1f out, not extended (11 to 8 fav op 5 to 4 tchd 6 to 4); 2 FARAWAY DANCER-(USA) (8-7, S Cauthen, 11), chased leaders, led over 2f out until over 1f out, ran on same pace (9 to 2 op 7 to 2 tchd 5 to 1); 3 MASHKOUR(USA) (8-7, W Ryan, 9), good headway over 3f out, every chance from 2f out, not quicken inside final furlong (14 to 1 op 12 to 1 tchd 16 to 1); 8 SHARROOD-(USA) (8-7, W Carson, 10), well placed until hampered and lost place over 2f out (11 to 2 op 5 to 1 tchd 6 to 1); 11 Ran. 1l, ½l, 6l, 2l, 6l. 1m 49.96s (a 11.06s). SR: 18/15/ 13/-/-/-.

Nov 1, Newmarket, 1m (2-y-o), firm, £3,844: 1 DANCING Bᴿ ᵛᴲ(USA) (9-2, G ᵗkey, 9) ⸗ᴸᵘᵗ   ⸗ₙ ₒᵤₜ

3.30 Derby Stakes
3-y-o
colts & fillies
1½m
£239,260

1-11 ALLEZ MILORD(USA) (9-0) b c
Tom Rolfe — Why Me Lord by Bold Reasoning. 1985, 1m good (Newmarket); 1986, 1½m heavy (Goodwood), 1m 1f good (Newmarket). £26,831 (£21,401).

May 21, Goodwood, 1½m (3-y-o), heavy, £16,934: 1 ALLEZ MILORD(USA) (8-12, G Starkey, 6), held up, progress 4f out, led approaching last 2f, pushed clear (5 to 6 op 5 to 4 tchd 4 to 5); 2 Badarbak (8-12, 1); 3 Laabas (8-12, 4); 8 Ran. 5l, 3l, 20l, 6l, not taken. 2m 53.68s (a 18.48s). SR: 46/36/30/ -/-/-.

May 1, Newmarket, 1m 1f (3-y-o), good, £4,467: 1 ALLEZ MILORD(USA) (9-6, G Starkey, 6), chased leaders, led 3f out ⸗ₑₙₑd   ⸗ᵗ ⸗ᵗ ₛₜₐᵥₑd on ⸗'

3.30—EVER READY DERBY STAKES (Group 1) (3-y-o colts and fillies) of £402.100; 1st 2nd £90,483, 3rd £44,241.50, 4th £20,115.50. One mile and a half.

SHAHRASTANI (USA), ch c Nijinsky-Shademah, by Thatch (Aga Khan) 9-0
           W R Swinburn 1 (10)
DANCING BRAVE (USA), b c Lyphard - Navajo Princess (K Abdulla) 9-0 .... G Starkey 2 (6)
MASHKOUR (USA), ch c Irish River - Sancta Rose (Prince Ahmed Salman) 9-0
           S Cauthen 3 (3)
Faraway Dancer (USA), 9-0
           W Ryan 4 (16)
Nisnas, 9-0 .... P Waldron 5 (11)
Flash Of Steel, 9-0 ... M J Kinane 6 (5)
Sirk, 9-0 .... P Robinson 7 (17)
Sharrood (USA), 9-0 .... W Carson 8 (1)
Mr John, 9-0 .... T Ives 9 (2)
Allez Milord (USA), 9-0
           C Asmussen 10 (14)
Nomrood (USA), 9-0 ...... T Quinn 11 (12)
Jareer (USA), 9-0 .... B Rouse 12 (4)
Then Again, 9-0 .... R Guest 13 (8)
Bold Arrangement, 9-0
           C McCarron 14 (13)
Arokar (Fr), 9-0 .. Y Saint-Martin 15 (15)
Fioravanti (USA), 9-0 .. C Roche 16 (9)
Wise Counsellor (USA), 9-0
           Pat Eddery 17 (7)
17 RAN. Off 3.44
Winner bred in USA by Owner; trained by M R Stoute at Newmarket. Distances: ½l, 2½l, hd, sht hd, ¾l, ¾l, 1l, hd, ½l, hd, 1l, 3l, 2½l, sht hd, 10l, not taken, (Photo 3rd). Official time: 2m 37.13s (a 2.13s).

STARTING PRICES

2 Dancing Brave(USA): Opened 5-2, touched 11-4. Bets of £5,500-£2,000 four times, £2,750-£1,000 twice, £5,000-£2,000, £2,500-£1,000 eight times, £13,500-£6,000, £9,000-£4,000 twice, £4,500-£2,000 six times, £2,700-£1,200, £2,250-£1,000 five times, £1,800-£800, £1,125-£500 three times, £2,125-£1,000 three times, £1,700-£800, and £4,000-£2,000 three times, including office money. Early afternoon bets of £15,000-£5,000, £6,000-£2,000, £3,000-£1,000 three times, £2,400-£800, £1,500-£500 three times, £11,000-£4,000 and £2,750-£1,000 five times.
11-2 SHAHRASTANI(USA): Opened 4-1, touched 6-1. Bets of £5,000-£800, £3,000-£500, £5,500-£1,000 twice, £4,500-£1,000 twice and £2,000-£500 each way. Early afternoon bets of £11,000-£2,000 and £3,200-£800.
8 Allez Milord(USA): Opened 6-1, touched 9-1 in places. Bets of £10,000-£1,200 twice, £5,000-£600 and £5,000-£700.
12 Bold Arrangement: Opened 12-1, touched 14-1. Bet of £18,000-£1,500.
12 Mashkour(USA): Opened 12-1, touched 13-1 in places and 10-1. Bets of £12,000-£1,000, £10,000-£800, £5,000-£400 five times and £10,000-£1,000 each way. Early afternoon business: 14-1 and 12-1 laid.
16 Jareer(USA): Opened 16-1, touched 20-1. Bets of £10,000-£600 twice and £8,000-£500.
16 Wise Counsellor(USA): Opened 12-1.
18 Arokar(Fr): Opened 16-1, touched 20-1. Bet of £4,000-£200 ... af-

3 **Mashkour (USA)**, switched right three out, good progress from two out, finished well.
4 **Faraway Dancer (USA)**, pressed leaders, every chance two out, stayed on final furlong.
5 **Nisnas**, with leader until weakened two out.
6 **Flash Of Steel**, ran on last three furlongs, never nearer.
7 **Sirk**, well behind until some progress last three furlongs.
8 **Sharrood (USA)**, spread a plate before start, never troubled leaders.
9 **Mr John**, started slowly, headway when not clear ran two and a half furlongs out, hampered one and a half did not recover.
10 **Allez Milord (USA)**, well in touch until no progress three out.
11 **Nomrood (USA)**, led for over nine furlongs, soon beaten.
12 **Jareer (USA)**, never dangerous.
13 **Then Again**, tracked leaders nine furlongs.
14 **Bold Arrangement**, never reached challenging position.
15 **Arokar (Fr)**, pressed leaders till over two out.
16 **Fioravanti (USA)**, in touch nine furlongs.
17 **Wise Counsellor (USA)**, well placed until weakened well over two out.

SHAHRASTANI (USA) ch

Shademah	Shamim	Le Haar	Vieux Manoir
			Mince Pie
		Diamond Drop	Charlottesville
			Martine
	Thatch	Forli	Aristophanes
			Trevisa
		Thong	Nantallah
			Rough Shod
Nijinsky b 1967	Flaming Page	Bull Page	Bull Lea
			Our Page
		Flaring Top	Menow
			Flaming Top
	Northern Dancer	Nearctic	Nearco
			Lady Angela
		Natalma	Native Dancer
			Almahmoud

DANCING BRAVE (USA) b

Navajo Princess	Olmec	Pago Pago	Matrice
			Pompilla
		Chocolate Beau	Beau Max
			Otra
	Drone	Sir Gaylord	Turn-To
			Something Royal
		Cap And Bells	Tom Fool
			Ghazni
Lyphard b 1969	Goofed	Court Martial	Fair Trial
			Instantaneous
		Barra II	Formor
			La Favorite
	Northern Dancer	Nearctic	Nearco
			Lady Angela
		Native Dancer	

Among the special features, Gerald Delamere's analysis for big-race meetings is penetrating, and also provides some long priced winners from time to time.

Racing Post — in choosing a tabloid form for a racing paper, I feel the *Racing Post* made a basic error. Since much of the paper consists of form details it makes page turning a tiresome task compared with looking at the broadsheet *Life*. The innovation of colour has, so far, had mixed success but one advantage colour has brought is in illustrating on big race days the racing colours of owners. Innovations have also been made in the actual presentation of card and form which, though not to everyone's taste, seem eminently clear to me:

Third Race 3.45 [£1]

The Royal Hunt Cup (Handicap)   Hcap0-75 1m Straight

Stakes: £25,000 added For: 3yo + rated 0-75 Penalties: winner since 14May 5lb, 1 £5,500 win 7lb Entries: 102 Weights published: 5 Jun Weights raised: 1lbs Minimum Weight: 7-07 Weight for Age: 3yo 9-01 4yot 10-00 Penalty Value 1st £28,326 2nd £8,531 3rd £

NO	LAST 6 RACES	HORSE & OWNER		TRAINER	AGE	WEIGHT		JOCKEY	DW NO	POST MARK
1	920/023	BOLD INDIAN BF SirPhilipOppenheimer		G.Wragg	5	9-10		S Cauthen	16	82
2	50L-272	SHMAIREEKH (USA) BF D MrHamdanAl-Maktoum		P.T.Walwyn	5	9-06		Paul Eddery	29	81
3	5111-20	TREMBLANT CD MrK.Abdulla		R.V.Smyth	5	9-03		Pat Eddery	13	80
5	48/544-2	HADEER MrW.J.Gredley		C.E.Brittain	4	8-13		C Asmussen	2	94
6	8211-41	SIYAH KALEM (USA)(7ex) D DanaStudLtd		J.L.Dunlop	4	8-10		W Carson	6	84
7	120-	KING'S HEAD (USA) MrA.P.Ward		G.Harwood	4	8-06		G Starkey	22	94
8	7-05500	QUALITAIR FLYER D QualitairEngineeringLimited	K.Stone	4	8-06(b)		T Ives	20	82
9	721-032	DORSET COTTAGE D MrsS.A.Randall		W.Jarvis	4	8-05(b')		B Rouse	9	85
11	141-639	TRULY RARE (USA) D SheikhMohammed		M.R.Stoute	4	8-04		W R Swinburn	1	82
12	d106501-	COINCIDENTAL MrR.E.Sangster		M.W.Dickinson	4	8-03		R Cochrane	30	77
13	8003-00	COME ON THE BLUES CD MrsC.Pateras		C.E.Brittain	7	8-02		P Robinson	32	82
14	570L-07	RED RUSSELL MrA.J.Duffield		G.A.Calvert	5	8-02		A Bond	24	82
15	670-094	OCTOBER (USA) MrCharlesH.Wacker III.	R.W.Armstrong	4	8-00		G Baxter	4	80
16	231-744	INDIAN HAL D MrsRogerWaters		P.T.Walwyn	4	7-13		N Howe	27	87
17	5424-44	BANK PARADE D MrsSallyLeggett		J.D.J.Davies	4	7-13		A Clark	25	82
18	11616-2	TELWAAH MrHamdanAl-Maktoum		A.C.Stewart	4	7-13		M Roberts	15	91
19	3411-20	PATRIACH BF D MrPeterS.Winfield		J.L.Dunlop	4	7-12		T Quinn	12	80
20	250-300	MANCHESTERSKYTRAIN C MrPhilBowditch	L.G.Cottrell	7	7-11		R Hills	18	80
21	310-670	GILDERDALE CD AvonIndustriesLtd		N.A.C.Vigors	4	7-09		S Dawson (3)	8	78
22	52-0060	ALL FAIR D MrsA.B.Dinsmore		P.C.Haslam	5	7-09		T Williams	7	79
23	4-84332	RANA PRATAP (USA) MrsGeorgieThornberry		G.Lewis	6	7-08		M L Thomas	3	84
24	125-030	ACONITUM CD MrJohnGalvanoni		J.D.Bethell	5	7-08		A Mackay	17	76
25	0-03361	CONMAYJO(5ex) MrJ.Gibbs		D.HaydnJones	5	7-07		D Williams (7)	31	79
26	0-65776	MOORES METAL D (Stoke-on-Trent)LtdMoores		R.Hollinshead	6	7-07★		A Culhane (7)	5	75
27	9-22100	READY WIT CD MrsR.Tennant		R.Hannon	5	7-07★		D McKay	26	80
29	7-96435	RUNNING FLUSH D MrN.Capon		D.A.Oughton	4	7-07★(v')		B Crossley	19	75
30	7028-60	SCOUTSMISTAKE D MrsG.Hallett		B.A.McMahon	7	7-07★		N Carlisle	14	71
31	46450-0	JOYFUL DANCER D VistaplanReferenceSystemsLtd		W.G.A.Brooks	6	7-07★		N Adams	10	69
32	402827	XHAI D MrM.H.Tompkins		M.H.Tompkins	4	7-07★(b')		R Morse (5)	28	77
33	31-0006	BUNDABURG D MrJ.F.Watson		M.McCourt	6	7-07★		J Lowe	23	71
36	80-0021	BACK MaxJackMaxwell		M.J.F-Godley	5	7-07★		L Charnock	11	79
39	370-441	THE GAME'S UP D MrBrandonChase		P.C.Haslam	5	7-07★		G French	21	69

DECLARED RUNNERS 32 ★ Long HandicapMoores Metal 7-06Ready Wit 7-06Running Flush 7-03Scoutsmistake 7-03Joyful Dancer 7-02Xhai 7-02Bundaburg 7-02Super Trip 6-13The Game's Up 6-10

| LAST YEAR COME ON THE BLUES MrsC.Pateras | | | C.E.Brittain | 6 | 8-02 | | C.Rutter(5) | 21 | |

SPOTLIGHT

TELWAAH proved best at 7f as a three-year-old, winning three times from five starts, but promises to get further this year and, from what looks a favoured draw, can score for Alec Stewart.

On his reappearance at Thirsk Telwaah was putting in all his best work at the finish when 3l second to Knights Secret. On the fast

ground he relishes, he is just preferred to **Dorset Cottage** who is, like the selection, a lightly-raced four-year-old. Dorset Cottage's second to Esquire at York last month marked him down as a certain future winner, and he is blinkered here.

Guy Harwood has laid out **King's Head** for this race, and admits he would have been happier had he been able to get a warm-up run into the colt.

Hadeer's second to Pennine Walk in the Diomed Stakes at Epsom was in advance of anything he had shown previously, and a line through the winner gives him a clear edge over **Truly Rare**.

Hadeer is weighted to reverse last season's Bunbury Cup placings with **Tremblant**. He represents a bigger threat than Clive Brittain's other runner, last year's winner **Come On The Blues**.

But a low draw may prove too big an obstacle to Hadeer, and I rule out **October** and **Rana Pratap** on the same grounds.

The Whitsun Cup has proved an outstanding guide to this race, and this year's winner **Siyah Kalem** is an obvious danger, though he could be hard-pressed to confirm Sandown form with **Indian Hal** and **Gilderdale**, who are 7lb better off here.

BETTING FORECAST: 8-1 Siyah Kalem, 9-1 Tremblant, 10-1 Hadeer, 12-1 Bold Indian, Indian Hal, 14-1 Rana Pratap, Telwaah, 16-1 Patriach, Kings Head, Truly Rare, Shmaireekh, 18-1 Gilderdale, 20-1 Dorset Cottage, October, 25-1 Aconitum, Bundaburg, Come on the Blues, Conmayjo, Super Trip, 33-1 bar

The betting forecasts, in particular, are excellent and *The Life*'s new rival has first-class coverage from George Ennor and Tim Richards, and the advantage of the well informed breeding articles of Tony Morris.

Timeform

This was the brainchild of Phil Bull who started *Timeform* in the late 1940s, using, as the name implies, time figures to back up his inimitable comments and shrewd observation of individual horses to arrive at a rating figure for every horse with form. *Timeform*, based at Halifax in Yorkshire, has blossomed into a great organisation now run by Reg Griffin as Managing Director, while Phil Bull is Governing Director. Its comments published in its weekly Black Book (which used to be pocket-size, and now is a hefty volume) are quite indispensable to any serious racegoer, but it may be as well that horses are unable to read ('a poor plater now', 'an arrant rogue', 'a jade'). The illustrations show how detailed *Timeform* is, both for Flat and Jumps, as well as its specially produced racecards overleaf.

SONIC LADY (USA) 3 b.f. Nureyev 131—Stumped 117 (Owen An- 130
thony 102) (1985 6f*) lengthy, medium-sized filly; showed a tremendous turn of foot when 2-length winner of Goffs Irish 1000
Guineas (from Lake Champlain) at the Curragh in May and Coronation Stakes (beating Embla) at Royal Ascot in June; successful
twice at Newmarket, always going very easily in Nell Gwyn Stakes
on reappearance and never looking likely to be beaten in Child
Stakes in July; sweating, third, ¾ length and a short head behind
Midway Lady and Maysoon, in General Accident 1000 Guineas
at Newmarket on second start; suited by 1m; yet to race on very
soft going but acts on any other; will prove extremely difficult to
beat (7d* 8g³ 8d* 8f* 8m*). M. Stoute.

WEST TIP 9 b.g. Gala Performance—Astryl (Vulgan) (1984/5 c24s   c154
c24s³ c29d* c25s* c25s* c25g* c36d^F c29f) big, strong, good-   —
topped gelding; very useful chaser; excellent second to Burrough
Hill Lad on unfavourable terms in Rehearsal Chase at Chepstow
in November; 8 lengths second to Door Latch in valuable SGB
Handicap Chase at Ascot the following month; ran moderately
next 2 starts but returned to his very best when winning handicap at Newbury on latest outing; rallied well to beat Beau Ranger
2½ lengths after being outpaced on home turn; disputing lead
and seemingly full of running when falling second Becher's in
Seagram Grand National at Liverpool on penultimate outing last
season (would probably have won); needs a good test of stamina;
needs some give in the ground to be seen to best advantage and
acts well in the soft, but is possibly unsuited by heavy; game
and genuine; not an easy ride, and is suited by strong handling;
normally a sound jumper; clearly in good heart (c24m c24d²
c24g² c30v c24v c25m c24d* Mar 22). M. Oliver.

The information on **THE TIMEFORM CARD** is concisely presented as below for practical use in winner finding.

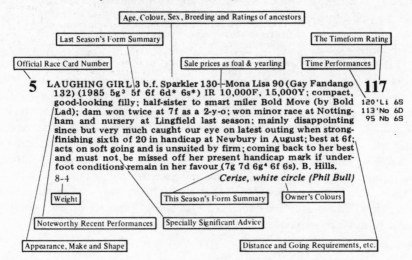

HOW TO USE THE TIMEFORM CARD

Start with the **RATINGS**. Of greatest importance in a race are the merits of the horses and their relative chances at the weights. That's what the ratings indicate. An outstanding rating implies an outstanding chance on previous form. But no horse will run to its rating if it is called upon to race at an inappropriate distance, or on unsuitable going, or over a track on which it cannot act. So for every horse with a good chance on the ratings it is necessary to check whether there is anything in its **COMMENTARY** to suggest that it might not be at home with the track, distance and going it has to face in today's race. Of the three things, the going is generally the most critical factor. Not infrequently it has more influence on the result of a race than the intrinsic merit of the horses or anything else, especially in handicaps, where the horses are supposed to be weighted to have equal chances. It pays to study the commentaries, for the performance of every horse is bound up with its merit *and* its racing character.

THIRD RACE   TRW 146 148 141 133 131

3.45   The Gold Cup (Group 1)   2½m

£60,000 added   WFA 4 9-10, 3 8-3

---

301 BOURBON BOY 4 br.g. Ile de Bourbon 133—Sofala 103 (Home   **113**
Guard 129) (1985 8g 12d* 14g* 15d* 16f 14d* 18f² 18m³) lightly-
built gelding; good mover; useful handicapper; successful last sea-   116'Nm18M
son at Ripon, Nottingham, Ayr and York and ran well when placed   109'Yo14D
in Doncaster Cup and Tote Cesarewitch; had stiff task when eighth   91'Ri12D
of 10, finding little under pressure, to Longboat in valuable race
at Sandown in May latest outing; suited by a test of stamina; probably acts on any going; best with waiting tactics (14d 16m). M.
Stoute.
9-0   *Maroon, white sleeves and star on cap*
                              (Sheikh Mohammed)

302 EASTERN MYSTIC 4 b.c. Elocutionist—Belle Pensee (Ribot 142)   **129**
(1985 12g² 12m² 12g² 12g* 12d² 14.6m* 13.3f*) big colt; very
useful performer; successful last season (not raced at 2 yrs) in ama-   126'Nb13F
teur ri̶d̶e̶r̶s̶ event a̶t̶ Newmarket £18.500 h̶a̶n̶d̶i̶c̶a̶p̶ Doncaster ¹⁵ 'No15M

moderate, ...en sweating up (12s 16m). G. Lewis.
9-0   *Dark blue, red chevron and cap, white sleeves*
                                                    (Mrs S. Khan)

305 LONGBOAT 5 b.h. Welsh Pageant 132—Pirogue 99 (Reliance II 137) **134**
(1985 16m* 14d⁴ 20m²) lengthy, attractive horse; smart performer; 101 Sa16M
successful in 1985 in Mono Sagaro Stakes at Ascot and excellent 91'As20M
second to Gildoran, beaten ½ length staying on strongly, in Gold 83'As16M
Cup; looking extremely well, stayed on strongly after leading under
2f out when winning 10-runner Mappin And Webb Henry II Stakes
at Sandown in May by 2½ lengths from Seismic Wave; suited by a
thorough test of stamina; suited by top-of-the-ground; sure to
continue running well in top company (13.3s 16m*). R. Hern.
9-0   *Crimson, silver braid (Mr R. D. Hollingsworth)*

306 ORE 8 ch.h. Ballymore 123—Minatonka (Linacre 133) (1985 NR) **128**
big. stro~ ~orse· sma~·   ~er (rated 11~   ~~~ 6-

The Black Books contain not only form figures and pithy comments, but excellent interviews with trainers, plans and details of racecourses.

Weekly papers

The Sporting Life Weekender and *Raceform Handicap Book* — both these publications in their different ways provide excellent service in filling out the day to day racing details, and providing background material, much of it fascinating and of value in assessing the immediate past and future. Both provide, in weekly instalments, form records which can be collected together to give a permanent record. For those who cannot afford the more established form books, this is more than useful, but the format means that the record is essentially for study at home rather than pocket-size reference on the racecourse. They also give good resumés of what the betting market has shown in the way of likely future winners during the preceding week. The *Handicap Book*, which celebrated its centenary in 1987, prints successfully in colour, while the *Weekender* scores with some first-class interviews with trainers, particularly the smaller ones. Full coverage is given to the racing immediately ahead with associated special features on big occasions, as well as sections on time figures, and updating of handicap ratings.

Racing and Football Outlook — an inexpensive little paper well worth its modest price. As the title suggests, football pool coverage in good detail shares the scene with racing, all supplemented by a *Weekend Special.* The only paper left where a back page column of tips, sometimes containing long priced winners, retains an Edwardian vocabulary ('one to keep on the right side is ...' and 'strong information concerns ...') hinting of touts still with binoculars at the ready on the Newmarket gallops and elsewhere — very refreshing in a computerised age.

Selected magazines

Pacemaker International (monthly) — incorporating the old *Stud and Stable*, this is a first-class glossy magazine, beautifully produced and with stunning colour photographs including those of the incomparable Gerry Cranham. In the past two decades, *Pacemaker* has built up a great reputation for authoritative comment, use of the foremost writers, and a sound coverage at a level not possible in daily or weekly publications of the entire racing scene, its personalities, and, notably, the ebb and flow of politics and policies in the bloodstock breeding world. It is expensive, but well worth it.

The European Racehorse (five issues per year) — rather more expensive, but, in real terms, nothing like as costly as its predecessor, *The British Racehorse*, used to be. This was a post-war venture with which that great racing personality, the late Tom Blackwell, was associated, and past editors include Bernard O'Sullivan, John Hislop and the late Michael Seth-Smith. The present version reflects the still expanding international aspect of racing, but, like *The British Racehorse*, concentrates on the breeding scene as well as maintaining a good sense of the history of the Turf with some first class contributions, and results with pictures and pedigrees of winners from the top-class meetings in the UK and Europe.

Horse and Hound (weekly) — well worth buying for the breeding articles of Peter Willett and others, Richard Pitman and the comment of the present Audax, John Oaksey, on current racing.

Racing Monthly — made its first appearance in April 1986 at 95p. It is rather reminiscent of the old *William Hill Racing Review* both in its A5 format and approach. This new magazine is aimed at a more popular readership than those of publications dealt with above.

Selected Annuals
To buy every one of the annuals listed below would leave no change out of about £200. Most of them are indispensable, however, to the serious follower of racing who would find the outlay easily recouped as a result of the information contained in these books, and nowhere else. Those considered most essential are marked with an asterisk.

*Ruff's Guide to the Turf — this oldest established racing annual, and the equivalent in racing terms of *Whitaker*, is now much fatter (and relatively more expensive) than it used to be, partly because it usefully incorporates *The Sporting Life Annual*, including all the previous season's Flat results and many other statistics, and partly because it has been much improved and expanded in scope in recent years with a much more up-to-date and lively presentation. *Ruff's* itself now has 556 pages (510 in total 20 years ago) plus a further 804 pages of *Sporting Life Annual*. Unrivalled in its comforting obesity as the racing man's most thumbed reference book, it contains chapter and verse of all Jockey Club rules, comprehensive breeding details, including a list of all the progeny of successful stallions, and sires of dams of winners, a huge range of statistics and reference lists of jockeys and trainers and their records, and much else besides, including features summing up the racing year, and a section of nearly 100 pages giving big race results, mostly back to 1900.

Trainers Review (Flat and National Hunt Editions) — is one publication without which the present day punter would be unable to grasp the significance of a previous season's form and apply the knowledge for future use. The book is divided between the trainers themselves, all the winners, kinds of races, percentages, profit and loss, with month by month analysis; and racecourses, giving leading trainers, jockeys and how the favourite fared. How does Willie Carson rate at Pontefract? Is it worth following Fred Winter at Devon and Exeter? Do the favourites at Hamilton Park show a profit? *Trainers Review* has it all, and the pages reproduced below (for O. Sherwood in the latest National Hunt edition, and for a racecourse chosen at random) give the style in which it does so.

O Sherwood (Upper Lambourn, Berks)

	Races Run	1st	2nd	3rd	4th	Unpl	Per cent	£1 Level Stake
Hurdles	110	27	7	8	14	54	24.5	+ 16.80
Chases	77	21	10	9	9	28	27.3	+ 10.98
Totals	187	48	17	17	23	82	25.7	+ 27.78

	W-R	%	£1 Level Stake		W-R	%	£1 Level Stake
August	0-7	-	- 7.00	January	2-24	8.3	- 13.50
September	1-7	14.3	- 2.50	February	1-4	25.0	- 2.20
October	4-8	50.0	+ 2.87	March	8-35	22.9	+ 5.63
November	6-27	22.2	- 1.27	April	10-23	43.5	+ 22.78
December	7-22	31.8	+ 12.88	May	9-30	30.0	+ 10.09

	W-R	%	£1 Level Stake		W-R	%	£1 Level Stake
Nov Hdles	17-82	20.7	- 19.45	Selling	0-0	-	0.00
H'cap Hdles	9-25	36.0	+ 26.25	Amateur	0-3	-	- 3.00
Nov Chses	8-34	23.5	- 12.44	Hunter Chses	8-14	57.1	+ 30.42
H'cap Chses	5-27	18.5	- 5.00	N H Flat	1-2	50.0	+ 11.00

Course Grade	W-R	%	£1 Level Stake	First Time Out	W-R	%	£1 Level Stake
Group 1	13-54	24.1	+ 16.92	Hurdles	5-29	17.2	+ 5.50
Gr⌐⌐p 2	8-30	⌐⌐.7	1.42	Chases	3-1⌐	23.1	+ 6.00

TAUNTON (Group 4)

Leading Trainers 1984-86

	Nov Hdles	H'cap Hdles	Nov Chses	H'cap Chses	Total W-R	Per cent	£1 Level Stake
M C Pipe	9-42	3-21	3-7	0-1	15-71	21.1	+ 7.27
R J Holder	2-11	4-6	0-1	0-0	6-18	33.3	+ 7.39
D R C Elsworth	4-18	1-5	0-3	0-0	5-26	19.2	- 2.46
L G Kennard	2-16	0-7	1-3	1-5	4-31	12.9	- 23.02
W G Turner	1-13	2-6	1-7	0-6	4-32	12.5	+ 38.00
J Thorne	1-10	0-5	2-10	1-9	4-34	11.8	- 6.50
R J Hodges	1-21	0-14	2-6	1-12	4-53	7.5	- 24.00
⌐ ⌐ ⌐e-Iudson	1-1	2-3	0-0	0 ⌐	3-4	75.0	+ 13.⌐⌐

Leading Jockeys

	1st	2nd	3rd	Unpl	Total Mts	Per cent	£1 Level Stake
C Brown	7	4	1	20	32	21.9	+ 8.55
P Leach	7	5	4	23	39	17.9	- 13.47
P Richards	6	2	3	19	30	20.0	+ 16.48
B Powell	6	6	6	38	56	10.7	- 39.35
J White	3	0	2	4	9	33.3	+ 3.50
P Murphy	3	0	0	9	12	25.0	+ 1.50
J Lower	3	2	1	7	13	23.1	+ 4.25
S Earle	3	0	1	19	23	13.0	+ 34.00
N Coleman	3	3	2	18	26	11.5	- 12.84
P Dever	3	2	4	21	30	10.0	- 20.87
M Pitman	2	2	0	2	6	33.3	+ 12.00
S Moore	2	0	2	4	8	25.0	+ 20.25

How the Favourites Fared

	W-R	Per cent	£1 Level Stake		W-R	Per cent	£1 Level Stake
Nov Hdles	22-53	41.5	- 2.85	Nov Chses	4-18	22.2	- 7.93
H'cap Hdles	3-21	14.3	- 13.96	H'cap Chses	8-23	34.8	- 3.19
Totals	25-74	33.8	- 16.81	Totals	12-41	29.3	- 11.12
All favs	37-115	32.2	- 27.93				

Trainers Record (Flat and National Hunt editions) — covers the same area as *Trainers Review* but in a different style, and with the opinions of its contributors on each trainer. Some of these are pretty unsparing, and others (like all opinions) open to dispute. That they add a dimension to the figures is undeniable, but the presentation and particularly the statistics themselves would be clearer and easier to appreciate if they were typeset.

*Raceform Horses in Training — another little book which has long been an automatic yearly addition to the shelf. Pocket-size, the title is self-explanatory. The 1986 edition contains details of 14,900 horses, 565 trainers (some in France and Ireland) both Flat and National Hunt or both, as well as useful details about racecourses, jockeys' weights and retainers etc. The illustration opposite gives a sample of the kind of information contained:

MR. N. A. GASELEE—continued

20 **KELLSBORO' JILL**, 5, ch m Rymer—Kellsboro' Jean
21 **KELLY'S BOY**, 6, b g Pitskelly—Ishtar Abu
22 **KING DAITHI**, 7, b g Linacre—Night Caller
23 **KING NIMROD**, 4, b g Kala Shikari—Princess Fair
24 **LADY KILLANE**, 4, ch f Reform—Cease Fire
25 **LAST ARGUMENT**, 12, b g No Argument—Last Dew
26 **LEADING ARTIST**, 11, b g Menelek—Suvonne
27 **MR DAWSON**, 7, ch g Ete Indien (USA)—Niamh Oir
28 **MR MOUSE**, 7, ch g New Member—Miss Mouswald
29 **MR PINKERTON**, 7, ch g Pauper—Chalk Slipper
30 **NUT ROYAL**, 4, b g Sagaro—Montelimar
31 **OLIVER ANTHONY**, 6, ch g Owen Anthony—Hergastangle
32 **PRIVATE VIEWS**, 5, b g Radical—Informal Vue
33 **PUCKS PLACE**, 5, ch g Midsummer Night II—Pirate's Cottage
34 **RECORD DANCER**, 6, b g Dancer's Image (USA)—Treacle
35 **THE CATCHPOOL**, 7, ch g The Ditton—Open Road
36 **WATFORD GAP**, 4, b c Dominion—Head Huntress

THREE-YEAR-OLDS

37 **NORHAM CASTLE**, b g Scott Joplyn—Gay Amanda

TWO-YEAR-OLDS

38 Gr c 30/3 Alias Smith (USA)—Northern Empress

Owners: H.R.H. The Prince Of Wales, Mrs R. W. S. Baker, Mr Julian Belfrage, Mr David Bill, Mr M. A. Boddington, Mr Edgar M. Bronfman, Lt. Col. F. J. Burnaby-Atkins, Lady Carden, Mrs E. Chappell, Mrs E. M. Charlton, Mr J. G. Charlton, Mr T. P. Charlton, Mr Charles Egerton, Mr T. E. S. Egerton, Mrs Derek Fletcher, Mr N. A. Gaselee, Capt J. A. George, Mr C. R. Glyn, Mr David A. Graham, Mr F. J. Haggas, Mrs B. P. Hall, Ld Hambleden, Imperial Inns & Taverns Limited, Mr R. J. Jenks, Mr M. S. Josephs, Sheikh Ali Abu Khamsin, Mrs R. L. Matson, Mr Neil A. McConnell, Mr N. G. Mills, Mrs G. N. Morris-Adams, Mr R. E. Morris-Adams, Maj R. F. Mortimer, Mr W. E. Norton, Mrs J. O'Brien, Mrs M. C. Peel, Mrs J. W. Phillips, Mr Ian Single, Mr A. D. Smith, Mr D. R. Stoddart, Mr Trevor Tyler, Mrs V. N. Wallis, Mrs F. Walwyn, Mrs G. Webb Bronfman, Mr Jeff Woodbridge.

Jockeys (NH): V McKevitt (10-0), P Scudamore (w.a.), S Smith-Eccles (10-3, w.a.).

Conditional: A Adams (9-4).

Lady Rider: Miss S Lawrence (9-7).

196   MR J. T. GIFFORD, Findon

Postal: **The Downs, Stable Lane, Findon, Nr.Worthing, Sussex, BN14 0RR.**

Phone: **FINDON (090 671) 2226**

1 **ADRAL (CHI)**, 5, ch g Apollo Streak (USA)—Falsia (CHI)
2 **ALEXANDRA PALACE**, 5, b g Warpath—Alexandra
3 **ARABIAN MUSIC**, 11, b g Gulf Pearl—Musical Watch
4 **AUGHRA BOURA**, 10, b g Brave Invader (USA)—Anno Domino
5 **BIT OF A DANDY**, 5, ch g Le Bavard (FR)—Fair People
6 **BLUE DART**, 6, ch g Cantab—Maisie Owen
.7 **BOLD YEOMAN**, 10, ~ ~ ~ Ruskins Bowes~

Racehorses of 19— and the yearly *Chasers and Hurdlers* — these Portway Press publications must be the most eagerly awaited annuals of all. They contain greatly expanded and rewritten versions of the *Timeform* Black Book comments on every horse that ran during the respective seasons, with illustrations, and make the most complete as well as enjoyable record to browse over and refer back to. *Racehorses* started in a modest way in the late 1940s as small green bound publications with a flat spine no more than an inch thick, which these days change hands for a hundred or so times their original cost. Like *Ruff's*, the *Timeform* annual has become stouter with age, but also, as well as branching out into National Hunt racing, larger all round, while maintaining outstanding value when judged in pence per page of shrewd and well written comment and information as shown overleaf.

FOR

to stay 2½m; probably acts on any going; usually wears blinkers; didn't run on on second outing. *J. Perrett.*

FOREST TRACK   4 b.f. Track Spare–Forest And Vale (March Past) (1984/5 16s^{pu} 16m) plating-class maiden at 2 yrs; well beaten in juvenile hurdle at —
Warwick in April. *Mrs S. Oliver.*

FOREVA GREY   4 gr.g. Averof–Roanette (Roan Rocket) (1984/5 20s 16v) well beaten on Flat, and both outings over hurdles. *A. Moore.*   —

FOREWARN   4 b.g. Fordham–Mark My Word (On Your Mark) (1984/5 16d^r 16s² 16d² 16v 18f*) fair sort; half-brother to winning hurdler Maujendor (by   118
Rose Laurel); winning stayer on Flat; sold out of J. Dunlop's stable 3,500 gns Newmarket Autumn Sales; held up when winning novice hurdle at Windsor in January and juvenile hurdle at Fontwell in April, latter by a head from Man O'Magic; jumped badly left at the last when beating Ace of Spies a short head in juvenile event at Chepstow on third outing, and was subsequently placed second; will stay 2½m; acts on firm going but best form with some give in the ground. *R. Akehurst.*

FORGE CLOSE   4 b.c. Swing Easy–Sweet Relief (Sweet Revenge) (1984/5 17h 16f⁴ 17g 17f) plater on Flat, stays 1m; poor form in early-season juvenile   85
hurdles. *J. Baker.*

FORGIVE N' FORGET   8 ch.g. Precipice Wood–Tackienne (Hard Tack) c166
(1984/5 c22s* c20s² c24g² c24d* c24g² c20d* c26g*)   —
    The cliff-hanging story of the fight to get Burrough Hill Lad fit for the Tote Cheltenham Gold Cup dominated the publicity in the run-up to the race. Burrough Hill Lad had been ante-post favourite for the 1985 Gold Cup since his victory in the event twelve months earlier, and for much of the latest season had been odds on. Seven days before the event a second Tote Cheltenham Gold Cup looked his for the taking but, as so often happens in steeplechasing, theory proved one thing, the fortunes of racing and training quite another. In no other branch of racing does injury confound so many hopes and expectations as it does in steeplechasing. Burrough Hill Lad, who injured himself at exercise the week before the Festival meeting, wasn't the only notable absentee from the Gold Cup line-up. Of fifteen horses quoted in the sponsor's ante-post betting at the end of October, only four actually ran in the Gold Cup. The 1984 runner-up Brown Chamberlin, joint-second favourite with Wayward Lad in late-October, missed the whole of the season, while Dawn Run, Observe, Lettoch and Forgive N' Forget's stable-companion Canny Danny were others ruled out by injury by the time Cheltenham came round. The participation of Forgive N' Forget was also in doubt for a time after heat was found in his off-fore foot three days before the Gold Cup. The trouble cleared up in time to allow Forgive N' Forget to take his chance, but wariness about removing the normal steel shoe on the affected foot resulted in his running in only three racing plates.
    Burrough Hill Lad's enforced withdrawal from the Tote Cheltenham Gold Cup robbed the race of some of its interest; but a thrilling finish—with sev‐
‘ the runne·   ‐ a ch‐ ‐e at the last—did much to r·   ‐he ·

Haig Superform Annual — another seasonal review, based on the Sussex-based *Superform* organisation's weekly form book, with ratings and commentaries on the first 10 horses in every race run during the previous season. Good back-up material here, although the book might be better organised and indexed.

Ladbrokes Flat Racing Companion — an excellent and very well-produced paperback with masses of information, and a little like a modern, more ambitious version of the old *Cope's Racegoers Encyclopaedia* (but without that little book's unique records of big races). The Ladbroke book contains good articles reviewing the previous season's flat racing, statistics, very useful information on racing organisations, and for those who like some fun with their betting, top tipsters' horses to follow.

Playfair Racing Annual — Christopher Poole and Valerie Burholt have gathered together an immense amount of information in this annual, with a first class section on racecourses. This is the book for anyone unable to afford *Ruff's*, and well worthwhile, in addition, for those who can.

Form books

The bedrock of finding winners is the form book in whatever form it takes. *Raceform* (and its National Hunt equivalent *Chaseform*) is the official record, published weekly in loose leaf form, the parts being put into a pocket size cord tied binder. *Raceform* is expensive (£223 for a season at present) but in return offers the fullest comments and description on how horses run. These are provided by race readers who go to every race meeting, headed by their senior man, John Sharratt, whose ability to 'read' and extract every worthwhile detail in running is unrivalled. He is backed up by a team including John Hanmer, Di Matthews, Ivor Markham and Alan Amies on a regional basis. The form book as we know it, however, has been in existence for less than half a century, and its development is greatly due to the work of an enormous, no nonsense Yorkshireman called Jack Topham, to whom John Sharratt was assistant in the late years of the 1940s, and for whom he is unstinting in his admiration: 'I think we have had some super race readers, but none to match the man I was lucky enough to be assistant to. Jack Topham was unquestionably the best race reader that the press room has ever seen. He made *Raceform* what it is today and anything I know is thanks to him.' Extracts from *Raceform* and *Chaseform* are reproduced below. (See Appendix B for meaning to abbreviations.)

Raceform

1845—1846   ASCOT, July 27, 1985

1639* Measuring *(IABalding)* 2-8-12 SCauthen (7) (hdwy 2f out: unable qckn ins fnl f) ... 1½.3
1528⁴ Dusty Dollar *(MajorWRHern)* 2-8-8 WCarson (4) (ev ch 2f out: r.o one pce) 6.4
1736 Hot Momma *(RBoss)* 2-8-8 BThomson (10) (hld up: ev ch 2f out: wknd 1f out) 2.5
1468* Little Pipers *(JRWinter)* 2-8-12 BRaymond (1) (hdwy 2f out: nvr nrr) nk.6
16⁰⁵² Security P°°⁰°⁰ '' ''Easterb⁰'' ¹² PWaldr°° '°' /°d °°°°°⁰r 4f) 7

1845 KING GEORGE VI & QUEEN ELIZABETH DIAMOND STKS (Gp 1) (C & F) £134274.00
          (£50528.20: £24499.10: £10918.70) 1½m   3-20 (3-22)

1526* **Petoski** *(MajorWRHern)* 3-8-8 WCarson (10) (lw: hdwy 3f out: swtchd & hrd rdn
          over 1f out: led wl ins fnl f: all out) .... —1
976* Oh so Sharp (Fav) *(HRACecil)* 3-8-5 SCauthen (6) (lw: 2nd st: hmpd 2f out: led
          wl over 1f out: hrd rdn: r.o wl) nk.2
1470² Rainbow Quest (USA) *(JTree)* 4-9-7 WRSwinburn (5) (lw: 3rd st: ev ch over 1f
          out: hrd rdn: r.o wl) ¾.3
1399a* Law Society (USA) *(MVO'Brien)* 3-8-8 PatEddery (8) (lw: hdwy 4f out: 5th st: ev
          ch over 1f out: unable qckn fnl f) 1½.4
1186³ Raft (USA) *(GHarwood)* 4-9-7 GStarkey (7) (hdwy fnl 2f: r.o) 1½.5
1574a* Strawberry Road (AUS) *(PLBiancone)* 6-9-7 YSaintMartin (1) (gd sort: hdwy 2f
          out: nvr nr to chal) hd.6
1399a⁴ Infantry *(BWHills)* 3-8-8 BThomson (11) (chsd ldr: led over 3f out: hung lft 2f out:
          one pce) 4.7
          Sirius Symboli (JPN) *(JRWinter)* 3-8-8 YOkabe (13) (w'like: scope: swtg: nvr
          nrr) 15.8
1574a³ Treizieme (USA) *(MZilber)* 4-9-4 ALequeux (2) (gd sort: 4th st: wknd wl over 1f
          out) 5.9
1526² Crazy (FR) *(RWArmstrong)* 4-9-7 LPiggott (4) (lw: a bhd) 2.10
1571a Princess Pati *(CCollins)* 4-9-4 PShanahan (3) (unf: prom 7f: hrd rdn: wknd 4f
          out) 6.11
1470⁴ August (USA) *(JTree)* 4-9-7 SRaymont (9) (swtg: led over 8f: 6th st: wknd over
          2f out) 5.12

4/5 Oh So Sharp, 3/1 Law Society (USA), 12/1 Rainbow Quest (USA), Strawberry Road (AUS), PETOSKI.
22/1 Crazy (FR), Raft (USA), 33/1 Infantry, 66/1 Treizieme (USA), 100/1 Sirius Symboli (JPN), Princess Pati.
1000/1 August (USA), CSF £20.80, Tote £13.90: £2.40 £1.30 £2.10 (£10.40). Marcia Lady Beaverbrook
(WEST ILSLEY) bred by Miss K Rausing. 12 Rn   2m 27.61 (U2.39)
                                                    SF—94/90/104/88'98 97

Chaseform

ATTITU...   ..., 14/1 .. ..arty(10/1—2.   ...ise...   ...... over, 100/1
Ors. CSF £46.36. Tote £11.30: £2.30 £2.10 £2.00 (£30.50). Mrs J. M. Magnier (IRELAND) bred by W.
Dower. 14 Rn   6m 45.9 (8.9)

2443   TOTE CHELTENHAM GOLD CUP (Chase)   £54900.00 (£20860.00: £10280.00:
£4760.00) 3¼m (22)   3-30 (3-32)

1834⁴ **Dawn Run** (Fav) *(MrPatrickMullins)* 8–11-9 JJO'Neill (mstkes 14th & 18th: led
2nd to 17th: led 2 out: rallied flat: drvn to ld nr fin) .... —1
1374* Wayward Lad *(MrsMDickinson)* 11–12-0 GBradley (hld up: hrd rdn 2 out: led
last: r.o wl) 1.2
1742⁴ Forgive'n Forget *(JGFitzGerald)* 9–12-0 MDwyer (hld up: led appr last: unable
qckn nr fin) 2½.3
1913³ Run and Skip *(JLSpearing)* 8–12-0 SSmithEccles (led to 1st: blnd 3rd & 13th: led
18th to 20th: one pce flat) 1.4
1319⁴ Righthand Man *(MrsMDickinson)* 9–12-0 REarnshaw (no hdwy fr 18th) 10.5
1742 Observe *(FTWinter)* 10–12-0 JDuggan (bhd fr 13th) 30.6
1742* Combs Ditch (bl) *(DRCElsworth)* 10–12-0 CBrown (bhd 15th tl carried out by
loose horse bef 20th) 0
1742³ Earls Brig *(WHamilton)* 11–12-0 PTuck (hmpd 7th: prom tl fell 15th) 0
1740 Von Trappe *(MOliver)* 9–12-0 RDunwoody (bhd whn fell 19th) 0
1834 Castle Andrea *(DJeffries)* 8–12-0 GMernagh (t.o tl p.u bef 15th) 0
1957² Cybrandian *(MHEasterby)* 8–12-0 ABrown (rdr lost irons and p.u bef 7th) 0

15/8 DAWN RUN. **7/2** Forgive'n Forget. **9/2** Combs Ditch. **15/2** Run and Skip. **8/1** Wayward Lad. **20/1**
Cybrandian. **25/1** Earls Brig. Von Trappe. Righthand Man. **50/1** Observe. **500/1** Castle Andrea. CSF £16.13.
Tote £2.50: £1.70 £1.70 £1.80 (£12.20). Mrs C. D. Hill (IRELAND) bred by J. J. Riordan. 11 Rn
6m 35.3 (1.9 under best: U1.7)
SF—99/102/97/95.75 15

Raceform also publishes a valuable service in its *Notebook*, sent weekly for filing, with a binder. This clarifies, expands, and puts into more readily understandable English the form book comments, and armed with this adjunct, not only is cryptology unnecessary in interpreting the book, but deeper significance is attached to abbreviations. Essentially the *Notebook*, the development of which has been a particular pride and responsibility of John Sharratt, is a guide to possible future winners. The simple 'Nt clr rn' ('Not clear run') of the basic form book, for example, may be turned in the *Notebook* to, 'His jockey unwisely stayed on the rails and must be considered an unlucky loser', or the horse 'didn't have the courage or the pace to battle out the situation'. Below is reproduced a page of the *Notebook*. Its comments for race 1139 can be compared with the form book. A good proportion of future winners are highlighted.

1139   Coventry Stks (Gp 3) (2y)   6f
£24,928

Cutting Blade   8-11   CAsmussen (12) ..—1
Polemos   8-11   AMurray (7) s.h.2
Amigo Sucio   8-11   SWhitworth (17) . s.h.3
Glory Forever (USA)   8-11   JLowe (14) ½.4
Brave Dancer   8-11   GStarkey (19) hd.5
Polonia (USA)   8-8   DGillespie (10) . 1½.6
19 Ran (LPiggott)   1m 17.14   (2.64)

992* Cutting Blade (b.c. Sharpo — Lady Of Renown (USA) by His Majesty (USA)) does get the six furlongs well and after this, when he looked in danger of being tightened up, his courage cannot be questioned. He was all out close home and the race was decided on the nod. (11/1: 8/1—12/1)

745* Polemos, making a great deal of his own running as he had done when winning at Doncaster, ran on in the bravest fashion inside the final furlong but could not prevent Cutting Blade turning the tables on him this time. (9/1)

ROYAL ASCOT, June 17

853* Amigo Sucio, winner of his races at Salisbury and Thirsk, had every chance from the distance. He edged a little to his left a furlong out but could not be faulted close home, with the race being decided on the nod. (20/1: op 12/1)

976 Glory Forever (USA) put in some solid work through the last furlong and a half and there was certainly no disgrace in this effort. (33/1)

1054* Brave Dancer did little wrong, having every chance from below the distance, and never flinched on the run to the line. (9/1)

819G* Polonia (USA), coming to race with the group on the stands' rails, only began to give best late inside the final furlong. Lean and hard fit, she looked very sensible on the way to post and in the race. (15/8 Fav.)

622 Someone Else (8-11 TIves: 4), running on at the finish, could not land a blow in time. (33/1)

848 ᴛ --ʰᵗ·   ᶦᵒ ₁₁ ᴍᵀᵀⁱˡˡⁱ· ᶦᵒ\ ʰₐ⁻ᵈ ᶦᵒ

A further Raceform service is the *Private Handicap* or *Yellow Book*, published daily. This gives the Raceform handicapper's assessment compared with the weights for any given race. Those at the top are considered to have the best winning chance.

AYR FRIDAY 20 JUNE 1986

5.0 Goukscroft H'cap 7f

Mr Jay-Zee	- 2	Moninsky	+ 2
Twicknam Garden	- 1	Qualitair King	+ 2
Lost Opportunity	- 1	Rossett	+ 2
Winter Words	- 1	Spring Pursuit	+ 3
Zio Peppino	-	Tit Willow	+ 3
Chablisse	-	Black Diamond	+ 3
Trade High	-	Barnes Star	+ 3
Abjad	+ 1	Warthill Lady	+ 3
Star's ᴰ⁻ˡⁱᵍʰᵗ	+ 1	ᶜᵒˡᵈᵉⁿ ᴰⁱˢᶜ	+ ᵒ

Aside from 'straight' form books, there are several other services, such as those provided by *Superform* (*Superform Weekly*), *Computer Racing Form*, *Juniorator*, and the *Professional Sporting Bureau*. The last named, based at Epsom, and run by Marten Julian, can be recommended particularly for its Bulletin Books which often contain good information, while all of them have individual approaches which help the business of winner finding. But for solid analysis the form book cannot be beaten, and is rivalled for value only by *Timeform* and its various publications.

Television and Radio
The service provided by television goes beyond the mere showing of the races. TV-am and Jim McGrath apart, which is well worth watching for a good racing preview, the paddock comments are of great value. The other valuable service is in showing up to the minute shifts in the betting market, in conditions far more comfortable than either the racecourse or betting shop. Television coverage, at the time of writing, appears to be shrinking, particularly that of the BBC. They still have a great team, however, including production man Ian Robertson, Julian Wilson, and the best commentator of them all, Peter O'Sullevan. This is complemented on radio by Peter Bromley's lively coverage on BBC Radio 2.

CHAPTER SIX

A Compendium of Bets

Men not given to Guessing, piled on the Dibs in such a way as to make Settling Day seem a remote possibility . . .

Royal Ascot, the Derby, the Grand National are all occasions to quicken the pulse, if not the typewriter. They are looked forward to, written about *ad nauseam*, and slaved at, in varying degrees, by professional racing correspondents who all harbour yet a dread in their hearts: the extra-runners, not the racecard variety, but those who are, more or less, colleagues from the distant reality of Fleet Street, a place infrequently visited, but which pays the wages.

Royal Ascot produces the hoorays from gossip columns, and charming diary ladies. The Derby flushes out a corps of reporters eager to apply substance to any rumour that the favourite has been got at. (The only good story I can recall on this marginal fringe concerns the occasion when the winning post was pinched the night before the race. This resulted in a *Daily Mirror* scoop for John Godley, who was roaming around as a freelance.)

The Grand National also brings its own battalion of reporters seen out only once a year. Among them was always Bernard McIlwaine, taking a break with his racing *alter ego* from his usual role as a *Mirror* Group film critic. He shared with me a fondness for the lines which appear at the head of this page, a *Sporting Pink* quotation with an unmistakable echo of fearless Plungers, and the riches and ruin of the Turf in Edwardian days. When, at the bar of the Lord Nelson Hotel, Liverpool, late on the Friday night before the race, I heard it whispered into my ear in a gravelly, laughing, Canadian accent, I knew that Bernie's train had arrived at Lime Street, and that the Grand National could take place. It was a merry, annual, consecrated experience; now Bernie is dead, but this chapter is very much his sort of territory.

Before listing some of the bets it is possible to pile the 'Dibs' on, there are various contingencies and other matters to deal with and clarify, such as betting tax, the definition of 'placed' horses and so on. The contingencies are covered by Tattersalls' Rules on Betting which appear in full in Appendix A, but which may be summarised in their relevant parts as follows:—

Horses withdrawn without coming under starter's orders
Tattersalls' rule 4(c) deals with this. If there is insufficient time to form a new market excluding the withdrawn horse, winning returns on the remaining horses which take part in the race are subject to deductions which vary in ratio to the odds of the absent horse at the time of its withdrawal. If the current odds are:

(a) 3/10 or longer odds on by 75p in the £.
(b) 2/5 to 1/3 by 70p in the £.
(c) 8/15 to 4/9 by 65p in the £.
(d) 8/13 to 4/7 by 60p in the £.
(e) 4/5 to 4/6 by 55p in the £.
(f) 20/21 to 5/6 by 50p in the £.
(g) Evens to 6/5 by 45p in the £.
(h) 5/4 to 6/4 by 40p in the £.
(i) 13/8 to 7/4 by 35p in the £.
(j) 15/8 to 9/4 by 30p in the £.
(k) 5/2 to 3/1 by 25p in the £.
(l) 10/3 to 4/1 by 20p in the £.
(m) 9/2 to 11/2 by 15p in the £.
(n) 6/1 to 9/1 by 10p in the £.
(o) 10/1 to 14/1 by 5p in the £.
(p) If over 14/1 the liability would be unchanged.
(q) In the case of two or more horses being withdrawn before coming under Starter's Orders, the total reduction shall not exceed 75p in the £.

Bets on the withdrawn horse are void and stakes are returnable, or, in certain instances, transferred to another horse (as, for example, in bets concerning unnamed favourites. If the original favourite is withdrawn, the shortest priced remaining horse becomes 'favourite' for this purpose).

Horses withdrawn, but under starter's orders at the time of withdrawal
This is a losing bet, the horse being treated as if it had taken part. No deductions are made from winning bets on the remaining horses.

Non-runners
If a horse is declared as a runner overnight and is withdrawn before racing, or is withdrawn, not under orders, immediately before a race, but in time for a new betting market to be formed, the bet becomes void, and stakes are returnable. Or, in certain instances, such as bets on unnamed mounts of jockeys, may be transferred: e.g. W. Swinburn appears in the morning papers as the rider of horse A. Horse A is withdrawn and Swinburn, instead, has a chance ride on horse B. If horse A is withdrawn and Swinburn has no other ride, the bet is then void. Any doubles on his unnamed mounts become singles, trebles become doubles, and so on. When two horses are nominated for a double and one of them does not run, the bet, to the same stake, becomes a single. When three horses are nominated for a treble, and one is a non-runner, the bet becomes a double to the same stake. If the remote chance occurs of two horses in the treble being non-runners, the stake becomes a single on the remaining horse. On the same principle, non-runners included in all other multiple bets, involving four, or five, or more runners, cause an automatic 'down-grading' of the bet.

Dead-heats
In a dead-heat for first place, stake money on each of the horses concerned will be divided by the number of runners in the dead-heat and full odds paid on the remaining stake. In a dead-heat for second, any place stakes are halved in races of six or seven runners. In a dead-heat for third, any place stakes are halved unless the first four home are being paid. In a dead-heat for fourth place, stakes are halved and full odds paid on the remaining stake.

Stakes wrongly calculated
If a wrong total is entered in the 'stakes' box of a betting slip (see Chapter Seven) and the betting shop clerk does not spot the error, the bet, if a winner, will usually be settled on a proportional basis, although bookmakers independent of the big chain firms may operate their own different rules, so here, once again, is a good reason for studying bookmakers' rules.

Betting disputes
Tattersalls' Committee are the arbiters in all betting disputes. In practice, only major disagreements (as well as cases of default) get as far as 'The Rooms'. *The Sporting Life* 'Green Seal' Service, costing a very small fee, acts as a mediator in most day-to-day differences arising between backer and bookmaker. This is the most readily accessible service in such matters, and one whose decisions bookmakers almost invariably abide by.

Betting tax
Betting tax amounted to £293 million on horseracing in 1983-84: a case of the Government taxing the same money over and over again, since taxed winnings or a proportion of them go forward as stakes to produce (if lucky) further winnings, which are then taxed, which then go forward etc. The tax gives much joy to puritanical hearts but does racing no good whatsoever. It is also a main reason for paring the professional backer's percentage on turnover to such an extent that their ranks, on the racecourse at least, have been much thinned in the past decade or so. There are clubs in existence where it is illegally possible to get a big bet on without tax, and these have become a refuge for some professionals in the constant quest to make a regular income out of racing.

Tax is levied at 4% on the racecourse on returns (i.e. winnings plus returned stakes) — a measure creating a differential between on-course and off-course tax which in turn is not very successfully aimed at making it more attractive to bet on-course than, say, in a betting shop. Off-course, the rate is 8%, but more commonly 10% is charged, the extra 2% being justified by bookmakers to help towards their levy contribution and 'overheads'. With the Tote, tax is deducted before dividends are declared. Some betting shops will advertise '8% deductions only' — but this will apply usually only to the amount deducted from gross returns. If the tax is paid in advance the common rate is 10%. (Detailed examples are given in other Chapters showing how, in detail, betting tax is deducted from individual bets.)

Place betting

The following are the general rules applied by bookmakers to determine the odds in place betting:

6-7	runners — 1/4 odds, 1st or 2nd	All races
8-11	runners — 1/5 odds, 1st, 2nd or 3rd	All races
12-15	runners — 1/4 odds, 1st, 2nd or 3rd	Handicaps only
16-21	runners — 1/5 odds 1st, 2nd, 3rd or 4th	Handicaps only
22+	runners — 1/4 odds, 1st, 2nd, 3rd or 4th	Handicaps only

In races where the favourite is odds-on, 1/5th the odds is paid with six or seven runners (1st or 2nd), 1/6th with eight or more runners (1st, 2nd or 3rd).

1st or 2nd in races of five to seven runners.

1st, 2nd or 3rd in races of eight or more runners.

1st, 2nd, 3rd or 4th in handicaps of 16 or more runners.

COMPENDIUM OF BETS

Where horses' names have been used in illustrations of how bets are settled, the names themselves are genuine enough. They have been chosen from both the recent and distant past history of the Turf, but no attempt whatsoever has been made to choose horses which in reality might have been included in the same bet, particularly with the more remote examples from the past. All bets, too, in the illustrations have been settled without deduction of the various levels of betting tax. (See p. 46 for a ready reckoner which is of practical use in calculation. The returns include stake back.)

One horse only involved

Single bets

Single bets offer by far the most reliable way of making betting pay.

Win only
(Bookmaker or Tote)

£1 staked on *Rataplan* to win, with Bookmaker Gus Demmy. Wins at SP of 10/1.

Gus Demmy returns £10 plus £1 stake back Return: £11 (less tax)

£1 staked on *Slip Anchor* to win the 1985 Derby, at Tote odds (some bookmakers will also settle at Tote odds off-course, if specified). *Slip Anchor* wins. Tote win dividend: £4.10.

Tote payout: £4.10 (including £1 stake back)

Place only (Tote only)	£1 staked on *Young Driver* to be placed in the 1986 Grand National. *Young Driver* is second. Tote place dividend £26.00.**	Tote payout: £26.00 (including £1 stake back)
Each way An equal amount staked to win and for a place (Bookmaker or Tote, but see Chapter Seven).	£1 e.w. (Total £2) staked on *Slip Anchor* to win or be placed in the 1985 Derby, with a bookmaker. *Slip Anchor* wins. SP returned 9/4 Favourite and ¼ those odds a place.	Bookmaker returns £2.25 + £0.56 + £2 stake back Return = £4.81 (less tax)
	£1 e.w. (Total £2) staked on *Slip Anchor* to win or be placed in the 1985 Derby, with the Tote. *Slip Anchor* wins. Tote win dividend: £4.10. Place dividend £1.60.***	Tote payout: £4.10 + £1.60 (including £2 stake back) Return = £5.70
	£1 e.w. (total £2) staked on *Gaye Brief* to win or be placed in the 1986 Champion Hurdle, with bookmaker. *Gaye Brief* is second at an SP of 14/1. Place odds are therefore ¼ × 14/1 = 7/2.	Bookmaker returns £3.50 + £1 place stake back, and keeps the losing £1 win stake. Return = £4.50 (less tax)
	£1 e.w. (total £2) staked on *Gaye Brief* to win or be placed in the 1986 Champion Hurdle, with the Tote. *Gaye Brief* is second. Tote place dividend: £3.60.	Tote payout: £3.60 (including £1 stake back, but the Tote keeps the losing £1 win stake) Return = £3.60

**An illustration of how the Tote often beats the book with prices of extreme outsiders. *Young Driver* was 66/1 SP (place odds of 16½/1) whereas the Tote place odds are 25/1.
***In this case, the Tote returns are better than SP. But over the entire season it is only about 50-50 as to whether Tote prices will beat the book or vice versa. The *Gaye Brief* example shows SP better than the Tote and the swings and roundabouts of the situation.

Two horses involved

Doubles

Bookmakers' rules should be carefully inspected to see that there are no time restrictions on multiple bets, e.g. 'There must be a minimum of 15 minutes between each race in a double, treble etc.'

| *Win double* (Bookmaker or Tote) Off-course | £1 is staked on *Ormonde* and *Bendigo* to win two separate races on the same afternoon, with a bookmaker. Both win, *Ormonde* at 2/1 SP and *Bendigo* at 6/1. | The bookmaker settles as follows. £2 won on *Ormonde* plus the original stake of £1 go forward as a stake of £3 on *Bendigo*. When he wins the winnings are thus £3 at 6/1 = £18. |

Simplified settling:

	$(2/1 + 1) \times (6/1 + 1)$ minus £1	plus	£3 stake
=	$(3/1) \times (7/1)$ minus £1	less	£1 original stake
=	£20 (i.e. a 20/1 Double)		£20
			(i.e. a 20/1 Double)

A double at Tote odds is similarly settled, the entire dividend from the winning first 'leg' going as stake on the second 'leg', and the winnings calculated according to the dividend on the winning second leg, e.g. the winning dividend of the first part of the double is £4.20. This goes on to the second horse, the winning dividend for which is £5.40. The winning return is therefore £4.20 × £5.40 = £22.68, i.e. a win double at approx 21½ to 1. This kind of double is not possible on the Tote at the racecourse, only with Tote off-course facilities, and with those bookmakers who will settle at 'tote prices'. The Tote used to run a popular bet called the daily double (as well as a daily treble) on nominated races on the card. These are now, sadly, defunct.

If, in the above example, *Ormonde* had won, and *Bendigo* been beaten the £1 stake would have been lost. In practice, it is not usual to have a win double bet without covering the two horses involved singly as well. So the *Ormonde-Bendigo* double plus two single £1 bets would cost £3, and if, again, *Bendigo* were beaten *Ormonde*'s win at 2/1 would exactly save the entire stake. More usually, a larger amount is staked singly on the two 'legs' of a double than on the double itself; and this can ensure a profit even if one of the horses is beaten.

Win doubles are also possible nominating favourites, jockey's mounts, trainer's runners e.g.: £1 Win double Favourite in the 2.30 at Bath with the favourite in the 3.00 at Folkestone. If there are joint-favourites the stakes are divided between the number of favourites which, effectively, at least halves the bet.

With jockeys and trainers, a permutation bet is often made:

e.g. Pat Eddery has four rides at Goodwood A B C D. Six bets are required to cover them all in win doubles: A with B, C & D; B with C & D; C with D. With an outlay of £6 in win doubles, a 5/1 double at least is required to break even. In the event, say, he has two winners at even money and 7/2, in which case there is a profit of £3. The bet is written: 'Full perm all Pat Eddery's mounts at Goodwood in win doubles. Stake 6 × £1'.

The method of calculating winnings on a double, and hence all multiple bets is very simple:

e.g. £1 Win Double

First 'leg' of the Double wins at 4/1

Second 'leg' of the Double wins at 6/1

Add one 'point' each to the respective winning odds (one betting unit is a 'point', thus 4/1 is one point greater than 3/1, and 3/1 is one point less than 4/1). So the winning double becomes (4/1 + 1) times (6/1 + 1) × £1 = 5/1 × 7/1 = £35 and the profit, therefore, having subtracted the original £1 stake becomes £34. A 34/1 Double in other words, or 34 points profit.

For the sake of explanation only, this is the somewhat cumbersome and complicated transaction on which the above simple method is based: the formula for settling a winning double: (first leg odds times original stake) plus original stake goes on the second leg as a stake. When this wins, the winnings become:

[(first leg odds times original stake) plus original stake] times second leg odds plus stake on second leg back, i.e. (first leg odds times original stake). The simplified way avoids all this, but in the case of fractional odds a pocket calculator is indispensable.

Each way double

Off-course only

— An equal amount staked on a win double and place double two horses in separate races, e.g. £1 each way double (stake £2) on *Beeswing* and *Alice Hawthorn*

Result: (a) *Beeswing* (3/1) and *Alice Hawthorn* (5/1) both win

Settled as follows: win double £(3/1+1) × (5/1 + 1) − £1 = £(4/1 × 6/1)

— £1 = £23

Place double say at ¼ the win odds £(¾ + 1) × (1¼ + 1) − £1 = £(1¾ × 2¼) − £1 = £2.94

Total £25.94

Results: (b)   *Beeswing* wins and *Alice Hawthorn* is placed

Alice Hawthorn wins and *Beeswing* is placed

The win double is lost, the place double pays out:

(−£1)   (+£2.94)

Profit £1.94

(c) Neither filly wins, but both are placed. The win double is lost, the place double pays out, as calculated above.

(d) *Beeswing* wins or is placed, *Alice Hawthorn* is unplaced
Alice Hawthorn wins or is placed, *Beeswing* is unplaced
The entire double goes down, and stake all lost.

Ante post doubles, win or each way
Off-course, credit, betting shop or Tote, or may be struck with bookmakers on the racecourse.
(See Chapter One for more about Ante post.)
Popular doubles are attempts to couple the winner of the 1000 and 2000 Guineas, Derby and Oaks, Spring Double and Autumn Double (see Chapter One). The doubles are settled as above at full multiplied odds.

Any to come
In this kind of bet at least two horses are nominated with the proviso 'any to come' or 'if win' or 'if cash' . . . so much on the next selection in the series. Any cash from previous bets in the series (winnings plus stakes) is used as stake on the succeeding selections. Many bookmakers limit the any-to-come part of such bets to double the original stake. Any tax pre-paid does not cover the any-to-come part of the bet. At its simplest it would be written £1 win *Spree*, A-T-C (if If cash or If win) £1 *Nortia*. Stake £1. *Spree* wins at 4/1, so £1 from the winnings goes on the *Nortia*.

Up and down double
This is an any-to-come bet in which the stake is carried forward, then back to give two win singles × 2. Also known as a Cross Bet, Vice-Versa, Stakes About, On and Off, or Reverse Bet. The cross symbol X between the horses on a betting slip indicates that up and down is required, but instructions should also be spelt out.
e.g. '£1 up and down win *Rakaposhi King* and *Mr Snugfit* — stake £2.'
Rakaposhi King wins at 2/1
Mr Snugfit wins at 10/1
The bet is settled:
£1 at 10/1 = £10
£1 at 2/1 = £2 × 2

Dual forecast
Tote bet, on-course and off-course. This is a bet in which the 1st and 2nd in a race have to be forecast in either order:
£1 dual forecast (sometimes written '£1 D/F') *Edwina Black* and *Baddesley Ensor*
Edwina Black is first, and *Baddesley Ensor* second so this is the result on which the dividend is paid. But had *Baddesley Ensor* won, and *Edwina Black* been second the same dividend would also have been paid.

The dividend is determined by the Tote by the total amount staked in any given race in the Tote dual forecast pool, divided by the number of winning bets, less deductions for the levy, overheads, and betting tax. The dividend is declared to a £1 stake, and the stake is included in the dividend. This can be a rewarding bet for fun, particularly if two successful outsiders are coupled in a biggish field.

Correspondingly, the forecast odds are usually not very high if the 1st and 2nd favourites are coupled successfully in smallish fields, and similarly are not likely to be astronomical if the favourite finishes in the first two, whatever the size of the field.

Record dual forecast dividend was achieved at Royal Ascot in 1986 when *Touch of Grey* beat *Manimstar* in a photo-finish for the Wokingham Stakes, and the payout was £3,414.70 to a £1 stake included in the dividend (the starting prices of the horses concerned were 20/1 and 33/1 respectively in a field of 28 runners). The record dual forecast pool was £24,398.50 on the 1986 Derby. In this case, however, there were also several thousand winners. The dividend was £7.00, odds of 6/1, for successfully coupling the 11/2 winner *Shahrastani* (2nd favourite) with *Dancing Brave*, the 2/1 favourite, who was second.

Computer straight forecast

Off-course bookmakers only. This bet (see also Chapter Seven) in which the 1st and 2nd in a race have to be forecast in the correct order: e.g. '£1 CSF *Shahrastani* to beat *Dancing Brave* Epsom 3.30.' The Tote used to run a straight forecast pool on the same basis as the dual forecast pool, but confined to smallish fields. This is no longer in their repertoire. The bookmakers' 'computer straight forecast', unlike the Tote pool, as far as declared dividend is concerned, bears no relation whatsoever to the amount of money staked or the number of winners. The pay-out is made according to a fixed scale 'computed' by a complicated formula on the basis, primarily, of the SP of the horses concerned in the forecast. Thus, in the example given above, the CSF dividend including £1 stake, was £15.16 (compared with the Tote's £7 for naming the correct horses, but in either order).

The bigger the odds of the horses involved in a computer straight forecast, the more likelihood there is of a Tote dual forecast proving better value. There are a fair number of examples throughout the season when it pays better to nominate two horses in either order, than attempt the correct forecast, the extreme example being in *Touch of Grey*'s astonishing dual forecast payout when coupled in either order with *Manimstar* in the Wokingham in 1986. As against the Tote's £3,414 for the dual forecast, the CSF for naming the two horses in correct order was only £509.96.

Three horses involved

Treble

Win or each way   A Treble seeks to clean up on the winners

Off-course only, Ante post   of three separate races
also   e.g. '£1 win Treble *Hyperion, Blue Peter,*
                                   Sea Bird II. Stake £1'.

If a winner, this is settled by the same method as for a double, i.e. a point is
added to the winning SP of each of the horses, and the three multiplied, with
the original stake deducted to give the winning treble odds. Say the winning
odds are 4/1, 6/1 and 6/4, then the treble is settled: £(5/1 × 7/1 × 5/2) − £1
= £86.50. Similarly, as explained above, each way trebles are settled, either
with the bookmaker or Tote. In order to succeed, all three horses must win;
two winners and a loser are no good. Correspondingly, an each way treble
will succeed only if all three horses are at least placed. The treble is a popular
bet, but the mathematical odds against winning are fairly high. In practice,
an 'uncovered' treble is not a usual bet. Rather better winning opportunities
are offered by covering the treble either with doubles, or, even better, with
singles and doubles, which although the total stake is increased, give more
chance of at least some success. Most common of these bets are the trixie,
and the patent.

Trixie
Win or each way   Form of bet involving one treble and three
Off-course only   doubles e.g. '£1 e.w. Trixie. *Sheila's*
                                  Cottage, National Spirit, Cottage Rake.
                                  Stake £8*
                                  (with racecourses/race-times),
                                  *Stake for a £1 win Trixie would be £4.

This bet is settled as for doubles and treble explained above. Two winners
out of three at multiplied odds (allowing for tax) for the one successful
double of about 7/2 are required to break even on this bet.

Patent
Win or each way   Probably the most popular, as well as the
(As for Trixie)   safest way of betting involving the treble.
                                  The bet is: one treble, three doubles and
                                  three singles and is written:
                                  e.g. '£1 Patent. *Orchardist, Marchakin, Creole*
                                  Stake £7* (with racecourses/race-times)'

One winner at 13/2 (allowing for tax) is enough to break even on this bet, or
two winners at even money and 6/4 (paying two singles and one double).

Tricast
Off-course bookmakers only

The tricast is a bet in which winner, second and third in certain big races
have to be forecast in correct order. The odds are computed in a similar way
to the computer straight forecast. The slip illustrated opposite is self-

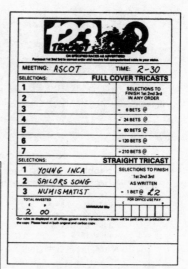

HOW TO MAKE YOUR TRICAST BET

Make your selections for the horses to finish 1st., 2nd. and 3rd. In the selected race. Enter your selections on the slip as illustrated. The example on the right shows a straight Tricast.

PERMUTATIONS INCREASE YOUR CHANCES

To increase your chances you can choose more than 3 horses in one race. The example on the left shows the selection of 5 horses; if any 3 of the 5 chosen occupy the first 3 places in any order you are guaranteed a return.

explanatory, and shows some of the possible permutations which are necessary in order to have the remotest chance of success. It also shows a minimum total stipulated, indicating that very small units are possible.

Forecast patent
Off-course bookmakers only

The tricast is difficult enough; the forecast patent appears to be sheer folly, adding the difficulties of sorting out a correct 1-2 forecast to those of combining the forecasts in a treble, three doubles and a single. A further complication may be added in by 'reversing' the forecasts, i.e. making them, at double the stake, either order forecasts, the illustration overleaf gives an example of this in the forecast patent plus, which, including 'bonus' is self-explanatory.

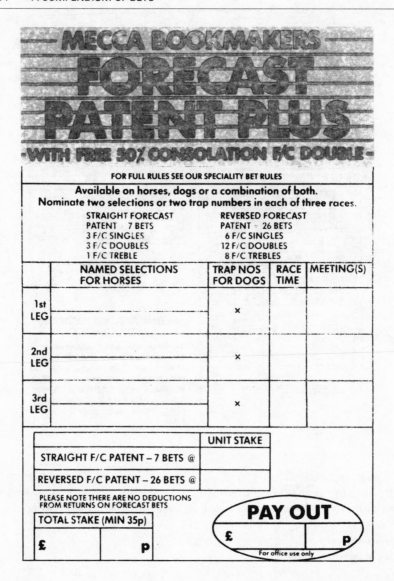

MECCA BOOKMAKERS

FORECAST

PATENT PLUS

- WITH FREE 50% CONSOLATION F/C DOUBLE -

FOR FULL RULES SEE OUR SPECIALITY BET RULES

Available on horses, dogs or a combination of both.
Nominate two selections or two trap numbers in each of three races.

STRAIGHT FORECAST	REVERSED FORECAST
PATENT 7 BETS	PATENT = 26 BETS
3 F/C SINGLES	6 F/C SINGLES
3 F/C DOUBLES	12 F/C DOUBLES
1 F/C TREBLE	8 F/C TREBLES

	NAMED SELECTIONS FOR HORSES	TRAP NOS FOR DOGS	RACE TIME	MEETING(S)
1st LEG		×		
2nd LEG		×		
3rd LEG		×		

	UNIT STAKE
STRAIGHT F/C PATENT – 7 BETS @	
REVERSED F/C PATENT – 26 BETS @	

PLEASE NOTE THERE ARE NO DEDUCTIONS
FROM RETURNS ON FORECAST BETS

TOTAL STAKE (MIN 35p)		**PAY OUT**	
£	P	£	P
		For office use only	

Union jack
Off-course bookmakers only

As the slip shows, with a full explanation, this bet, consisting of eight trebles, win or each way, or place only at Tote odds, follows the pattern of the red and white stripes in the British Union Flag. Anyone who has played noughts and crosses will see how it works, as well as appreciating that it is possible to achieve the not unremarkable feat of picking no fewer than five winners out of nine selections, and still lose the entire stake, as the losing illustration

UNION JACK

ALL TRANSACTIONS ARE ACCEPTED SUBJECT TO OUR RULES
CLAIMS WILL ONLY BE PAID ON PRESENTATION OF THE COPY

THE UNION JACK BET CONSISTS OF 9 SELECTIONS MAKING 8 TREBLES.
TO HAVE A WINNING TREBLE YOU MUST HAVE 3 WINNERS IN A LINE AS
ILLUSTRATED.

WINNING TREBLES

1	2	3
4	5	6
7	8	9

1	2	3	4	5	6	7	8	9
1	4	7	2	5	8	3	6	9
1	5	9		3	5	7		

ANY OTHER COMBINATION IS A LOSING BET

1st SELECTION	2nd SELECTION	3rd SELECTION
WINNER	WINNER	LOSER
MEETING	MEETING	MEETING

4th SELECTION	5th SELECTION	6th SELECTION
LOSER	WINNER	WINNER
MEETING	MEETING	MEETING

7th SELECTION	8th SELECTION	9th SELECTION
WINNER	LOSER	LOSER
MEETING	MEETING	MEETING

8 WIN BETS @	PER LINE	TOTAL INVESTMENT	RETURNS
8 PLACE BETS @	PER LINE	£	£

above demonstrates. A bet for the very optimistic on Bank Holidays with a dozen or so meetings.

Round robin
The slip overleaf explains what the bet is. It is settled as one treble, three doubles, six up and down singles.

Round the clock
Involves at least three selections. Settled as follows:

Horse A   £1 Win
           Any to come £1 win B. Any to come £1 win C.
Horse B   £1 Win
           Any to come £1 win C. Any to come £1 win A.
Horse C   £1 Win
           Any to come £1 win A. Any to come £1 win B.

If all three selections win there will be three times as much going on to each

10 Win Bets		23 Win Bets	
20 Each Way Bets		46 Each Way Bets	
From 3 Selections		From 4 Selections	
Giving		Giving - 6 Doubles	
3 Doubles		4 Trebles	
1 Treble		1 Accumulator	
6 Single Stake		12 Single Stake	
Cross Bets		Cross Bets	
3 Selections Only		**4 Selections**	
1		1	
2		2	
3		3	
All Bets Accepted Subject To Our Rules Payment Only on Presentation of the Copy		4	
10 Win Bets of £ : p Units		23 Win Bets of £ : p Units	
20 E.W. Bets of £ : p Units		46 E.W. Bets of £ : p Units	
Stake	Tax	Total Stake	Returns
£ p :	£ p :	£ p :	£ p :

M.P. (0532) 444454

winner as was originally staked. Some smaller firms stop this bet at a loser, so rules should be checked.

Four or more horses involved
Accumulator
Win or each way,
Off-course bookmakers,
or Tote

A treble is technically an 'accumulator' involving the winnings from each horse successively going on to the next, but the the term is more usually applied in cases of four horses or more. The specific term for a four-horse accumulator is a four-timer.

Four-timer

In practice, only the foolhardy would simply make a straight bet in the expectation of four winners, and this kind of accumulator is normally covered with a combination of singles, doubles, and trebles, as, in particular the yankee, perhaps the most popular Saturday betting shop wager.

We are now in the area where most off-course bookmakers make a good profit. What Crockford invented more than a century and a half ago has been refined, embellished and honed to the fine art of temptation of big profits for a very small outlay, the Achilles heel of all small gamblers (and some big ones, too) and today the betting scene in the high street offers a bewildering variety of bullseyes, round robins, lucky fifteens, sweet sixteens, Dundee shuffles, and so on, some of which are explained below. When there is a big pay out on a multiple bet there is inevitably appropriate publicity as the cutting reproduced below demonstrates:

Ladbroke's sale boosts punter

A MANCHESTER punter won £47,019 with a 5p Heinz yesterday, despite picking a loser.

And, thanks to Ladbroke's Glorious Goodwood Sale, he received £11,525 more than if his bet had been settled at starting prices.

Ladbrokes increased the prices of Goodwood winners yesterday and plan to do the same today. They added one point to a horse priced 10-1 and over, two points to a 20-1 chance and over, and five points to outsiders chalked up at 30-1 and over.

The fortunate punter picked 33-1 winner Gemini Fire, settled at 38-1, Royal Loft (14-1 settled at 15-1), Murillo (10-1), Green Ruby (20-1 settled at 22-1), loser Mudisah and Star Cutter, who obliged at 7-2.

The bet was placed at Ladbroke's Miles Platting betting shop in north Manchester, and was 10p understaked at £3.25 since he also had a 25p each-way equally divided accumulator on the same horses.

The punter also lost out on another £5,000 or so as he did not pay the tax, but he probably will not be too worried when he collects his money.

Stop at a winner
Another series bet. The first win in the sequence ends the bet with the total paid as a single to the winning odds. '£1 each *Mailman, Sonic Lady, Longboat, Moon Madness.* Stop at a Winner. Possible Stake £4.' They all win: 7/1, 6/4 on, even money, and 8/1. But the bet stops with *Mailman*'s gallant effort at 7/1.

Yankee (Win or each way)
The most popular Saturday bet for small punters involving four selections and 11 bets. Written simply '£1 Yankee ... and names of four horses involved. Stake £11.' Involves six doubles, four trebles, one four timer.

Yankee plus Lucky fifteen

A YANKEE WITH FOUR SINGLES = FIFTEEN BETS
A <u>RETURN</u> FOR <u>ONLY ONE WINNER</u>
IF ONLY <u>ONE</u> WINNER WE PAY <u>DOUBLE S.P. ODDS</u>
TWO & THREE WINNERS OR ANY NON-RUNNERS
ORDINARY RULES APPLY
**10% BONUS ADDED TO WINNINGS IF
ALL FOUR SELECTIONS CORRECT**
ALL BETS ACCEPTED SUBJECT TO OUR RULES.
CLAIMS PAID ONLY ON PRESENTATION OF COPY.

1
2
3
4

15 BETS IN	STAKE	TAX	TOTAL STAKE	RETURN
£ p	£ p	£ p	£ p	£ p
Units :	:	:	:	:

A YANKEE WITH FOUR SINGLES = FIFTEEN BETS
A <u>RETURN</u> FOR <u>ONLY ONE WINNER</u>
IF ONLY <u>ONE</u> WINNER WE PAY <u>DOUBLE S.P. ODDS</u>
TWO & THREE WINNERS OR ANY NON-RUNNERS
ORDINARY RULES APPLY
**10% BONUS ADDED TO WINNINGS IF
ALL FOUR SELECTIONS CORRECT**
ALL BETS ACCEPTED SUBJECT TO OUR RULES.

15 BETS IN	STAKE	TAX	TOTAL STAKE	RETURN
£ p	£ p	£ p	£ p	£ p
: Units	:	:	:	:

Involves four selections and 15 bets. Same as yankee but with the addition of four covering single bets.

Canadian super yankee
Involves five selections and 26 bets in 10 doubles, 10 trebles, five four-timers, one five-horse accumulator.

Heinz
Involves six selections, and, as the name implies 57 bets. It was a Heinz that gave Ladbroke's client in Miles Platting (see earlier in Chapter) his big win. The bet is settled as: 15 doubles,
20 trebles,
15 four-timers
6 five-horse accumulators
1 six-horse accumulator

Anyone who succeeds with a Heinz deserves the money, a remark which may be made with even greater force in the case of the Goliath.

MECCA BOOKMAKERS
SWEET SIXTEEN
PLUS FREE 50% CONSOLATION

FOR FULL RULES SEE OUR SPECIALITY BET RULES

5 Selections – Win or Each Way – Horses, Dogs or a combination of both.
10 Trebles, 5 Fourfolds, 1 Fivefold = 16 Win Bets – 32 Each Way Bets.

	SELECTION (ONE PER RACE)	TIME	MEETING
1			
2			
3			
4			
5			

	UNIT STAKE
WIN SWEET SIXTEEN – 16 BETS @	
EACH WAY SWEET SIXTEEN – 32 BETS @	

	£	p
STAKE (MIN 80p)	£	p
TAX PAID	£	p
TOTAL STAKE	£	p

PAY OUT

£	p

For office use only

Sweet sixteen
Involves five selections and 16 bets in 10 trebles, five four-timers, one five-horse accumulator.

Bullseye
Involves five selections and 13 bets.
The 'banker' bet goes in the middle here. Settled as shown on the slip in five singles, six trebles (must include the 'banker' for a winning treble of any kind) one four-timer, one five-horse accumulator.

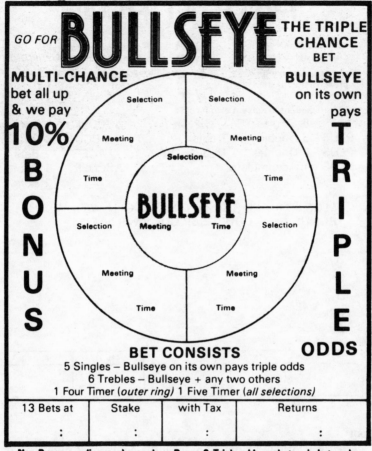

GO FOR BULLSEYE **THE TRIPLE CHANCE BET**

MULTI-CHANCE bet all up & we pay 10%

B O N U S

BULLSEYE on its own pays

T R I P L E ODDS

Selection — Selection

Meeting — Meeting

Selection — Time — Time

BULLSEYE — Meeting — Time

Selection — Meeting — Time — Selection

Meeting — Meeting

Time — Time

BET CONSISTS
5 Singles — Bullseye on its own pays triple odds
6 Trebles — Bullseye + any two others
1 Four Timer (*outer ring*) 1 Five Timer (*all selections*)

13 Bets at	Stake	with Tax	Returns
:	:	:	:

Non Runners ordinary rules apply.   Bonus & Triple odds apply to win bets only

Goliath
Involves seven selections and 120 bets.
The bet is settled as: 21 doubles
35 trebles
35 four-timers
21 five-horse accumulators
7 six-horse accumulators
1 seven-horse accumulator

Patent plus
Involves six selections in 22 bets. The settling of this bet is fully explained by the slip.

PATENT PLUS

Any non-runners
ordinary rules apply

A
B C D
E
F

Bets will be settled
in strict order as written **ONLY**

Claims paid only on
presentation of the copy

Please hand in set
intact

All bets accepted subject to our rules

6 Singles	ABCDEF	6 Bets
PLUS - 3 Doubles - 1 Treble	BCD	4 Bets
PLUS - 6 Doubles - 4 Trebles - 1 Acc	ACEF	11 Bets
PLUS - 1 Accumulator	ABCDEF	1 Bet
		22 Bets

PLUS
BONUS -

If Selection C is the Only Winner
DOUBLE SP ODDS will be Paid

A

B

C

D

E

F

22 BETS IN	STAKE	TAX	TOTAL STAKE	RETURN
£ p	£ p	£ p	£ p	£ p
Units	:	:	:	:

Jackpot

A Tote bet which may be done on or off the course with the Tote, or with bookmakers off-course who accept bets specifying Tote odds. The requirement is to nominate all six winners on the card.

The jackpot started in the 1960s. The biggest one-day total staked in the jackpot pool remains that at Goodwood on 28 July, 1967 and stands at £253,741. The record win was £73,217.95 to a 50p stake at Ascot on 21 June, 1986, and the biggest consolation dividend, £8,331-odd to the old five shilling (25p) stake, also at Ascot, in 1967.

Placepot

The Tote placepot operates exactly in the same way as the jackpot, but has a less stringent requirement. Six placed horses on the jackpot card have to be nominated in sequence.

The biggest placepot dividend was a handsome £4,317.75 to a 50p stake at Liverpool on Grand National Day, 1986.

t⊙te JACKPOT

SELECT THE WINNER IN EACH OF THE 6 RACES
PERMUTATIONS OR 50p SINGLE ENTRIES
JACKPOT RACES 1 - 6
ENTER HORSE NUMBER OR 'FAV'

							NO OF BETS
RACE 1							**X**
RACE 2							**X**
RACE 3							**X**
RACE 4							**X**
RACE 5							**X**
RACE 6							

	No. of Bets	TOTAL INVESTED	
3194805	× ======= Stake	= £	p

SUBJECT TO RULES OF HORSERACE TOTALISATOR BOARD

HOW TO ENTER - SEE REVERSE COPY

JACKPOT GUIDE

1. Enter your selections on this coupon using the horse numbers shown on the racecard or in your newspaper.

2. Take the coupon to any Tote cash building, counter or kiosk. The operator will retain the top two copies and return the bottom copy to you after acceptance together with a printed receipt.

3. Please do not leave it until the last moment and risk disappointment. Tote windows are open 45 minutes before the first race, earlier at big meetings.

4. To win the Jackpot you must pick all six winners. If there is no outright winner the gross pool will be carried forward to the next Jackpot meeting.

5. If you select a favourite or non-runner the S. P. favourite will be substituted. If there is more than one favourite, the favourite with the lowest racecard number is substituted.

6. The usual stake per line is 50p. Permutations of less than 50p per line in multiples of 5p are accepted down to a minimum stake of 10p provided they total not less than £5 in value.

7. Dividends are declared to a 50p stake. Part-stake winners receive an amount in proportion to the stake. For example, a 10p winning line would receive 1/5th of the dividend.

8. Winnings are paid ONLY on presentation of the printed receipt at the Kiosk or Building where the bet was struck.

t⊙te PLACEPOT

JUST PICK A PLACE IN EACH PLACEPOT RACE
PERMUTATIONS OR 50p SINGLE ENTRIES
PLACEPOT RACES 1 - 6
ENTER HORSE NUMBER OR 'FAV'

RACE 1								
RACE 2								X
RACE 3								X
RACE 4								X
RACE 5								X
RACE 6								X

5188838	No. of Bets × = Stake	TOTAL INVESTED £ | p

**IN RACES WHERE NO PLACE DIVIDEND IS DECLARED
THE WINNING HORSE WILL QUALIFY**

SUBJECT TO RULES OF THE HORSERACE TOTALISATOR BOARD
HOW TO ENTER - SEE REVERSE COPY

PLACEPOT GUIDE

1. Enter your selections on this coupon using the horse numbers shown on the racecard or in your newspaper.

2. Take the coupon to any Tote cash building, counter or kiosk. The operator will retain the top two copies and return the bottom copy to you after acceptance together with a printed receipt.

3. Please do not leave it until the last moment and risk disappointment. It is better to place your Jackpot and Placepot bets before betting on the first race. Tote windows are open 45 minutes before the first race, sometimes earlier at big meetings.

4. To win the Placepot your selections must be "placed" in all six races. A horse is "placed" if it finishes: 1, 2, 3 or 4 in any handicap of 16+ runners; 1, 2 or 3 in any race of 8+ runners; 1 or 2 in any race of 5, 6 or 7 runners. If less than 5 runners you must pick the winner.

5. If you select a favourite or non-runner the S. P. favourite will be substituted. If there is more than one favourite, the favourite with the lowest racecard number is substituted.

6. The usual stake per line is 50p. Permutations of less than 50p per line in multiples of 5p are accepted down to a minimum stake of 10p provided they total not less than £5 in value.

7. Dividends are declared to a 50p stake. Part-stake winners receive an amount in proportion to the stake. For example, a 10p winning line would receive 1/5th of the dividend.

8. Winnings are paid ONLY on presentation of the printed receipt at the Kiosk or Building where the bet was struck

CHAPTER SEVEN

How to Get 'On'

This section is especially for all those who are daunted by the notion of going into a betting shop, and for those who, on Grand National and Derby days, would so much like a bet, but have no idea how to go about it. Betting shops do, of course, vary but sadly, perhaps, they have never quite shaken off the image of some of the shops which flourished in the 'sixties, and cashed in briefly on the amendment to the betting laws which permitted public betting in cash. Often these were unbelievably squalid back-street dumps, complete with a cast of derelicts, layabouts and drunks; and rip-off limits scrawled so high on the wall they could not be read, but if deciphered revealed that not much was allowed in the way of winnings. There are still surviving versions in this category, but not too many, since Hill's, Ladbroke's, Coral's, and Mecca between them effectively control the betting shop operation up and down the country, with some good independent rivals. The smaller gaffes have been bought out and refurbished with immense benefit to the off-course punter. You still don't see many women in betting shops, though, which I feel has nothing to do with a male monopoly of the desire to have a bet, but because betting shops are still stuck with the old image despite the improvements. They do vary, of course, but mostly it's between the carpeted establishments of the West End of London and other cities, complete with banks of video, television, armchairs, no unreasonable limit on winnings and provision of almost every amenity except money to bet with, and the median grade of shop, which, without being exactly an annexe to the nearest Hall of Temperance or branch of the Chase Manhattan Bank, provides reasonably clean and tidy facilities, particularly before racing begins. Afterwards, depending on the area, things get a little more lively, though rarely unpleasant.

Here then is a step by step procedure for the betting shop, which may look long, but is extremely simple:

1. First have an inspection of the local betting shops; there's often more than one to choose from, so find one which appears to have the best atmosphere, and also shop around to see if the rate of tax payable on the winnings varies and which has the most favourable rules.
2. Next, if it's Grand National Day or Derby Day, weigh the possibilities up as early as possible, and prepare to make the bet *in the morning*, before the action, noise and queues start in the shop. On Grand National Day it can be like being in the Post Office when everybody in front is paying the telephone bill, water rates, *and* relicensing at least two cars. The morning, in fact, is a good time to bet anyway if not too worried about following the market changes which are chalked up, or appear on the video during racing.

3. Write out the intended bet beforehand on a slip of paper and take it to the betting shop.

4. Most important, take a ball-point pen (and a spare, if nervous that one might expire in mid-bet). This is the most *vital* piece of kit. Some betting shops used to provide pens, and some, outside my knowledge, may still do so but most have abandoned the practice.

5. Once in the betting shop, first have another careful look at the rules. With the big chains the rules are not desperately prohibitive, but it's worth a look in all cases to see what, if any, restrictions are placed on the amount that can be won in a single afternoon or single bet.

The newspapers, sporting or otherwise, are pinned round the walls, open at the various racecards for the day. This gives an opportunity for a final check that horse's names are correct (though, in practice, unless the name is wildly mis-spelt, the betting shop settler won't mind), as well as on the correct racecourse and time of race. Also on view, either marked up on big display boards, or on the video screens, will be the latest ante post prices, or early prices available up to the time of the first show of betting from the racecourse, in most cases. These are known in the shop as board prices, and if a selection is considered to be better to back at board prices rather than trust to the SP (i.e. if it is considered the SP is likely to be shorter than the price on offer) this is the time to decide whether to take what it is hoped might turn out to be a bargain price, such as 8/1 a horse that could well come in to 4/1 favourite. Judgement is required here, but then, the whole business is concerned with judgement.

6. Next take a betting slip. These are dispensed from machines, operated by the turn of a knob at the side, and situated above the ledges round the walls which are used for writing out bets. Alternatively, the slips may simply be contained in small racks in a similar position.

7. The kind of plain slip is illustrated below. It will have a carbon attached to it, which, after the bet has been written and presented, will be returned as a copy.

8. Next, write the bet following the slip of paper made earlier. Examples are given below, but write, or even better, print:
   (a) How much is to be staked on each bet.
   (b) What kind of bet, e.g. win only, each way (e.w.), double, treble etc. In the case of more complicated bets which the bookmaker will take immense delight in accepting, it is best to use one of the special slips usually provided, illustrated in Chapter Six.
   (c) Horses' name(s).
   (d) Name of racecourse or suitable abbreviation, more usually, and time race is due to start.

9. The total amount to be staked should then be added and entered in the box at the bottom of the slip.

10. Finally, as far as writing is concerned, 10 per cent of the stake should be calculated and entered in the tax box next to the stake. Some shops

C. Racing Services

£5 WIN

    SUGAR PALM

       (3.45 Leicester)

£5 WIN

    BARCLAY STREET

       (4.45 Leic.)

£1 e.w. Double

    Above Two

Stake	£12		TOTAL RETURN		
Tax Paid (if required)	£1.20		It is your responsibility to write your Bet correctly.		
Total	£13.20		All Bets Subject to Rules.		

advertise only the eight per cent betting tax required by law, but this usually applies only in the case of tax deducted from returns. The going rate for pre-paid tax is 10 per cent though exceptions may be found. It is strongly advised to pre-pay the tax (after all, the bet is being made in the expectation of a winner). e.g. £10 staked to win plus £1 tax pre-paid. The bet wins at an SP of 10/1

Winnings £100 less £1 tax pre-paid.   Return net £99.00
£10 staked to win. Tax not pre-paid. The bet wins at an SP of 10/1
Winnings £100 less £8.80 tax deducted at eight per cent
on returns (stake plus winnings)   Return net £91.20
or at 10 per cent rate similarly, £11 tax deducted.   Return net £89.00

11. Take the completed betting slip and stake money to the counter, usually with a glass screen, and specifically to the part marked 'bet here' or a similar instruction.

12. (a) If the selections are intended to be paid out, if winners, at SP simply hand the slip and cash under the glass. On the other side it will be checked through primarily to see the bet is readily understood, and there are no obvious mistakes, and that the amount staked (and tax)

STAKE	SELECTIONS	TIME & MEETING

£5 each to WIN

MR. SNUGFIT ⎫
CORBIERE ⎬ Grand
DOOR LATCH ⎭ National
(3.20)

£5 e.w. INSPIRED
(Hereford 2.0)

3 x £1 e.w Doubles
Same Horses

	£	p.	FOR OFFICE USE ONLY						
STAKE	46	00							
TAX	4	60	£		PAY		p		
TOTAL INVESTED	50	60							

Our Rules as displayed in all offices, govern every transaction.
A claim will be paid only on production of the copy.
PLEASE HAND IN BOTH ORIGINAL AND CARBON COPY.

are correct (also to see that a second mortgage hasn't been raised, and an enormous bundle staked, in which case the boss may be called from the back-room to negotiate, depending on the locality of the shop and how well known the punter is). Next, the slip will be time-stamped by clock-machine, imprinting also on the carbon which is handed back as a receipt so there can be no argument about the time the bet was placed.

(b) If board price is required rather than SP, simply say, for example, 'I'll take board price *Rataplan* at 10/1,' at which the board price of *Rataplan* will be checked and 10/1 written against the selection on the slip, and ringed. So, whatever the SP *Rataplan* is returned, if a winner, 10/1 is the price at which it will be paid out.

Nothing more need be done, except to tuck the receipt away in a safe place and wait for the results. Finally, assuming the happy circumstances of a winner, what to do then? Essentially, just present the receipt at the 'payment here' section of the betting shop counter and the original slip will be found, and the cash remitted. Before collecting, however, it's as well to calculate what is expected from the winning bet. If the amount paid out doesn't tally with what is expected, point out that a mistake appears to have been made. Settlers *can* make mistakes; equally, so can punters, particularly when miscalculating the odds payable on a place bet, or, even more likely, on a complicated multiple bet.

One point about pay-out on big race-days such as the Grand National: because of the likely amount of business, a notice may appear in the 'bet here' window saying something like: 'No winning bets on the Grand National paid until 5 o'clock'. This is not because the bookmaker is planning to hammer spikes into his shoes in the event of a big liability, and leg it to the hills, but because the Grand National always generates more business than any other one day of the year (the Derby comes next; Cheltenham in March, and Ascot in June are also busy times). Particularly in the instance of a popular winner, depending on the size of the shop, and how many settlers are calculating the losses in the back room and transferring them to individual winning slips, it may well be 5 o'clock before a pay-out is possible, by which time queues are forming. This is very much the case with small betting shops, though not the bigger ones. It may well be better to wait to be paid out until the next available day. Because winnings are not collected on the day it does not mean the money will not be paid out. Winning slips are put in dated racks if the cash has not been collected on the day. They are kept for several weeks, and if not collected by then are sent on, in the case of big chains, to head office, to which application can be made. The obverse of this, of course, occurs on normal days when winnings can be collected soon after the 'weighed in' call has come over the loudspeaker.

Betting on the racecourse
1. *With a bookmaker*
    Many bookmakers operate 'minimum stake' limits. In Tattersalls at present these vary from as little as £2 up to £10, though a few at the back will happily accept £1 stakes. Some bookmakers also stipulate 'win only' or 'each way taken'. Some bookmakers are not interested in taking big amounts on an outsider, but will happily lay the favourite to the same sort of money. If it happens that a bet is refused or halved, there are always other bookmakers along the line, some of whom may not bat an eyelid at the amount. For the ordinary punter, however, there are no real problems about getting 'on'.

    If a bet on a horse running *at a different meeting* is wanted there are usually one or two bookmakers at the back or side specialising in this sort of bet. They will also, normally, bet at SP if stipulated. They can be located in Tattersalls by the time-honoured shout of 'AT the other meeting'. Also 'Nah then, who wants this favourite at Ponty ... have you

all done, now. They're off Ponty ... yes, sir, which one do you want ...?'
Ted Murrell used to be a great specialist, a colourful figure in straw hat,
making a book at the 'away' meetings. There is a story that Ted used to
have a telephone on his joint (unconnected to anything but the floor of
the Ring) and in order to liven things up would get his clerk to make it
ring, at which the following 'conversation' would take place: Ted: 'Yes,
your Lordship ... a pony on which one ... oh a monkey ... (aside to his
clerk) ... George, scrub off all that nine to two ... yes, your Lordship,
you've got 2000 to five the favourite ...' Another story, well documented,
concerns his operations in shirt sleeves on hot sunny days at southern
meetings when, say, he was making a book on the Warwick meeting. At
some point Ted would say to his clerk, again to attract the business in:
'Put the umbrella up, George'. 'The umbrella, guv?' 'Yes, the umbrella.
It's raining at Warwick.'

It is also sometimes possible to get *a bet in running* on the course in the
closing stages of a race when, say, the favourite looks as if he's not going
to make it in the last furlong or so. From the bookmakers the shouts will
go up 'I'll lay five hundred to one this favourite'. Fred Binns, who can
read a race better than most, used to be a great specialist in this sort of
bet which is certainly not for the amateur. There also used to be a
bookmaker at the smaller jumping meetings who would take bets up to
the last fence, and was similarly able to spot a tiring or unwilling
favourite approaching the final jump. He had a good line of patter:
'Come on now ladies and gents ... up to the last fence ... you can have
anything you want, Green Shield Stamps, Omo Coupons, Savings
Cerstificates, anything you like ... here, six to one this favourite, sixes ...
up to the last fence ... oh, that's done it ... the favourite's down, yer
money's on the floor ...' As far as ordinary betting is concerned the
procedure on the racecourse could hardly be simpler. All that has to be
done is to go up to the bookmaker and say how much is wanted on any
given horse at the price quoted on the board: e.g. if, say, *Rataplan* is

quoted at 4/1, and a fiver is wanted on it, the exchange of words goes like this: Punter: 'Twenty pounds to five, *Rataplan,* or simply 'A fiver *Rataplan.*' Bookmaker: 'Twenty pounds to five *Rataplan,* ticket number 361.' The fiver is handed over in exchange for the ticket; the cash disappears into the satchel; the bookmaker's clerk notes the bet and ticket number in the field book; and you're on, not forgetting, however, to make a note of the exact odds and bet on the back of the ticket. Should *Rataplan* win, the bookmaker will pay out when the 'weighed in' flag is run up on the numbers board, or a public address announcement is made. On the particular example above, when the ticket is given back to the bookmaker, he will pay out £24, made up as follows: £20 winnings plus £5 stake returned less £1 betting tax at 4 per cent on total returns of £25.

2. *On the Tote*
Close-circuit television is the usual method used now to give the approximate odds that may be expected if a bet is had 'on the machine'. In general, the Tote often pays out a longer price than the book on outsiders.

The Tote operation has been computerised and the betting windows much simplified in recent years. The procedure again is very simple, and rather like buying a railway ticket, only quicker except at the big Ascot and Cheltenham meetings.

No horses' names are involved in betting with the Tote; everything is done by reference to numbers on the racecard. These are self-evident in the case of meetings where the jackpot or placepot is not operating. When those pools *are* operating the racecard number to be used in ordinary Tote bets is the bold type part of the number on the card — the first number of the three digits given should be ignored as this simply refers to the number of the race. Thus the racecard number to be used in ordinary Tote bets becomes, for example, 14 from 1*14*, from 20*6*, 22 from 5*22* and so on. Having chosen which horses are required, go to any Tote window marked 'sell', with the cash and say:

	'£2 Win Number 8'	(Stake £2)
or	'£5 each way Number 22 and £25 win Number 4'	(Stake £35)
or	'£2 Forecast Number 6 and Number 10'	(Stake £2)
or	'£10 Forecast Numbers 2, 8, and 24'	(Stake £30)
	(This couples 2 and 8	
	2 and 24	
	8 and 24	
	in Dual Forecasts)	

and so on.

Whatever the bet, the Tote operator behind the window will take the cash, press various buttons, and a ticket of the kind illustrated overleaf will be issued.

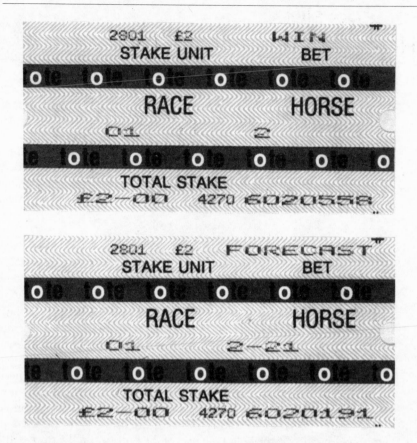

If the bet is a winning one, the pay out takes place after the weighed in signal at the pay windows, the tax having been deducted already. So, if £2 has been staked to win on a successful selection for which the win dividend declared is £6.20, the actual odds are £5.20 to £1, and the pay out will be £12.40, which includes £2 stake returned.

CHAPTER EIGHT
Horses for Courses

When the straight was reached there were only two horses left with a chance, Brown Jack and Solatium. As they headed for home it sounded as if everyone on the course was cheering for Brown Jack . . . as he passed the post he was two lengths clear . . . in every enclosure hats were in the air but many who would have liked to cheer were rendered speechless by an inconvenient lump in the throat. Dignified individuals whom one would never have suspected of displaying their feelings in public, unashamedly wept.

The above was written by Roger Mortimer describing (*Twenty Great Horses*) the final appearance at Ascot in 1934 of *Brown Jack*, then a 10-year-old, when he was winning the Queen Alexandra Stakes, at 2¾ miles the longest race in the calendar (originally the Alexandra Stakes) for the sixth year running. Altogether in his long career *Brown Jack* won 25 races including the Goodwood Cup, Doncaster Cup, Chester Cup and the Champion Hurdle, but he reserved his most heroic feats for the Ascot crowds who loved him. Altogether he ran there 11 times, winning seven times, and being runner-up once. If ever a horse illustrated the saying about 'horses for courses' it was *Brown Jack*. His performances at Ascot captured the public's imagination and affection in a way that those of few horses have ever done. In more recent times *Arkle* and *Dawn Run* are the only equivalents. At Ascot, *Brown Jack* is honoured still and remembered (in the same way as the deeds of *Arkle* and *Dawn Run* are commemorated at Cheltenham). There is a statuette of him outside the weighing room, and a race named after him. True, the race, which used to be over the Queen Alexandra distance of 2¾ miles, has been shortened, but it still bears his name.

Less exalted than Ascot and *Brown Jack*, there is another horse whose name, nonetheless, is forever associated with one racecourse, and which still, over the years, is equally capable of conjuring a measure of affection at the memory: his name was *Cider Apple*, and his fondness for a course was reserved for the now defunct Alexandra Park. This, the last remaining metropolitan racecourse, was more familiarly known as Ally Pally, and if you were never knocked over by the gaol delivery from the Scrubs trying to get 9/2 a 2/1 chance at this curious racecourse, you haven't lived.

Ally Pally had a conformation that was quite unique: the horses started in front of the stands, galloped away up the straight, went round and round a very tight circle at the end (how many times depended on the distance of the race) and returned the way they came towards the winning post. It was called 'racing round the frying pan, and up the handle' and horses that ran there supposedly 'finished dizzy.' *Cider Apple* developed a liking for Ally Pally, not matched, perhaps, by the majority of its patrons. As quite an old horse he was still capable of giving the younger ones a trouncing over its longest distance of 1 mile 5 furlongs and a few yards, and he won there so many times that a race was named after him. Sadly, *Cider Apple*'s name is no longer commemorated because racing ceased at Alexandra Park in 1969 (a few years before the great glass palace and original home of BBC television was gutted by fire), but *Cider Apple* is another instance of a horse who developed a pronounced preference for a particular course just as *Denikin* could invariably be relied on on the Rowley Mile (nine victories) in the early 1950s; *Operatic Society* showed a preference for Epsom and Brighton; and old *Certain Justice* became the definition of a course specialist at Fontwell in the 1960s with an astonishing 13 wins there.

More recently, the *Timeform* comment on *Corbiere*, the 1983 Grand National winner was 'about 21 lb inferior away from Liverpool nowadays ...' And, at random among the 1985 Flat race records can be found several horses with more than one win at a particular course. For example, the sprinter *Al Amead* ran a dozen times during the season being unplaced in all his races except at Lingfield where he ran six times, winning three times, and was never out of the first four and finishing second, third and fourth on the remaining occasions. In July the following year he recorded his seventh victory on the course, and broke the six furlong track record for good measure. *Show of Hands*, meanwhile, was equally fond of Edinburgh (seven wins), while by 1987 *Peaty Sandy*, 13-y-o, had achieved the incredible record by being unbeaten over jumps at Newcastle, with ten victories to his credit.

So, there is some truth in horses for courses. It is therefore important to take note of a horse's course and distance times printed alongside its name in the newspaper racecard usually as C & D3 or CD3, or, say 'course 4, distance 3' (C4D3).

It is also important to study whether a horse has a liking for (or, perhaps more important, an aversion to) a left-handed or right-handed track. *Timeform* will often make a note on this point. There are countless examples, some of them notable horses, including Lester Piggott's first Derby winner, *Never Say Die*. *Never Say Die* used to hang to the left. All sorts of ironmongery had been put on his bit to try and correct the tendency. At Lester's suggestion these were left off for the Derby, which, after all, takes place on a left-handed course, and *Never Say Die* was an easy winner. Unfortunately, *Never Say Die*'s next race was in the King Edward VII Stakes at Royal Ascot, a week or two later, Ascot being a right-handed course. It was this race which gave rise to Lester's most unjust suspension. He himself (*Lester* by Dick Francis), says of *Never Say Die*'s tendency: 'He was perfectly all right on a left-handed course, but if you were going the other way he was inclined to come out. There are certain horses that don't go one way at all. You run them one way and they're useless, and the other way they're champions. You try to tell people it makes all that difference and they don't believe you, but it's a fact!'

Another significant factor in the relationship between horse and course is its stamina in relation to the particular track. A horse which barely lasts out a mile on an easy track such as Kempton Park will almost certainly not be able to get more than seven furlongs on a stiff, galloping course such as Ascot or the Newmarket Rowley Mile (see Chapter Nine). A horse's breeding may suggest that he should be able to get a mile, but if he fails to do so in a truly run race it will be said that 'he didn't get the trip'.

Depending on the particular course, the draw, particularly in sprint races, may be a crucial factor in the outcome. In handicap terms, a bad draw in a big field can mean, in effect, a 'penalty' of several pounds inflicted on a horse purely by chance. The draw for places at the start, i.e. which starting stall each horse and jockey occupies is a further complication (in Flat racing only) in the relationship between horse and course: it is *the* random factor in a sport full of random factors. On most courses it makes little or no difference, but on others it is of crucial significance. A bad draw increases in significance in proportion to the number of runners; the greater the field, the greater the effect of a bad draw. The importance of the draw is also in ratio to the shortness of the race. For example, in races up to a mile on the straight at Ascot, and on the Rowley Mile, the draw should be studied in big fields. Both are wide, galloping courses, and when there are a lot of runners, the field very often splits into two groups, thus making two races out of one. The pace and whether the going is better on the far side or on the stands side then also enter into calculations, and which side is more favourable can only be told (if at all) by noting what has happened in previous races on the programme (a big race will usually be third or even fourth on the card). Thus it can be seen (Chapter Nine) that at Ascot, for instance, middle numbers in the draw in the 6 furlong Wokingham Stakes which normally attracts a big field do not do very well. The small circuit at Chester is a case where the draw assumes importance for shorter races, low numbers being usually best. Here are the results at the main Chester Cup meeting in 1985, with (some very surprising) starting prices:

			Winners		Runners-up	
Dist.	Race	Runners	Draw	SP	Draw	SP
5f	Lily Agnes Stakes (2-y-o)	5	2	2/1 jtF	4	7/2
7f	Holsten Diat Pils Hcp	14	2	9/1	1	8/1
5f	Prince of Wales Hcp (3-y-o)	11	1	9/2	2	25/1
5f	Philip Cornes Nickel Alloy Stakes (2-y-o)	11	3	6/4F	1	8/1
7f	Sefton Stakes (Mdn 3-y-o F)	11	4	5/2F	10	11/4
7f	Roodeye Stakes (3-y-o C & G)	6	2	2/1	3	12/1
5f	EBF Sceptre Stakes (Mdn 2-y-o F)	7	2	9/1	5	14/1
7f	Ladbroke Hotels Hcp (3-y-o)	8	2	11/4	1	5/2F
5f	Oulton Hcp	9	6	9/2	3	7/2F

At least the off-course punter, these days, is forewarned about the draw, as it is now made the day before the race and is published on the racecard in the newspapers. Before this came about, the draw was made by the Clerk of the Scales dipping his hand into a bag and pulling out the numbers less than an hour before each race.

Finally, in assessing a horse's chance on a particular course, one factor above all affects all horses on all courses. That is the going, the importance of which cannot be over emphasised. It is said that a good horse can act on any going, but this is an over simplification. The extremes, really heavy mud, and bone-shaking rock hard ground, are really not the best conditions for any horse, although there are some jumpers, in particular, who love the mud. The best way of finding out if a horse has a preference for a particular kind of going is by consulting the *Timeform Black Book* or *Racecard*. Many more horses do not run because of firm or hard conditions than soft. In a hot dry summer, on the rare occasions this happens in England, the fields invariably become small because trainers will not risk horses' legs in the conditions. When it rains overnight, transforming the going from good to heavy, a trainer is faced with having to re-assess his plans, and take a difficult decision in the case of a well backed horse, say, which the public have supported in the ante post market. Such a horse was the 2000 Guineas and Derby winner *Crepello* who was favourite to win the King George VI and Queen Elizabeth Stakes at Ascot in 1957. Although a champion, *Crepello* had suspect forelegs and used to race with support bandages. Noel Murless really had little option when the going changed that day at Ascot, and he wisely withdrew *Crepello* an hour before the big race. Sadly, the Triple Crown which might have been *Crepello*'s did not materialise. In his preparation for the St Leger, he broke down.

Apart from *Timeform*, the newspapers also publish plenty of information on the subject of going, illustrating how vital it is in determining trainers' intentions for their horses. Look out for, 'He'll only run if it's soft,' or conversely, 'He's no good on anything but good ground, and we'll only run if we get that.' One last word: there are some courses which are affected by rain more than others. At Newmarket, for instance, it very rarely becomes worse than soft. Good ground or good to soft in the spring and autumn on the Rowley Mile are usually the prevailing states of going, however much rain has fallen. Liverpool, where the turf is old and springy, is another course where it does not often become heavy — 1980 was an exceptional year for the National with only four finishers because of the demanding conditions.

CHAPTER NINE
Records and Analyses of Principal Courses and Big Races

The course descriptions are based on those appearing in *Ruff's Guide to the Turf*. The race analyses are intended for use as much for narrowing down possibilities as providing a likely group from which a winner might come. The races dealt with are: the Classics — St Leger, the Derby, the Oaks, 2000 Guineas, 1000 Guineas — the Royal Hunt Cup, the Wokingham Stakes, the Champion Hurdle, the Cheltenham Gold Cup, the Lincoln Handicap, the Stewards' Cup, the Cambridgeshire, the Cesarewitch, the Ebor Handicap, and a race on its own — the Grand National.

ASCOT   Right-hand   Flat and National Hunt

> Draw: On the straight Royal Hunt Cup course, when there are big fields, both high and low numbers have an advantage over middle numbers. The side which has the ultimate advantage will be determined, if the field splits into two groups, by the pace on the stands side or opposite rails which in turn may be affected by slight differences in going. Ascot has an artificial watering system which, though operated with expertise and the best will in the world, can produce this slight difference between stands side and far rails. When the going is soft high numbers in any case hold a very slight advantage.

Ascot, under Captain Nicky Beaumont, the Clerk of the Course, has become an increasingly popular racecourse with an average of nearly 22,000 people coming to the races on any given day. It has lost much of the starchiness of former days and the facilities are superb, although because of the sheer numbers attending, particularly at the main summer meetings, the view of the finish, for many, is remote and angled. At the four day Royal meeting in mid-June with the best racing possible, over-crowding has meant that Grandstand admission has now to be booked in advance. This great event apart, Ascot also stages the following month, the King George VI and Queen Elizabeth Diamond Stakes, sponsored at present by De Beers Consolidated Mines which is one of the two most important tests for 3-y-o and 4-y-o and upwards in Europe (the other being the Prix de l'Arc de Triomphe). Racing throughout the year, however, is of a consistently high standard and in the autumn there are some significant two-year-old events, while September 1987 sees the first 'Festival of British Racing', with the biggest amount of prize money, in the region of £630,000, ever competed for in one day on the British Turf. The Queen Elizabeth II Stakes alone is upgraded to Group One and prize money of nearly a quarter of a million, and a cup presented by HM The Queen.

National Hunt racing has taken place at Ascot since 1966, the hurdles and chase courses being laid out on the inside of the triangle. In the shadow of the huge stands it hardly possesses the intimacy of an afternoon's jumping at, shall we say, Plumpton, but it makes up for that in quality and in early to mid-season there are valuable prizes such as the Crockfords Trophy Hcp Chase and SGB Chase. The Ascot fences are quite stiff and provide good trials for both the Cheltenham Festival and Grand National, in particular the three mile Whitbread Trial Chase in February. As might be expected with the overall high prizes for both Flat and National Hunt, the leading trainers in the country do best at Ascot. On the Flat (1983-86) the Newmarket trainers Michael Stoute (31 winners) and Guy Harwood (23) are in front. But on a percentage basis (ratio of winners to runners) Jeremy Tree comes out best, having turned out 14 winners from 53 runners from Beckhampton (26.4 per cent), while £1 level stake on all Harry Thomson Jones's runners from Newmarket would have produced £42.92 profit at an outlay of £56. On the National Hunt front Fred Winter, Josh Gifford and Fulke Walwyn have trained most winners.

Ascot is a triangular course of 1 mile and just over 6 furlongs: the first half of it is nearly all on the descent, and the last half, which is called the Old Mile, is exactly one mile and is uphill the greater part of the way. The Swinley Course is the last mile and a half. The comparatively short (2½ furlongs) run in from the sharp final bend to the winning-post puts a big premium on jockeyship. If a horse is not in a good position at this final turn it is goodbye to any chance. Experienced jockeys are a prerequisite here, and now that Lester Piggott is no longer able to demonstrate the art of Ascot race-riding, Willie Carson is now top of the list, followed by Pat Eddery, Steve Cauthen, Greville Starkey and Walter Swinburn, although Brent Thomson has made his mark quickly at Ascot. The Royal Hunt Cup course is one mile straight: a gentle switchback with overall uphill gradient. This is a tough galloping track which, particularly when the going is soft, finds out any stamina limitations a horse may have.

1 mile Hcp			Royal Hunt Cup, Royal Ascot, June			
	Winner	*Age*	*Wt.*	*Trainer*	*Jockey*	*Ran*	*Price*
1960	Small Slam	5	8.2	G. Barling (Newmarket)	R.P. Elliott	26	28/1
1961	King's Troop	4	8.4	P. Hastings-Bass (Kingsclere, Berks)	G. Lewis	39	100/7
1962	Smartie	4	7.9	R. Mason (Northants)	J. Sime	31	22/1
1963	Spaniards Close	6	8.6	F. Winter (Newmarket)	L. Piggott	38	25/1
1964	Zaleucus	4	8.2	G. Brooke (Newmarket)	D. Smith	30	100/7
1965	Casabianca	4	8.7	N. Murless (Newmarket)	L. Piggott	26	100/9
1966	Continuation	4	7.9	S. McGrath (Ireland)	J. Roe	30	25/1
1967	Regal Light	4	7.6	S. Hall (Middleham, Yorks.)	G. Sexton *5	15	100/9
1968	Golden Mean	5	8.4	D. Smith (Newmarket)	F. Durr	26	28/1
1969	Kamandu	7	8.6	F. Carr (Malton, Yorkshire)	L. Piggott	24	7/1
1970	Calpurnius	4	7.13	J.W. Watts (Newmarket)	G. Duffield	18	33/1
1971	Picture Boy	6	7.13	G. Todd (Manton, Wiltshire)	J. Wilson	18	11/1
1972	Tempest Boy	4	8.1	J. Sutcliffe Jr (Epsom)	R. Hutchinson	20	20/1
1973	Camouflage	5	7.9	J. Dunlop (Arundel, Sussex)	D. Cullen	20	14/1

1974	Old Lucky	4	8.8	B. van Cutsem (Newmarket)	W. Carson	30	8/1
1975	Ardoon	5	8.3	G. Pritchard-Gordon (Newmarket)	D. Maitland	18	9/1
1976	Jumping Hill	4	9.7	N. Murless (Newmarket)	L. Piggott	16	6/1F
1977	My Hussar	5	8.10	J. Sutcliffe (Epsom)	W. Carson	15	10/1
1978	Fear Naught	4	8.0	J. Etherington (Malton, Yorkshire)	M. Wigham	19	12/1
1979	Pipedreamer	4	8.5	H. Candy (Wantage)	P. Waldron	24	12/1
1980	Tender Heart	4	9.0	J. Sutcliffe (Epsom)	J. Mercer	20	13/2
1981	Teamwork	4	8.6	G. Harwood (Pulborough, Sussex)	G. Starkey	20	8/1
1982	Buzzards Bay	4	8.12	H. Collingridge (Newmarket)	J. Mercer	20	14/1
1983	Mighty Fly	4	9.3	D. Elsworth (Hants)	S. Cauthen	31	12/1
1984	Hawkley	4	8.6	P. Haslam (Newmarket)	T. Williams	18	10/1
1985	Come on the Blues	6	8.2	C. Brittain (Newmarket)	C. Rutter *5	27	14/1
1986	Patriarch	4	7.12	J. Dunlop (Arundel, Sussex)	T. Quinn	32	20/1

*Apprentice allowance claimed

Favourites   The Royal Hunt Cup is very much a prestige handicap, one of the centrepieces of the Royal Ascot meeting, and consistently attracts a good quality field. One favourite during the period under review may suggest it is a difficult race for backers, but this is not so. Only an occasional shock outsider turns up as winner. In the past decade the race has been won (with the sole exception of the 1986 winner *Patriarch*) by a well-backed horse in the first four or so in the betting.

Trainers   Newmarket: 12 winners. John Sutcliffe (Epsom): 3 winners. John Dunlop (Arundel): 2 winners.

No outstanding jockey

Age   4-y-o is the predominant age group and provides 58 per cent of the average entry for the race, but 67.5 per cent of the winners. Next is 5-y-o, but older horses also do quite well — a 15 per cent average entry produces the same percentage success. 3-y-o do not do well.

Weights   The brackets 8 st 2 lb to 8 st 6 lb have provided 11 out of 27 winners and 7 st 9 lb to 7 st 13 lb a further eight out of 27.

Draw   As in the Wokingham, but to a less pronounced degree, the far side or the stands rails are favoured.

---

6 furlong Handicap	The Wokingham Stakes, Royal Ascot, June

First run 1874, this race is a feature of the final afternoon at Royal Ascot.

	Winner (Draw)	Age	Wt.	Trainer	Jockey	Ran	Price
1960	Silver King (25)	4	7.11	S. Hall (Middleham, Yorks.)	J. Sime	29	15/2F
1961	Whistler's Daughter (4)	4	8.6	S. Hall (Middleham, Yorks.)	J. Sime	28	10/1F
1962	Elco (28)	4	8.13	D. Whelan (Epsom)	W. Williamson	35	20/1
1963	Marcher (14)	3	7.12	D. Hanley (Lambourn)	R. Hutchinson	27	100/8
1964	No race						
1965	Nunshoney (24)	3	7.2	G. Beeby (Compton, Berks.)	D. East	25	33/1
1966	My Audrey (7)	5	8.2	E. Cousins (Tarporley, Ches.)	G. Cadwaladr *5	33	20/1
1967	Spaniards Mount (2)	5	8.6	J. Winter (Newmarket)	D. Smith	19	100/6
1968	Charicles (1)	3	7.6	E. Lambton (Newmarket)	D. East	21	100/7
1969	Sky Rocket (4)	4	7.3	M. Pope (Streatley, Berks.)	P. Eddery *7	21	20/1
1970	Virginia Boy (3)	4	7.4	Doug Smith (Newmarket)	D. McKay	28	100/9
1971	Whistling Fool (3)	5	7.7	Doug Smith (Newmarket)	D. McKay	21	11/2
1972	Le Johnstan (7)	4	9.5	J. Sutcliffe Jr (Epsom)	G. Lewis	17	9/1
1973	Plummet (17)	4	8.2	J.E. Sutcliffe (Epsom)	W. Carson	21	11/1
1974	Ginnie's Pet (16)	4	8.6	J.E. Sutcliffe (Epsom)	L. Piggott	22	7/1
1975	Boone's Cabin (USA) (6)	5	10.0	M.V. O'Brien (Ireland)	L. Piggott	20	6/1

	Winner (Draw)	Age	Wt.	Trainer	Jockey	Ran	Price
1976	Import (1)	5	9.4	W. Wightman (Upham, Hampshire)	M.L. Thomas	12	4/1F
1977	Calibina (11)	5	8.5	P. Cole (Lambourn)	G. Baxter	13	14/1
1978	Equal Opportunity (3)	4	7.12	P. Arthur (Aston Tirrold, Berkshire)	R. Curant	24	20/1
1979	Lord Rochford (5)	4	8.8	B. Swift (Epsom)	S. Raymont *5	28	16/1
1980	Queen's Pride (19)	4	7.13	P. Cole (Lambourn)	G. Baxter	29	28/1
1981	Great Eastern (30)	4	9.8	J. Dunlop (Arundel, Sussex)	W. Carson	29	16/1
1982	Battle Hymn (2)	3	7.7	G. Harwood (Pulborough, Sussex)	A. Clark *3	24	14/1
1983	Melindra (22)	4	7.5	D. Elsworth (Whitsbury, Hampshire)	A. McGlone *5	27	7/1F
1984	Petong (18)	4	9.6	M.A. Jarvis (Newmarket)	B. Raymond	28	11/1JF
1985	Time Machine (2)	4	7.12	P. Hughes (Ireland)	W. Carson	30	10/1
1986	Touch of Grey (13)	3	8.8	D. Thom (Newmarket)	M.L. Thomas	28	20/1

*Apprentice allowance claimed

Favourites   The Wokingham is a highly competitive hell-for-leather dash over the tough Ascot 6 furlongs, the last 6 furlongs, in fact, of the straight Royal Hunt Cup course. This is no course for short runners, and run at a strong pace throughout, tests a sprinter to its limit. Despite the attractive prices (because of big fields, normally) of the winners shown in the table, the Wokingham is *not* a race for outsiders. Well-backed horses usually win.

Trainers   Epsom trainers, in particular the Sutcliffe family, have done well in this race, with five winners since 1960. Newmarket have sent out half a dozen winners, but all from smaller training establishments. Paul Cole should be noted as saddling the winner twice in recent years.

Jockeys   Claiming apprentices (five winners including that ridden by Pat Eddery back in 1969) have an excellent record, as well as light-weight jockeys.

Age   Since the 1939-45 war:

    3-y-o   20 per cent of winners
    4-y-o   62.5 per cent of winners
    5-y-o   17.5 per cent of winners

The only horse of over 5-y-o to have won this century was *Galleot* (6-y-o) in 1910.

Weight   With the raising of the minimum handicap weight it is a difficult to draw a useful conclusion. In the entire post-war period since 1945 the 7 st 7 lb to 8 st 8 lb bracket has provided approximately 50 per cent of all winners, but whereas it used to be the middle part of the handicap, it is now the lower. One point of significance may be emerging, and that is the increased proportion of higher-weighted winners — four carrying 9 st 4 lb or more since 1975.

Draw   The Wokingham is yet another race (see also the Cambridgeshire) where the draw is commonly supposed not to matter very much. This is not so, as a look at the draw diagram will show. This is based on the draw expressed as a percentage of the total number of runners each year, which portrays the spread of the draw across the start, although a horse drawn one in a field of 20, for example, is expressed at 5 per cent, and draw one in a field of 30 becomes 3 per cent.

From this it can be seen that 13 winners of the 26 since 1960 (50 per cent) came from the 0-21 per cent area, and a further seven from the 80-100 per cent sector. The message, in general, therefore, is to ignore middle numbers (significantly, perhaps, it took Lester Piggott, on two occasions, to beat the low-high draw pattern) when making a choice, and concentrate on the extremes. 75 per cent of the winners in the period are contained in the following draw brackets:

Field	Draw
15	1-3 and 12-15
20	1-4 and 16-20
25	1-5 and 20-25
30	1-6 and 24-30
35	1-7 and 28-35

The main reason for the Wokingham draw being so oriented is, of course, that the field invariably splits, and, in a fast start, horses drawn in the middle lose ground getting over to either side. The positioning of the starting stalls must also be taken into account.

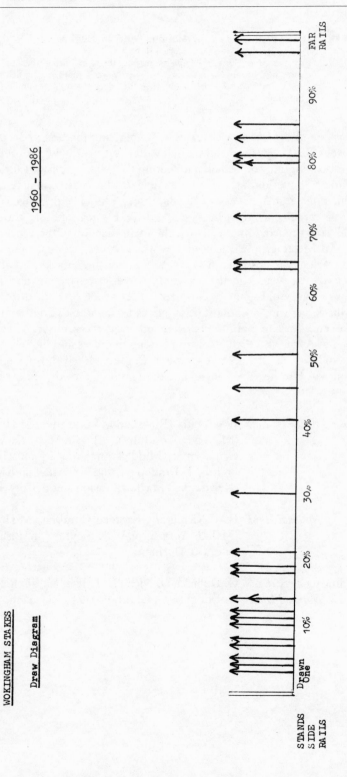

WOKINGHAM STAKES

Draw Diagram

1960 – 1986

AYR   Left-hand   Flat and National Hunt

Draw: Because of the long left-handed bend after the start, low numbers are favoured in races of 7 furlongs and 1 mile, particularly when there are big fields. Again, on the straight course in big fields when the going is soft, high numbers in contrast are preferable.

Ayr is one of the finest racecourses in Britain, and the best in Scotland. It is an oval of just over a mile and a half with easy turns, and the round course joins the 6 furlong course half a mile from the winning post. 11 furlong races start on a chute joining the main course on the far side. There are minor undulations, but Ayr is essentially flat throughout. The drainage is excellent and it is rare to encounter heavy going there. Having said that, the exception to the rule occurred in 1985 when the main meeting of the year, called the Western Meeting, in September was wrecked by torrential rain. Only one day's racing was possible, in heavy going, and three days were abandoned because of a waterlogged course! The Western Meeting features the 6 furlong Ayr Gold Cup, sponsored by Ladbrokes, and this invariably produces big fields and big starting prices for a gamble. The Land of Burns Stakes and the Tote Sprint Trophy are other big races at Ayr. National Hunt racing at Ayr is also high-class, and among the races are the Scottish Grand National (which was taken over when Bogside closed down) and Scottish Champion Hurdle. The course, like the Flat one, provides an excellent and fair test.

Leading trainers: *Flat* J.W. Watts (Richmond, Yorkshire), M.H. Easterby (Malton, Yorkshire), J. Hindley (Newmarket), C. Thornton (Middleham, Yorkshire), B. Hills (Lambourn), J. Dunlop (Arundel, Sussex) and M. Stoute (Newmarket) who has an astonishing 50 per cent 'strike rate'.

National Hunt G.W. Richards (Greystoke, Cumbria), M.H. Easterby (Malton, Yorkshire), W.A. Stephenson (Bishop Auckland, Co. Durham)

Leading jockeys: *Flat* G. Duffield, D. Nicholls, T. Ives, M. Birch, K. Darley
National Hunt N. Doughty, C. Grant, P. Tuck, T.G. Dun

BRIGHTON   Left-hand   Flat only

Draw: There is a slight advantage to low numbers, particularly in sprints, but *Raceform* adds the proviso except in very wet conditions.

Ever since Graham Greene wrote *Brighton Rock*, his novel containing a race gang episode on Brighton racecourse, the reputation for having a Tattersalls' Ring full of villains still lurks uneasily round this Corporation-owned track. Quite unjustified, of course, but there is no doubt that the course, like Brighton itself, does have a breezy, slightly raffish atmosphere. The racing is moderate but the holidaymakers, to say nothing of the punters who rattle down from the 'smoke' within an hour on the Brighton Belle, all enjoy it. At least the latter, when the naps have been turned over, can get back all their losses playing nap with strangers on the train on the way home.

The track is 1½ miles long, starting in the distance on the downland, and pursuing a course shaped roughly like a battered cooking-pot seen in cross section. In between the start and the stands is a kind of depression which was used as the location for filming *Oh What A Lovely War*. The first three furlongs are slightly uphill. There is then a slight descent and rise to about 4 furlongs from home when the ground falls more steeply until 2 furlongs from the finish when there is another rise, with the final hundred yards level. The bends are fairly innocuous, but with this conformation the course does not favour horses which like to stride out. Handy horses do well at Brighton, as well as horses that are fast out of the stalls and can make all the running. Being on chalk downland, Brighton is another course which is lucky with its going and seldom becomes testing.

Leading trainers: J. Dunlop (Arundel, Sussex), G. Harwood (Pulborough, Sussex), P. Cole (Whatcombe, Berkshire), R. Hannon (Marlborough, Wiltshire)

Leading jockeys: G. Starkey, B. Rouse, P. Eddery, T. Quinn, S. Cauthen

CHELTENHAM   Left-hand   National Hunt only

Cheltenham is the show case of National Hunt racing, the equivalent of Newmarket 'headquarters' on the Flat, without the training, a place of pilgrimage for the hardy followers of the winter game, and its great Festival meeting in March has been called the Royal Ascot of jumping. The Festival Meeting is packed with wonderful racing in the spectacular setting below Cleeve Hill. Apart from the Gold Cup (sponsored by the Tote), the Champion Hurdle (sponsored by Waterford Crystal) and the Triumph

Hurdle for four-year-olds (rescued, revived and sponsored by the *Daily Express* from the time a year or two after Hurst Park closed in 1962) there is not a race lacking top class contestants and strong betting markets. Novice hurdlers and chasers, 2 mile chasers, long distance hurdlers, hunter-chasers, amateur riders, all are catered for at this three day bonanza. But the racing throughout the year at Cheltenham is superb, with prize money to match. The big races include the 2½ mile Mackeson Gold Cup in November, Still Fork Trucks Gold Cup Handicap Chase and Bula Hurdle (same sponsor) in December, and the Kennedy Construction (formerly the Massey-Ferguson) Gold Cup.

Cheltenham racecourse is, in fact, two racecourses. In the late 1950s a new course was added to the old one and both courses are now used, both approximately 1½ mile ovals, with special chutes for the starts of races run of 2½ miles, 3¼ miles and 4 miles. There used to be a chute, out of sight of the stands, for the start of the Gold Cup; also, 4 mile races used to disappear for a time somewhere beyond the stands and behind the car park. But that has all been changed. Quite unchanged, however, are the Cheltenham gradients including a severe uphill run-in of 257 yards from the last of the demanding fences, making this course a stiff test of both stamina and courage. One of the greatest heroes of Cheltenham is *Arkle*, a magnificent chaser, whose memory is now commemorated by a bronze statue. More recently, the Cheltenham crowd took to their hearts another Irish horse called *Dawn Run*. This outstanding mare is the only horse ever to win both the Champion Hurdle and the Gold Cup, a feat she achieved in 1984 and 1986, before cruelly meeting her death shortly afterwards while attempting to win the French Champion Hurdle for the second time. Her statue, unveiled in 1987, faces that of *Arkle*.

Leading trainers:	Fred Winter and Fulke Walwyn (whose astonishing Cheltenham record includes four Gold Cups, two Champion Hurdles, six Cathcart Challenge Cups, three Waterford Crystal Stayers' Hurdles, a Sun Alliance Novices' Hurdle, Mackeson Gold Cup, and Massey-Ferguson Gold Cup), N. Henderson, J.R. Jenkins, Mrs M. Rimell
Leading jockeys:	S. Smith Eccles, P. Scudamore, R. Linley, S. Sherwood

---

2 miles   Champion Hurdle, Cheltenham, March

Like the Cheltenham Gold Cup, also run at the Festival Meeting, this is the National Hunt equivalent of a 'Classic' race, and decides the Hurdles Championship of the year. The distance has varied over the years (up to 200 yards beyond 2 miles) but is now fixed at 2 miles. Horses carry the following weights: 4-y-o 11 st 6 lb; older horses (except mares) 12 st (the majority of runners). Mares 11 st 9 lb. The race was first run in 1927 as the Champion Hurdle Challenge

Cup, and, sponsored since 1978 by Waterford Crystal, is now called the Waterford Crystal Champion Hurdle Challenge Trophy. Prize to the winner in 1986 was £41,435.

	Winner	Age	Trainer	Rider	Ran	Price
1960	Another Flash	6	P. Sleator (Ireland)	H. Beasley	12	11/4F
1961	Eborneezer	6	H.R. Price (Findon, Sussex)	F. Winter	17	4/1
1962	Anzio	5	F. Walwyn (Lambourn)	G.W. Robinson	14	11/2
1963	Winning Fair	8	G. Spencer (Ireland)	Mr A. Lillingston	21	100/9
1964	Magic Court	6	T. Robson (Greystoke, Cumbria)	P. McCarron	24	100/6
1965	Kirriemuir	5	F. Walwyn (Lambourn)	G.W. Robinson	19	50/1
1966	Salmon Spray	8	R. Turnell (Ogbourne, Wiltshire)	J. Haine	17	4/1
1967	Saucy Kit	6	M.H. Easterby (Malton, Yorkshire)	R. Edwards	23	100/6
1968	Persian War	5	C. Davies (Chepstow, Mon.)	J. Uttley	16	4/1
1969	Persian War	6	C. Davies (Chepstow, Mon.)	J. Uttley	17	6/4F
1970	Persian War	7	C. Davies (Chepstow, Mon.)	J. Uttley	14	5/4F
1971	Bula	6	F. Winter (Lambourn)	P. Kelleway	9	15/8F
1972	Bula	7	F. Winter (Lambourn)	P. Kelleway	12	8/11F
1973	Comedy of Errors	6	F. Rimell (Kinnersley, Worcs.)	W. Smith	8	8/1
1974	Lanzarote	6	F. Winter (Lambourn)	R. Pitman	7	7/4
1975	Comedy of Errors	8	F. Rimell (Kinnersley, Worcs.)	K. White	13	11/8F
1976	Night Nurse	5	M.H. Easterby (Malton, Yorks.)	P. Broderick	8	2/1F
1977	Night Nurse	6	M.H. Easterby (Malton, Yorks.)	P. Broderick	10	15/2
1978	Monksfield	6	D. McDonogh (Ireland)	T. Kinane	13	11/2
1979	Monksfield	7	D. McDonogh (Ireland)	D. Hughes	10	9/4F
1980	Sea Pigeon	10	M.H. Easterby (Malton, Yorks.)	J.J. O'Neill	9	13/2
1981	Sea Pigeon	11	M.H. Easterby (Malton, Yorks.)	J. Francome	14	7/4F
1982	For Auction	6	M. Cunningham (Ireland)	Mr C. Magnier	14	40/1
1983	Gaye Brief	6	Mrs M. Rimell (Kinnersley, Worcs.)	R. Linley	17	7/1
1984	Dawn Run (Mare)	6	P. Mullins (Ireland)	J.J. O'Neill	14	4/5F
1985	See You Then	5	N. Henderson (Lambourn)	S. Smith Eccles	14	16/1
1986	See You Then	6	N. Henderson (Lambourn)	S. Smith Eccles	23	5/6F

About 3¼ miles 22 Fences   The Cheltenham Gold Cup

The Cheltenham Gold Cup, centrepiece of the final day of the Festival Meeting, is to National Hunt racing what the Derby is to the Flat. Since *Red Splash* was the first winner, in 1924, the race has provided the entry to steeplechasing's hall of fame, and some illustrious names embellish its records, after many a thrill on the way to so doing: *Easter Hero* and *L'Escargot* (twice each), *Cottage Rake* and *Arkle* (three times each), and *Golden Miller* (five times), although the number of victories gives no indication of the immeasurable superiority of *Arkle* as the greatest of all chasers, and, before him, that of *Golden Miller*. Among other famous names, *Mandarin* won in 1962 not long before his sensational victory with a broken bridle in the Grand Steeplechase de Paris; the game little ex-hunter-chaser *Halloween* (partnered, like *Mandarin*, by the incomparable Fred Winter) was placed four times without winning; while *The Dikler* set the seal on his career and Fulke Walwyn's high opinion of him at the fourth attempt. Most recently, *Dawn Run*, amid enthusiasm and sentiment not witnessed since *Arkle*'s day, became only the fourth mare to win, and the first horse to have succeeded in both Gold Cup and Champion Hurdle; *Burrough Hill Lad* and *Forgive 'N Forget* each have chances still to extend their tally of victories beyond one apiece; while in 1982, Michael Dickinson saddled the winner, *Silver Buck*, and runner-up, *Bregawn*, and the following year improved on that by being trainer of all five horses to finish, this time *Bregawn* being the winner, and *Silver Buck* finishing fourth. In 1924, the value to the winning owner was £685; sponsored by the Tote, the equivalent figure in 1986 was £54,900.

	Winner	Age	Wt.	Trainer	Jockey	Ran	SP
1960	Pas Seul	7	12.0	R. Turnell (Marlborough, Wiltshire)	W. Rees	12	6/1
1961	Saffron Tartan	10	12.0	D. Butchers (Epsom)	F. Winter	11	2/1F
1962	Mandarin	11	12.0	F. Walwyn (Lambourn)	F. Winter	9	7/2
1963	Mill House	6	12.0	F. Walwyn (Lambourn)	G.W. Robinson	12	7/2F

	Winner	Age	Wt.	Trainer	Jockey	Ran	SP
1964	Arkle	7	12.0	T. Dreaper (Ireland)	P. Taaffe	4	7/4
1965	Arkle	8	12.0	T. Dreaper (Ireland)	P. Taaffe	4	100/30 on
1966	Arkle	9	12.0	T. Dreaper (Ireland)	P. Taaffe	5	10/1 on
1967	Woodland Venture	7	12.0	F. Rimell (Kinnersley, Worcestershire)	T. Biddlecombe	8	100/8
1968	Fort Leney	10	12-0	T. Dreaper (Ireland)	P. Taaffe	5	11/2
1969	What A Myth	12	12.0	Ryan Price (Findon, Sussex)	P. Kelleway	11	8/1
1970	L'Escargot	7	12.0	Dan Moore (Ireland)	T. Carberry	12	33/1
1971	L'Escargot	8	12.0	Dan Moore (Ireland)	T. Carberry	8	7/2JF
1972	Glencaraig Lady*	8	12.0	F. Flood (Ireland)	F. Berry	12	6/1
1973	The Dikler	10	12.0	F. Walwyn (Lambourn)	R. Barry	8	9/1
1974	Captain Christy	7	12.0	P. Taaffe (Ireland)	H. Beasley	7	7/1
1975	Ten Up	8	12.0	J. Dreaper (Ireland)	T. Carberry	8	2/1
1976	Royal Frolic	7	12.0	F. Rimell (Kinnersley, Worcestershire)	J. Burke	11	14/1
1977	Davy Lad	7	12.0	M. O'Toole (Ireland)	D. Hughes	13	14/1
1978	Midnight Court	7	12.0	F. Winter (Lambourn)	J. Francome	10	5/2
1979	Alverton	9	12.0	M.H. Easterby (Malton, Yorkshire)	J.J. O'Neill	14	5/1JF
1980	Master Smudge	8	12.0	A. Barrow (Bridgwater, Somerset)	R. Hoare	15	14/1
	(Tied Cottage finished first, disqualified)						
1981	Little Owl	7	12.0	M.H. Easterby (Malton, Yorkshire)	Mr J. Wilson	15	6/1
1982	Silver Buck	10	12.0	M. Dickinson (Harewood, Yorkshire)	R. Earnshaw	22	8/1
1983	Bregawn	9	12.0	M. Dickinson (Harewood, Yorkshire)	G. Bradley	11	100/30F
1984	Burrough Hill Lad	8	12.0	Mrs J. Pitman (Lambourn)	P. Tuck	12	7/2
1985	Forgive 'n Forget	8	12.0	J. Fitzgerald (Malton, Yorkshire)	M. Dwyer	15	7/1
1986	Dawn Run*	8	11.9	P. Mullins (Ireland)	J.J. O'Neill	11	15/8F

*Mares.

Favourites   Not, overall, a race for favourites, nor, altogether a good race for backers. Despite a fairly strong ante post market for several months before the race, betting on the Gold Cup is not a particularly profitable activity. Against this, the race itself invariably provides a spectacle well worth watching for itself alone, and without the necessity for extra *angst* through the wallet or handbag.

Trainers   Of present day trainers, Fulke Walwyn (Lambourn) has the most impressive individual record, and while Ireland has provided most winners overall during the period, it is encouraging that out of the last eight Gold Cups, Yorkshire trainers have saddled the winners of no fewer than five.

CHEPSTOW   Left-hand   Flat and National Hunt

Draw: A slight advantage to high numbers on the straight course

Chepstow racecourse is only 60 years old and has come up in the world since its early days. For this the enterprise and imagination of its present Clerk of the Course, John Hughes, must be thanked, particularly in the area of attracting sponsors; also the opening of the Severn Road Bridge has brought easy access via the M4, not least for competing horses, in particular those from the Lambourn training area. Picturesque parkland surroundings and good racing make for an enjoyable time at Chepstow races. There is a mile course, quite straight, with undulations and the round course is an oval joined to the straight course about two miles in circumference. National Hunt racing takes place on the oval course and as a result of its switchback nature the going can vary from fast down the back straight to wet in the dips. The undulating nature of the course in the home straight also presents problems and demands on riding skill at the fences, last of which is right in front of the stands. And for the horse on the Flat there is a stiffish 2 furlong rise where the two courses join. Big races include: (Flat) Welsh Derby, (National Hunt) Coral Welsh Grand National, in December, Finale Junior Hurdle, Persian War Novices Hurdle, Racing Post Hurdle, Welsh Novices' Championship Chase, and Blue Circle Welsh Champion Hurdle. The average prize money for National Hunt racing is far greater than for Flat racing at Chepstow and the quality of the jumping races quite outstanding. Horses that like to make the running do well over the jumps here.

Leading trainers: *Flat*   H. Thomson Jones (Newmarket), P. Walwyn (Lambourn), Sir M. Prescott (Newmarket)

National Hunt   Mrs M. Rimell, F. Winter (Lambourn), T. Forster (Letcombe Bassett, Berkshire), J. Gifford (Findon, Sussex)

Leading jockeys: *Flat*   P. Cook, P. Eddery, T. Quinn, G. Duffield, A. McGlone

National Hunt   P. Scudamore, S. Smith Eccles, S. Sherwood, J. Duggan

---

CHESTER   Left-hand   Flat only

Draw: The draw is of crucial importance on this course. Because of the conformation of the track, low numbers are very much favoured in races from 5 furlongs to 7 furlongs 122 yards. Conversely, if there is a biggish field for a sprint, a high number draw is often the kiss of death.

Racing began in Chester on the Roodeye within the city walls in 1540, the prize being a silver bell. Chester thus boasts the oldest racecourse in the land, as well as the smallest, the most unusual, and, these days, one of the three most popular. Only Ascot and York among racecourses staging flat racing have a higher daily average attendance. Matching the bustling prosperity of the city, with its thriving tourist trade and crowded shops, racing on the Roodeye has seen bigger and yet bigger crowds over the past few years. The number of spectators in 1985 averaged 12,607, while for one evening meeting the following year, more than 17,000 packed themselves into this little course.

At one time there was only one three day meeting at Chester, centred round the 2¼ mile-plus Chester Cup, first run in 1824, and including among its winners famous stayers such as *Brown Jack*, *Trelawny* and *Sea Pigeon* (twice). This meeting, in May, is still the big event of the year, and, although not all the shops now put up their shutters on Chester Cup day as once used to happen, many still do. In addition to the main meeting, however, there are additional fixtures, including evening racing, in July and August. The course is usually described as circular (which makes it unique in this country), 1 mile 73 yards round (which makes it the smallest circuit), with a straight side from the 7 furlong start, and a short very slightly curving run-in of only 2 furlongs from the final proper bend. This, quite apart from making the draw important, also means that a horse which likes to make all the running is well suited at Chester. The conformation of the course also dictates an advantage to the horse who gets a fast start in sprints, which start on the bend.

The Chester Cup (sponsored by Ladbrokes) was worth £16,952 to the winner in 1985. It is invariably run at a cracking pace from start to finish and therefore, despite the sharpness of the track, is an exceptional test of stamina in which the runners pass the stands three times. Valuable Group III events in May are: the Chester Vase, the Cheshire Oaks, the Ormonde Stakes and the Dee Stakes. The Chester Vase, in particular, has long been used as a try out race for Classic candidates, and, despite the emergence of other trials, is still so used today. Chester Vase winners who have gone on to win the Derby are Lord Derby's great racehorse *Hyperion* (1933), *Windsor Lad* (1934) and, more recently, *Henbit* (1980) and poor, ill-fated *Shergar* (1981), while in 1951 *Supreme Court* (not entered in the Classics) became the first winner of what is now the King George VI and Queen Elizabeth Stakes.

Leading trainers: W.R. Hern (West Ilsley, Berkshire), B. Hills (Lambourn), G. Wragg (Newmarket)

Leading jockey: W. Carson, but B. Thomson, the young New Zealand-born jockey has ridden no fewer than eleven winners at Chester in the short time he has been over here

---

DONCASTER   Left-hand   Flat and National Hunt

Draw: Difficult to assess accurately because recent course alterations may change the old pattern of advantage. For years on the straight mile (where the Lincoln Handicap is run) high numbers had a distinct pull except in soft going. But in recent years this has not been the case, and low numbers now seem to enjoy an advantage.

Records of racing at Doncaster go back as far as 1595. The oldest Classic, the St Leger, was first run here in 1776 and was won by the Marquis of

Rockingham's strangely named filly *Allabaculia*. Despite the superb racing the facilities at Town Moor were rather spartan until Alderman Cammidge put his ambitious plans for improvement into action. These have come to fruition, and now there can be no complaints about conditions for the spectators at this historic course which stages the first and last fixtures of the Flat season. The course is a very fair one, a pear-shaped oval about 1 mile 7 furlongs in circumference, flat throughout, except for a slight hill on the far side about 1¼ miles from the winning post. There are two mile courses, a straight mile on which the Lincoln Handicap is run, and one which starts on an arm at a tangent to the round course. Because Town Moor has a sandy subsoil, the course becomes heavy only after prolonged rainfall. It very much favours long striding stayers with its great width, and long run-in of nearly 5 furlongs. The final and longest Classic of the season, the St Leger is only one of several top class races at the September meeting which features the Doncaster Cup over 2¼ miles, which with the Ascot Gold Cup and Goodwood Cup forms a corner of the triple crown for stayers. Horses since the war to have won all three in the same season are *Le Moss* who, incredibly, performed the feat two years running (1979 and 1980), *Souepi* who dead-heated for his Doncaster Cup in 1953, and *Alycidon* (1949). Other top stayers to have won during the period include *Raise You Ten* (1963), *Proverb* (1974) and *Ardross* (1982).

These races apart, the Doncaster programme is particularly rich in valuable 2-y-o events which include, at the St Leger meeting, the Laurent Perrier Champagne Stakes (7f), the May Hill Stakes (1 m, fillies only, won in 1985 by *Midway Lady* who went on to take the 1000 Guineas and Oaks) and the Brian Swift Flying Childers Stakes (5f), and later in the season, the 1 m William Hill Futurity (worth more than £43,000 in 1985), a race originated by Phil Bull of *Timeform*, and the EBF Nursery. Other good races are the Unipart Handicap (1¾ m), Battle of Britain Handicap (1 m) and well-proven older established events like the Park Hill Stakes for staying 3-y-o fillies, and the 5f Portland Handicap, both at the St Leger meeting.

The steeplechase course is also one of the fairest in the country. Its main feature used to be the Great Yorkshire Chase, now sponsored by William Hill, and won by *Freebooter* in 1950 before winning the Grand National, and *Knock Hard* in 1953 before winning the Cheltenham Gold Cup. With competition from other courses around the same date, and bad luck with the weather, the race has lost some of its importance as a trial, but (frost permitting) it is still a marvellous race to watch and has been joined by other big jumping events in the Sheila's Cottage Chase, the Freebooter Novices' Chase (both in December) and the Rossington Main Novices Hurdle.

Leading trainers: *Flat* M. Stoute (Newmarket), H. Cecil (Newmarket), W.R. ˙Hern (W. Illsley, Berkshire), B. Hills (Lambourn)

National Hunt H. Wharton (Wetherby, Yorkshire), G.W. Richards (Greystoke, Cumbria), W.A. Stephenson (Bishop

Auckland), J.G. Fitzgerald (Malton, Yorkshire)

Leading jockeys: *Flat* W. Carson, S. Cauthen, G. Starkey, P. Eddery, T. Ives

National Hunt N. Doughty, M. Dwyer, M. Bowlby, P. Corrigan

---

1 mile Hcp   The Lincoln Handicap, Doncaster, late March

Originally the Lincolnshire Handicap, and the first big handicap of the Flat season which used to open at Lincoln on the Carholme, this race was first run in 1853 and is the first leg of the Spring Double. When racing ceased at Lincoln, in 1964, the race was transferred to the present opening fixture at Doncaster, and retains its popularity as the first big handicap gamble on the Flat. Since 1979, the race has been sponsored by the William Hill Organisation.

	Winner (Draw)	Age	Wt.	Trainer	Jockey	Ran	Price
1965	Old Tom (20)	6	8.7	M.H. Easterby (Malton, Yorkshire)	A. Breasley	38	22/1
1966	Riot Act (45)	4	8.3	F. Armstrong (Newmarket)	A. Breasley	49	8/1F
1967	Ben Novus (12)	5	7.10	W. Hide (Ludlow, Salop)	P. Robinson	24	22/1
1968	Frankincense (31)	4	9.5	J. Oxley (Newmarket)	G. Starkey	31	100/8
1969	Foggy Bell (9)	4	7.11	Denys Smith (Bishop Auckland, Co Durham)	A. Barclay	25	20/1
1970	New Chapter (15)	4	8.1	F. Armstrong (Newmarket)	A. Barclay	23	100/9
1971	Double Cream (20)	4	8.9	W. Elsey (Malton, Yorkshire)	E. Hide	26	30/1
1972	Sovereign Bill (6)	6	8.12	P. Robinson (Newmarket)	E. Hide	21	9/2F
1973	Bronze Hill (22)	4	7.9	M.H. Easterby (Malton, Yorkshire)	M. Birch	26	50/1
1974	Quizair (22)	6	7.13	R. Jarvis (Newmarket)	M.L. Thomas	26	28/1
1975	Southwark Star (18)	4	7.3	G. Peter-Hoblyn (Marlborough, Wiltshire)	R. Fox *5	24	33/1
1976	The Hertford (14)	5	8.6	B. Swift (Epsom)	G. Lewis	26	20/1
1977	Blustery (24)	5	7.11	R. Smyly (Lambourn)	D. McKay	26	20/1
1978	Captain's Wings (6)	5	7.10	R. Boss (Newmarket)	M. Wigham *5	25	13/2F
1979	Fair Season (15)	5	8.10	I. Balding (Kingsclere, Berks.)	G. Starkey	23	8/1
1980	King's Ride (2)	4	8.12	W. Wightman (Upham, Hampshire)	G. Baxter	18	10/1
1981	Saher (9)	5	8.12	R. Sheather (Newmarket)	R. Cochrane *5	19	14/1
1982	King's Glory (22)	4	8.3	P. Mitchell (Epsom)	B. Crossley *3	26	11/1
1983	Mighty Fly (5)	4	8.4	D. Elsworth (Whitsbury, Hampshire)	S. Cauthen	26	14/1
1984	Saving Mercy (8)	4	8.9	Dermot Weld (Ireland)	W. Swinburn	26	14/1
1985	Cataldi (8)	4	9.10	G. Harwood (Pulborough, Sussex)	G. Starkey	26	10/1F
1986	K-Battery (12)	5	8.4	W. Elsey (Malton, Yorkshire)	J. Lowe	25	25/1

*Apprentice allowance claimed

Favourites   Only four winning favourites (prices 9/2–10/1), and a large proportion of winners (47.7 per cent) at 20/1 and over, does not inspire great confidence in the Lincoln as a way for the average backer to make money. Well-backed horses, including two of the favourites, have won all but twice in the past 10 runnings and this trend may be connected with the diminished importance of the draw (see below). Beware the winner of the previous season's Cambridgeshire being made favourite for the Lincoln. The last Cambridgeshire success to win the Lincoln the following season was *Long Set* in 1911-12 and before that *Winkfield's Pride* in 1896-97 when the professional commissioner Charlie Mills backed the horse down from 66/1 to favouritism for the Cambridgeshire on behalf of the Hermits of Salisbury Plain (see Chapter Three) and there was a big gamble again on him for the Lincolnshire when he started at 7/2 favourite again.

Trainers   Newmarket stables lead with seven winners, but, as might be expected, Yorkshire and the north are also strongly represented. Both trainers who have saddled more than one winner are, in fact, from Yorkshire: M.H. Easterby (2) and W. Elsey (2) whose father, Capt Charles Elsey, saddled three winners of the old Lincolnshire Handicap, including one war-time substitute run at Pontefract.

Jockeys   Greville Starkey has the best performance figure. He has ridden three winners, a record for this century shared with Joe Sime and Eddie Hide. Claiming apprentices also do quite well with four winners since 1965.

Age   4-y-o: 12 (54.5 per cent)
5-y-o: 7 (31.8 per cent)
6-y-o: 3 (13.7 per cent)

Weight   The going is often soft for the Lincoln and this helps to explain the relatively poor showing of horses with big weights. Only two winners carrying over 9 st appear in the entire record of the race since it was transferred to Doncaster. One of them, *Cataldi*, in 1985, was made favourite and stormed through soft going with heavy patches to make every yard of the running — a brave exception to the rule. Neither is the Lincoln a race for very low weights. All but four of the winners were contained within the handicap range 7 st 10 lb two (two winners) to 8 st 12 lb (three winners).

Draw   The draw used to be of crucial importance both in the old Lincolnshire on the Carholme, Lincoln, and when the race was first run at Doncaster. Improvements to the course and to drainage now seem to have successfully countered the big advantage once enjoyed by high numbers in the draw, making the race fairer all round. In recent years there have been winners from all sectors of the draw. The draw diagram on page 152, expressing the draw number as a percentage of the total field, shows the overall spread over the past 20 or so years.

1¾ miles   St Leger, Doncaster, September

The oldest classic, sponsored since 1985 by Holsten Pils.

	Winner	Sire	Trainer	Jockey	Ran	Price
1960	St Paddy	Aureole	N. Murless (Newmarket)	L. Piggott	9	4/6F
1961	Aurelius	Aureole	N. Murless (Newmarket)	L. Piggott	13	9/2
1962	Hethersett	Hugh Lupus	W.R. Hern (W. Ilsley, Berks.)	W.H. Carr	15	100/8
1963	Ragusa	Ribot	P.J. Prendergast (Ireland)	G. Bougoure	7	2/5F
1964	Indiana	Sayajirao	J.F. Watts (Newmarket)	J. Lindley	15	100/7
1965	Provoke	Aureole	W.R. Hern (W. Ilsley, Berks.)	J. Mercer	11	28/1
1966	Sodium	Psidium	G. Todd (Manton, Wilts.)	F. Durr	9	7/1
1967	Ribocco	Ribot	F.J. Houghton (Blewbury, Oxfordshire)	L. Piggott	9	7/2JF
1968	Ribero	Ribot	F.J. Houghton (Blewbury, Oxfordshire)	L. Piggott	8	100/30
1969	Intermezzo	Hornbeam	H. Wragg (Newmarket)	R. Hutchinson	11	7/1
1970	Nijinsky (Can)	Northern Dancer	V. O'Brien (Ireland)	L. Piggott	9	2/7F
1971	Athens Wood	Celtic Ash	H. Thomson Jones (Newmarket)	L. Piggott	8	5/2
1972	Boucher	Ribot	M.V. O'Brien (Ireland)	L. Piggott	7	3/1
1973	Peleid	Derring-Do	W. Elsey (Malton, Yorks.)	F. Durr	13	28/1
1974	Bustino	Busted	W.R. Hern (W. Ilsley, Berks.)	J. Mercer	10	11/10F
1975	Bruni	Sea Hawk	H.R. Price (Findon, Sussex)	A. Murray	12	9/1
1976	Crow	Exbury	A. Penna (France)	Y. Saint-Martin	15	6/1JF
1977	Dunfermline (f)	Royal Palace	W.R. Hern (W. Ilsley, Berks.)	W. Carson	13	10/1
1978	Julio Mariner	Blakeney	C. Brittain (Newmarket)	E. Hide	14	28/1
1979	Son of Love	Jefferson	R. Collet (France)	A. Lequeux	17	20/1
1980	Light Cavalry	Brigadier Gerard	H. Cecil (Newmarket)	J. Mercer	7	3/1
1981	Cut Above	High Top	W.R. Hern (W. Ilsley, Berks.)	J. Mercer	7	28/1
1982	Touching Wood	Roberto	H. Thomson Jones (Newmarket)	P. Cook	15	7/1

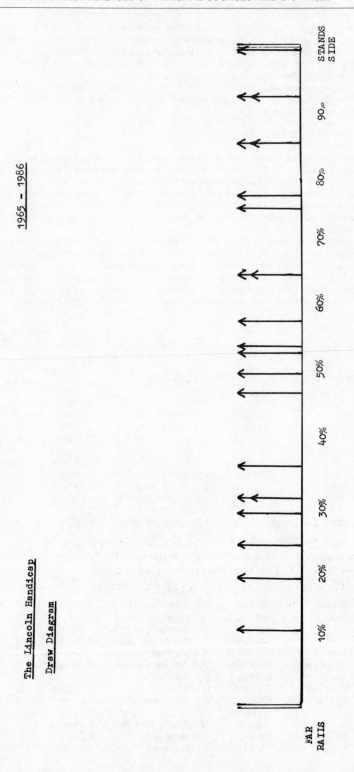

The Lincoln Handicap

Draw Diagram

1965 – 1986

1983	Sun Princess (f)	English Prince	W.R. Hern (W. Ilsley, Berks.)	W. Carson	10	11/8F
1984	Commanche Run	Run the Gantlet	L. Cumani (Newmarket)	L. Piggott	11	7/4F
1985	Oh So Sharp (f)	Kris	H. Cecil (Newmarket)	S. Cauthen	6	8/11F
1986	Moon Madness	Kalamoun	J. Dunlop (Arundel, Sussex)	P. Eddery	8	9/2

(f) filly

The declining prestige of the St Leger is discussed elsewhere, notably in Chapter Eleven. As a betting race, although there is still an ante post market on it, it is not as popular as other classics, but that is no reason for not trying to find the winner. The prerequisite, of course, is a colt or filly who will stay the tough Doncaster 1¾ miles, to which breeding and past performance are the clues: there have been notable failures of horses who, before the St Leger, had not attempted the distance. Seven clear favourites, and two joint or co-favourites won in the period from 1960, but there were no fewer than five winners at over 20/1, so a certain amount of caution is dictated. The St Leger is certainly not as good a race for backers as the Derby, or as the Guineas.

The trainer to follow *par excellence* is Major Dick Hern (W. Ilsley, Berkshire) with no fewer than six winners, but Newmarket has an excellent record, the most successful trainer from there being Henry Cecil with two winners. Now Lester Piggott (eight winners) has retired, only Willie Carson among present jockeys has ridden more than one winner. Nevertheless, the race is invariably taken by a top jockey. In recent years, too, fillies have an outstanding record against the colts.

EPSOM   Left-hand   Flat only

Draw: Low numbers up to 1¼ m; middle numbers for the Derby course.

Epsom is synonymous with Derby Day, and Frith's great painting of that title, in the Tate Gallery, still has power to conjure up that particular atmosphere of peculiarly English carnival existing on that and no other day in the year. The costume has changed since Victorian times, but the faces haven't, nor the gipsies with lucky white heather, the unimaginable crush round the bookmakers in the centre of the course, and the sense that one horse will go into the history books within an hour or so. Added today are the jellied eel stalls, the helter-skelters, the blare of fairground music, but still, also, the dips, the wide boys, the tipsters. Epsom, still a considerable training centre, is as integral to the British racing scene as Newmarket, but so very different. The Derby winner occupies a place in Turf history as no other horse ever does. To see it all in perspective it is quite an experience to walk up the course to near Tattenham Corner station and see the start of a two-year-old race such as the Woodcote Stakes, or a 5 furlongs sprint, the stalls rattle asunder, the horses plunge down the dip, and disappear in a blur of silks towards the winning post in the far distance. From here you get a hint of the challenge of the Derby. Tattenham Corner itself is an enormous test to jockeyship and the balance of a horse which is unique in racing. It used to be sharper than it is today. Even George Fordham (known alternatively as 'The Terror' or 'The Demon' or 'The Kid') could not kid other jockeys at Tattenham Corner, where he was not very demon-like, and his fear of the course gave his rival Fred Archer an advantage over and above his own riding skill. Epsom is still a place for courageous and good jockeys. As well as the Derby, there are also the Oaks and Coronation Cup over the same course. The spring meeting features the Blue Riband Trial Stakes, which is used (less frequently these days than in the past) as a Derby trial, the City and Suburban Handicap, and the Great Metropolitan Handicap. These races provide early examples of sponsorship. In the mid-19th century Epsom was having difficulty in finding funds for its new race, the Great Metropolitan. So one Samuel Beeton, a publican in Cheapside, opened a subscription list in his ale-shop. A collection of £300 was raised; the following year, £500. With this race a success, suburban pubs joined in later, and in 1851 a further race, the City and Suburban was made possible. Other races include the Princess Elizabeth Stakes (3-y-o fillies, 1 m 110 yds) Perrier-Jouet Champagne Hcp (3-y-o, 1½ m) Diomed Stakes (1 m 110 yds) Northern Dancer Handicap (1½ m), Moet and Chandon Silver Magnum Hcp (amateur riders) Steve Donoghue Apprentice Hcp.

Leading trainers: G. Lewis (Epsom), R. Hannon (Marlborough, Wiltshire), J. Dunlop (Arundel, Sussex), H. Cecil (Newmarket)

Leading jockeys: Pat Eddery, W. Carson, S. Cauthen, P. Waldron

An indispensable guide to the drama of the Derby over more than two centuries is Roger Mortimer's brilliant *History of the Derby Stakes*. Just as indispensable in attempting to put the finger on the winner is the Form Book. With its help, and taking some other factors into consideration, this is not the impossible task that is sometimes imagined. A great deal of ballyhoo surrounds the Derby, and rightly so because of its prestige, value as a unique test of the thoroughbred and its high prize money (in 1986, sponsored by Ever Ready, it was worth a record £239,260 to the winning owner). Yet if the following points, based on an analysis of the past decade are carefully evaluated in relation to the race, a fair proportion of winners can be guaranteed in the future.

Form
Recent 3-y-o form is of greater importance these days than 2-y-o form, and previous winning form at 3-y-o is essential. Of the ten winners considered, all had won at least one race, and none had been out of the first three at this age. All had raced at least twice, and none more than three times at 3-y-o. Five were unbeaten in their run-up to the Derby, each with two victories apiece.

The most important races to study in early to mid-May are the Heathorn Stakes (Newmarket, 1 m 2 f) the winner of which went on to take the Derby on three occasions, and, more traditionally, the Dalham Chester Vase (1 m 4 f), the Highland Spring Derby Trial (Lingfield, 1 m 4 f), and the Mecca

Dante Stakes (York 1 m 2½f) — each of which provided two subsequent Derby winners in the period. The Lingfield Trial (over the same distance and a course which has a resemblance to Epsom, though not so tricky) has a consistent record of success over the years. However, earlier than these, the best pointer of all in recent years has been the Guardian Classic Trial (1 m 2f) in late April at Sandown. Four of its winners and a runner-up went on to win the Derby.

Should there be French runners the Prix Hocquart (1 m 4f) and Prix Lupin (1 m 2½f) both at Longchamp in May are worth looking at, but no one Irish Trial stands out.

With the exception of *Shirley Heights* (four runs) all were very lightly raced as 2-y-o, and with the exception of *Henbit* (4th in the Chesham Stakes at Royal Ascot the previous June) none made their first racecourse appearance until the autumn, most frequently in a 7f or 1 m race. Eight of the ten won at least one 2-y-o race, but the value of the form did not always amount to much. Fashions change among trainers, and although *The Minstrel* won the William Hill Dewhurst Stakes (Newmarket, 7f) and *Shirley Heights* won the Royal Lodge Stakes (Ascot, 1 m) these and other important 2-y-o races at the back-end are losing significance as pointers to the following year's Derby. These days, the Epsom winner is more likely to have made his appearance in a fairly ordinary 2-y-o event at Newbury, a maiden race at Newmarket, or even at Nottingham. This makes the form difficult to assess and, in turn, a word of warning is necessary about the ante post prices available on the Derby months in advance. The bookmakers still tend to base their prices on the results of older-established autumn 2-y-o races. Study of the form of such races, as well as the available prices, used to be a profitable pastime for the punter on a cold January evening. It is less so today, and the winter favourites for the Derby are far more of a trap than was once the case.

Stamina and breeding

No less an authority than Vincent O'Brien, who is the outstanding modern Derby trainer, considers that the ideal horse for Epsom is a top-class 1 m 2f colt. He certainly proved it (with the help of Lester Piggott) with *Sir Ivor*, and it will be noted that most of the 'trial' races above are run at that distance. Much of the pre-race discussion in the press as to whether or not a colt will stay the Derby distance (if he has not already proved it on the racecourse) will be settled only on the day, partly by breeding but also by the pace and the way in which the Derby is run. Vincent O'Brien's contention aside, of the ten most recent winners under review, five had won at 1 m 4f before Derby day, and five had never before attempted the distance. But there were clues in the breeding of all of them. Four of those winners were bred from a sire who had himself won the Derby — *Shahrastani* (by *Nijinsky*), *Slip Anchor* (by *Shirley Heights*), *Golden Fleece* (by *Nijinsky*) and *Shirley Heights* himself (by *Mill Reef*). A further three were sired by stallions (*Northern Dancer* and *Great Nephew*) who had already produced a previous Derby winner.

Jockeyship

Top jockeys dominate the Derby, and it is pointless looking beyond them. Lester Piggott's record of nine winners will take some beating, and Pat Eddery, Willie Carson and Walter Swinburn with two apiece are the nearest rivals. Post-race pictures of Tattenham Corner nearly always show the winner in a good position, handy in the first half dozen, and this owes as much to jockeyship, especially in the tricky early stages, as to a colt's ability to come down the left-handed hill into the straight, where, for good measure, the horse must be properly balanced to cope with the run-in which is not only uphill but also sloping across the track.

Trainers

The Derby is similarly dominated by top trainers. Vincent O'Brien is out in front with half a dozen winners, but Major Dick Hern and Michael Stoute have each trained two. The French, who very successfully raided in the post-war years have not had a winner since 1976. Epsom trainers have not had a success at their 'local' meeting since *April the Fifth* was an enormously popular win in 1932 for his owner and trainer, the actor Tom Walls.

Fillies

Only six fillies have ever won, the last being *Fifinella* in 1916, and the most recently placed *Nobiliary* in 1975.

Betting

Despite the vivid memories of occasional very long-priced winners such as *Psidium* at 66/1 and *Snow Knight* at 50/1, the Derby in recent years has been an excellent race for punters concentrating on the best-backed horses — provided they have not jumped in too early on the ante post market. When the various trials are sorting themselves out is the time to have a bet. In the ten years under review the favourite won four times, and the second favourite five times. A £1 level stake on the favourite during this decade would have given a small profit of £4.66 before tax; a similar amount on every second favourite would have yielded £22.00 profit before tax, allowing for splitting the stake to 50p when in 1978 *Shirley Heights* was joint second favourite with *Whitstead*.

1½ mile	The Derby, Epsom, early June

Sponsored by Ever Ready and with guaranteed price money for 1987 of £450,000.

	Winner	Sire	Trainer	Jockey	Ran	Price
1960	St Paddy	Aureole	N. Murless (Newmarket)	L. Piggott	17	7/1
1961	Psidium	Pardal	H. Wragg (Newmarket)	R. Poincelet	28	66/1
1962	Larkspur	Never Say Die	M.V. O'Brien (Ireland)	N. Sellwood	26	22/1
1963	Relko	Tanerko	F. Mathet (France)	Y. Saint-Martin	26	5/1F
1964	Santa Claus	Chamossaire	M. Rogers (Ireland)	A. Breasley	17	15/8F
1965	Sea Bird II	Dan Cupid	E. Pollet (France)	P. Glennon	22	7/4F
1966	Charlottown	Charlottesville	G. Smyth (Lewes, Sussex)	A. Breasley	25	5/1

1967	Royal Palace	Ballymoss	N. Murless (Newmarket)	G. Moore	22	7/4F
1968	Sir Ivor	Sir Gaylord	M.V. O'Brien (Ireland)	L. Piggott	13	4/5F
1969	Blakeney	Hethersett	A. Budgett (Whatcombe, Berkshire)	E. Johnson	26	15/2
1970	Nijinsky (Can)	Northern Dancer	M.V. O'Brien (Ireland)	L. Piggott	11	11/8F
1971	Mill Reef (USA)	Never Bend	I. Balding (Kingsclere, Berkshire)	G. Lewis	21	100/30F
1972	Roberto (USA)	Hail to Reason	M.V. O'Brien (Ireland)	L. Piggott	22	3/1F
1973	Morston	Ragusa	A. Budgett (Whatcombe, Berkshire)	E. Hide	25	25/1
1974	Snow Knight	Firestreak	P. Nelson (Lambourn)	B. Taylor	18	50/1
1975	Grundy	Great Nephew	P. Walwyn (Lambourn)	P. Eddery	18	5/1
1976	Empery (USA)	Vaguely Noble	M. Zilber (France)	L. Piggott	23	10/1
1977	The Minstrel (Can)	Northern Dancer	M.V. O'Brien (Ireland)	L. Piggott	22	5/1
1978	Shirley Heights	Mill Reef (USA)	J. Dunlop (Arundel, Sussex)	G. Starkey	25	8/1
1979	Troy	Petingo	W.R. Hern (W. Ilsley, Berks.)	W. Carson	23	6/1
1980	Henbit	Hawaii	W.R. Hern (W. Ilsley, Berks.)	W. Carson	24	7/1
1981	Shergar	Great Nephew	M. Stoute (Newmarket)	W. Swinburn	18	10/11F
1982	Golden Fleece	Nijinsky (Can)	M.V. O'Brien (Ireland)	P. Eddery	18	3/1F
1983	Teenoso	Youth (USA)	G. Wragg (Newmarket)	L. Piggott	21	9/2F
1984	Secreto	Northern Dancer	D. O'Brien (Ireland)	C. Roche	17	14/1
1985	Slip Anchor	Shirley Heights	H. Cecil (Newmarket)	S. Cauthen	17	2/1F
1986	Shahrastani (USA)	Nijinsky (Can)	M. Stoute (Newmarket)	W. Swinburn	17	11/2

1½ mile   The Oaks, Epsom, early June

First run as the Oakes Stakes in 1779, for 3-y-o fillies only. The weight carried is 9 st, and has been since 1892, but previously there were several fluctuations, from 8 st 4 lb originally, down to 8 st, then progressively upwards. During both World Wars the race was transferred to the Newmarket July Course and run as the New Oaks Stakes. Sponsored since 1984 by Gold Seal, the prize to the winner in 1986 was £119,952.

	Winner	Sire	Trainer	Jockey	Ran	Price
1960	Never Too Late II	Never Say Die	E. Pollet (France)	R. Poincelet	10	6/5F
1961	Sweet Solera	Solonaway	R. Day (Newmarket)	W. Rickaby	12	11/4F
1962	Monade	Klairon	J. Lieux (France)	Y. Saint-Martin	18	7/1
1963	Noblesse	Mossborough	P.J. Prendergast (Ireland)	G. Bougoure	9	4/11F
1964	Homeward Bound	Alycidon	J. Oxley (Newmarket)	G. Starkey	18	100/7
1965	Long Look	Ribot	M.V. O'Brien (Ireland)	J. Purtell	18	100/7
1966	Valoris	Tiziano	M.V. O'Brien (Ireland)	L. Piggott	13	11/10F
1967	Pia	Darius	W. Elsey (Malton, Yorkshire)	E. Hide	12	100/7
1968	La Lagune	Val de Loir	F. Boutin (France)	G. Thiboeuf	14	11/8F
1969	Sleeping Partner	Parthia	Doug Smith (Newmarket)	J. Gorton	15	100/6
1970	Lupe	Primera	N. Murless (Newmarket)	A. Barclay	16	100/30F
1971	Altesse Royale	Saint Crespin	N. Murless (Newmarket)	G. Lewis	11	6/4F
1972	Ginevra	Shantung	H.R. Price (Findon, Sussex)	A. Murray	17	8/1
1973	Mysterious	Crepello	N. Murless (Newmarket)	G. Lewis	10	13/8F
1974	Polygamy	Reform	P. Walwyn (Lambourn)	P. Eddery	15	3/1F
1975	Juliette Marny	Blakeney	J. Tree (Beckhampton, Wilts.)	L. Piggott	12	12/1
1976	Pawneese	Carvin	A. Penna (France)	Y. Saint-Martin	14	6/5F
1977	Dunfermline	Royal Palace	W.R. Hern (W. Ilsley, Berks.)	W. Carson	13	6/1
1978	Fair Salinia	Petingo	M. Stoute (Newmarket)	G. Starkey	15	8/1
1979	Scintillate	Sparkler	J. Tree (Beckhampton, Wilts.)	P. Eddery	14	20/1
1980	Bireme	Grundy	W.R. Hern (W. Ilsley, Berks.)	W. Carson	11	9/2
1981	Blue Wind	Lord Gayle	D. Weld (Ireland)	L. Piggott	12	3/1JF

	Winner	Sire	Trainer	Jockey	Ran	Price
1982	Time Charter	Saritamer	H. Candy (Wantage, Oxon)	W. Newnes	13	12/1
1983	Sun Princess	English Prince	W.R. Hern (W. Ilsley, Berkshire)	W. Carson	15	6/1
1984	Circus Plume	High Top	J. Dunlop (Arundel, Sussex)	L. Piggott	16	4/1
1985	Oh So Sharp	Kris	H. Cecil (Newmarket)	S. Cauthen	12	6/4F
1986	Midway Lady	Alleged (USA)	B. Hanbury (Newmarket)	R. Cochrane	15	15/8F

Favourites   Only one filly has won at a price longer than 12/1 in period going back more than 15 years. This is very much a Classic where the first choice in the market should be respected.

Even more than for the 1000 Guineas, the Hoover Mile at Ascot the previous September has consistently pointed the way to a good Oaks performance. *Scintillate, Circus Plume* and *Oh So Sharp* all won after being placed in or winning the Hoover Mile, while Hoover Mile winners *Leap Lively, Acclimatise,* and *Untold* were all placed in the Oaks.

GOODWOOD

Right-hand, but long-distance races starting in the straight swing left-handed first   Flat only

Draw: High numbers in sprint races, except in soft going.

Goodwood earned its title of 'Glorious' because of the exceptional racing during its big meeting, its unmatched pastoral setting on a fold of the Sussex Downs with distant views of hay-making, the fizz of champagne and creaking open of luncheon baskets, and (except when storm clouds gathered over Trundle Hill) a sense of unending summer — the Panama Hat to the Grey Toppers of Ascot and Derby Day. Today, the racing is better than ever, spread over five days for the main meeting and with other fixtures throughout the season, and no fewer than 11 Pattern races to attract enthusiasts. Yet a great deal of the old charm went when the new grandstand went up, bringing with it a degree of regimentation, priority for private boxholders, and having to fight the crowds for a good place from which to view the racing. The course, laid out on the Duke of Richmond's estate five miles from Chichester, and with which Lord George Bentinck had much to do in the beginning, is a complicated one, full of bends and turns on the downland loop, favouring handy horses, and a fast switchback and downhill stretch for the 6 furlong straight. Jockeyship is of enormous importance on the part of the track away from the sprint course, and top jockeys win most of the races. The main races include: Sussex Stakes (*the* race for milers to win), Goodwood Cup (one of the three 'legs' of the stayers' crown), Waterford Crystal Mile, the King George Stakes (a top race for sprinters), Nassau Stakes (fillies over 1¼ m), Gordon Stakes (three-year-olds over 1½ m), the Stewards' Cup (see opposite) and classic trials such as the Lupe Stakes, and Predominate Stakes. The last-named commemorates a Goodwood favourite, *Predominate* (see Chapter One, under *Aged*).

Leading trainers: G.   Harwood   (Pulborough,   Sussex),   W.R.   Hern

W. Ilsley, Berkshire), H. Cecil (Newmarket), L. Cumani (Newmarket)

Leading jockeys: Pat Eddery, W. Carson, G. Starkey, S. Cauthen, W. Swinburn

6 furlongs Hcp	The Stewards' Cup, Goodwood, late July

First run in 1840, the race has been sponsored since 1982 by the William Hill Organisation.

	Winner	Age	Wt.	Trainer	Jockey	Ran	Price
1960	Monet	3	8.5	J. Tree (Beckhampton, Wilts.)	J. Lindley	18	20/1
1961	Skymaster	3	8.12	G. Smyth (Arundel, Sussex)	A. Breasley	22	100/7
1962	Victorina	3	8.9	P. Nelson (Lambourn)	W. Williamson	26	10/1
1963	Creole	4	9.1	J. Jarvis (Newmarket)	S. Smith	25	20/1
1964	Dunme	5	7.12	R. Read (Lambourn)	P. Cook*	20	9/1
1965	Potier	3	8.5	J. Jarvis (Newmarket)	R. Hutchinson	20	100/7
1966	Patient Constable	3	7.7	R. Smyth (Epsom)	R. Reader	25	33/1
1967	Sky Diver	4	7.5	P. Payne-Gallwey (U. Lambourn)	D. Cullen	31	20/1
1968	Sky Diver	5	7.6	P. Payne-Gallwey (U. Lambourn)	T. Sturrock	18	100/6
1969	Royal Smoke	3	7.9	W. O'Gorman (Newmarket)	M.L. Thomas	15	100/7
1970	Jukebox	4	8.11	H. Wallington (Epsom)	L. Piggott	24	100/6
1971	Apollo Nine	4	9.5	P. Nelson (Lambourn)	J. Lindley	26	14/1
1972	Touch Paper	3	8.2	B. Hobbs (Newmarket)	P. Cook	22	25/1
1973	Alphadamus	3	7.11	M. Stoute (Newmarket)	P. Cook	27	16/1
1974	Red Alert	3	9.2	D. Weld (Ireland)	J. Roe	25	16/1
1975	Import	4	8.0	W. Wightman (Upham, Hampshire)	M.L. Thomas	21	14/1
1976	Jimmy the Singer	3	7.8	B. Lunness (Newmarket)	E. Johnson	17	15/1
1977	Calibina	5	8.5	P. Cole (Wantage, Oxon)	G. Baxter	24	8/1
1978	Ahonoora	3	8.0	B. Swift (Epsom)	P. Waldron	23	50/1
1979	Standaan	3	7.10	C. Brittain (Newmarket)	P. Bradwell*	16	5/1
1980	Repetitious	3	7.2	G. Harwood (Pulborough, Sussex)	A. Clark*	28	15/1
1981	Crews Hill	5	9.9	F. Durr (Newmarket)	G. Starkey	30	11/1
1982	Soba	3	8.4	D. Chapman (Yorkshire)	D. Nicholls	30	18/1
1983	Autumn Sunset	3	8.2	M. Stoute (Newmarket)	W. Carson	23	6/1
1984	Petong	4	9.10	M. Jarvis (Newmarket)	B. Raymond	26	8/1
1985	Al Trui	5	8.1	S. Mellor (Lambourn)	M. Wigham	28	9/1F
1986	Green Ruby	5	8.12	G.B. Balding (Weyhill, Hants.)	J. Williams	24	20/1

*Apprentice allowance

Favourites   The Stewards' Cup is a fairly typical big handicap sprint at the main Goodwood summer meeting, unfailingly attracting big fields which start out of sight in a dip in the course, and are first seen in full cry as if in full pursuit of General Custer when they breast the rise. Wokingham failures are often backed for the Stewards' Cup and several have done well recently without winning. We have to go back to *Creole* in 1963 before finding a horse that was placed in the Wokingham and went on to take the Stewards' Cup the following month. Wokingham winners in recent years which have gone on to complete the double in the Stewards' Cup have been *Calibina*, 1977 and *Petong*, 1984.

Only one favourite winning since 1960 and a fair share of 20/1 and over winners (25.9 per cent) make the Stewards' Cup the sort of race that led to the advice 'Never bet in a handicap', although well-backed (5/1–10/1) horses including the successful 9/1F *Al Trui* in 1985 have won the race on a further 25.9 per cent of occasions.

Trainers   Newmarket: 9 winners. Lambourn: 7 winners. Epsom: 3 winners. Michael Stoute has two Stewards' Cup winners to his credit.
Jockeys   P. Cook: 3 winners. M.L. Thomas: 2 winners.
Weights and Draw   The winning weights cover the entire handicap range with no preponderant group. The draw similarly defies analysis, so altogether, this information has little use when deciding on a bet.

HAYDOCK PARK   Left-hand   Flat and National Hunt

Draw: Races over 6 furlongs and further, low numbers. When the ground is soft, high numbers have an advantage over five and six furlongs.

An attractive course in the industrial hinterland of Lancashire with particularly pleasant paddock and good amenities, making it a favourite day out from Manchester or Liverpool, or farther afield with easy access from the M6 motorway. Racing is always entertaining, and National Hunt especially is excellent, making Haydock one of the leading jump courses in the country. The circuit is undulating and one which suits a galloper. There is a gradual rise over the 4 furlong run in; and the fences, which have a slight drop on the landing side, make Haydock a good course for an Aintree preliminary, because they are also fairly stiff. Some main races: Flat — Cecil Frail handicap (three-year-olds over 1 m), John of Gaunt Stakes (7 f), Lancashire Oaks (three-year-old fillies, 1½ m), Vernons Sprint Cup (6 f), Brooke Bond Oxo Amateur Riders Championship Final, Old Newton Cup (1½ m Hcp).

National Hunt: Edward Hanmer Memorial Hcp Chase, Ladbroke Northern Hcp Hurdle, Premier Long Distance Hurdle, Haydock Park Champion Hurdle Trial, Peter Marsh Chase, Greenall Whitley Breweries Chase, Timeform Chase, De Vere Hurdle, Victor Ludorum Hurdle, Swinton Insurance Brokers Trophy.

Leading trainers: *Flat*   H. Cecil (Newmarket) (with 42 per cent of his runners winning), J. Dunlop (Arundel, Sussex), R. Hollinshead (but with a 6.7 per cent success rate from a tremendous number of runners)
National Hunt   J. Fitzgerald, Mrs M. Dickinson, M.H. Easterby

Leading jockeys: *Flat*   W. Carson, J. Lowe, S. Cauthen, W. Ryan
National Hunt   G. Bradley, M. Dwyer, C. Hawkins

NEWBURY   Left-hand   Flat and National Hunt

Draw: Doubtful advantage.

With its own railway station alongside the course, and easy access to the M4 motorway, the big and attractive Berkshire course is deservedly popular with London racegoers, and equally so with the great number of trainers whose stables are also in very easy reach from the Lambourn area. Another reason for its popularity and the size of its fields is that the oval track, and one mile straight which joins it are wide and only gently undulating, providing an extremely fair test of a horse but one which, with a long run-in, favours the horse that likes to stride out. The steeplechase and hurdle courses are similarly fair, and spectators can see all the running from the stands. Newbury racecourse was the idea of the great trainer John Porter of nearby Kingsclere, where Ian Balding now trains. His original plan was turned down by the Jockey Club, but, supported by King Edward VII, was later adopted and racing began in September 1905. During both World Wars the course was turned over to the military, and after the 1939-45 War, when a huge American Supply Depot had submerged the precious turf in concrete, barrack blocks, hard standing, and 35 miles of railway line, prodigious feats of demolition, restoration and re-turfing had to be achieved before racing could start again. This did not take place until 1949. Some main races: Flat — Greenham Stakes, Fred Darling Stakes — these are both races over 7 furlongs for 3-y-o only, the latter confined to fillies, run in the spring and regularly providing reliable trials for the 2000 Guineas and 1000 Guineas. The Horris Hill stakes in the autumn, for 2-y-o only over 7 furlongs 60 yds, is one to watch for possible Classic horses and stayers for the following season. Older horses: Hungerford Stakes (7f approx), Lockinge Stakes (1 m), John Porter Stakes (1½ m), St Simon Stakes (1½ m), Geoffrey Freer Stakes (1 m 5f approx). In addition, and most important, Newbury stages a great number of maiden races for two-year-olds and three-year-olds throughout the season. These normally attract outsize fields with horses especially from stables close by. A notebook can fairly quickly be filled with likely future winners. National Hunt — Hennessy Cognac Gold Cup Chase, Mandarin Chase, Challow Hurdle, Tote Gold Trophy (Hcp Hurdle), Fairview Homes Novices Chase, Philip Cornes Saddle of Gold Hurdle, Tote Credit Hurdle. In addition there are numerous novice hurdles and novice chases which, like the equivalent maiden races on the Flat, also pay future dividends if an intelligent eye is kept on them.

Leading trainers: *Flat* H. Cecil, I. Balding, W.R. Hern, B. Hills, M. Stoute
   National Hunt T. Forster, F. Winter, J.R. Jenkins, J. Gifford

Leading jockeys: *Flat* S. Cauthen, W. Carson, P. Eddery, W. Swinburn, G. Starkey
   National Hunt H. Davies, P. Scudamore, S. Smith Eccles

NEWCASTLE   Left-hand   Flat and National Hunt

Draw: No advantage, if the going is good. Low numbers are best on the straight course if the ground becomes soft, and progressively more so if the going becomes heavy.

There is a long history of high-class racing at Newcastle dating back at least to the 17th century and well maintained at Gosforth Park today. *Beeswing* is the most celebrated horse at this course, commemorated by the valuable 7 furlong event for 3-y-o and upwards named after her. Ballads have also been written about the exploits of this remarkable 19th century race mare who won 51 races in eight seasons, and not a few pub signs also bear her name. As her owner-breeder, William Orde, of the ancient Durham-Northumbrian family said: 'She belongs to the people of Northumberland'. The most famous event is the Northumberland Plate, a handicap for stayers, first run in 1833, and known as 'The Pitmen's Derby', when the course is packed. The track itself is pear-shaped, with a 7 furlong straight joining it four furlongs from the finish. A steady rise from the final turn to the winning post, bends which are banked and can be taken at top speed thus giving no opportunity for a breather, and, in general, an uncompromising test make Newcastle no course for a horse lacking either stamina or will to win on the Flat or over jumps. Drainage in recent years has improved the going. Some main races, other than those already mentioned: Flat — Virginia Stakes (3-y-o, 1¼ m), Northumberland Sprint Trophy, XYZ Handicap (3-y-o, 1¼ m), Gosforth Park Cup; National Hunt — Pintail Hcp Chase, Eider Hcp Chase, Vaux Breweries Novices Chase Final, Fighting Fifth Hurdle.

Leading trainers: *Flat*   M. Stoute (Newmarket), J. Etherington (Malton, Yorkshire), B. Hills (Lambourn), J.W. Watts (Richmond, Yorkshire)

       National Hunt   M.H. Easterby, W.A. Stephenson, Mrs M. Dickinson

Leading jockeys: *Flat*   M. Birch, S. Cauthen, J. Lowe, W. Swinburn, T. Ives
       National Hunt   T.G. Dun, P. Tuck

NEWMARKET   Right-hand   Flat only

Draw: For most races, no appreciable effect. (But see below for effect of the Draw in the Cambridgeshire.)

Enough has already been written to obviate the necessity for rehearsing the history of Newmarket again, as well as to leave no doubt of its importance as Turf 'headquarters'. Anyone who loves horses and racing derives a quite specific enjoyment from the meetings on its two courses, both from the sense of the continuity of Turf history, and from the no-nonsense professional aspect of the racing particularly on the Rowley Mile Course. This is the course (where, in fact, there are races of much longer than a mile) which stages the spring and autumn meetings. At the time of writing, the stands were undergoing a massive and ambitious transformation, but no amount of reconstruction will solve Newmarket's main problem, that is that the courses were laid out at a time when it was not thought necessary for grandstand spectators to follow every yard of the running (because, in any case, this object could be achieved by following the races on horseback). Thus many races in their early stages are out of range of even the most powerful binoculars an extreme instance being the Cesarewitch which, starting down by the Devil's Dyke, runs much of its course unseen to all but television and close circuit watchers. Fortunately, to the enthusiast, this is a shortcoming easily forgiven by the quality of racing and, additionally, the fact that most of the real action is well within range, and intensified as the horses reach 'the Bushes' and go into 'the Dip' (traditional marker points in the final furlongs of the Rowley Mile). Of the meetings on this course, the Craven Meeting, first of the season, can be recommended for those who want a look at early 2-y-o, and see how 3-y-o have developed physically during the winter. As to atmosphere, Sir Alfred Munnings best captured for ever on canvas what a Rowley Mile meeting is like, in the clear East Anglian light, and between the infinite horizons of the Heath.

The July Course, which stages the important meeting in July (hence the name) as well as the regular weekend meetings during the summer (and took over Rowley Mile fixtures during rebuilding), has a more relaxed atmosphere, an effect heightened by its thatched buildings. The early stages of races on both courses are run over the same ground, before joining the Rowley Mile proper, or branching on to the final mile of the July Course. Both courses provide a comprehensive test of the thoroughbred and horses require undoubted stamina to make the grade at the various distances. Some main races: *Rowley Mile* — Craven Stakes, Free Handicap, Nell Gwynn Stakes (fillies), 2000 Guineas, 1000 Guineas (all 3-y-o); Middle Park Stakes (6 f), Cheveley Park Stakes (6 f fillies), Dewhurst Stakes (7 f), Houghton Stakes (7 f) (all 2-y-o); Jockey Club Stakes, Palace House Stakes, Sun Chariot Stakes, Jockey Club Cup, Champion Stakes, Bisquit Dubouché Challenge Stakes, Cambridgeshire Handicap, Cesarewitch. *July Course* — July Cup (top-class sprint), July Stakes (2-y-o, 6 f), Princess of Wales' Stakes, Child Stakes, Bunbury Cup, Van Geest Stakes, Cherry Hinton Stakes (2-y-o fillies, 6 f), Sweet Solera Stakes (2-y-o fillies, 7 f), Colmans of Norwich Nursery (2-y-o).

Leading trainers: Newmarket races naturally attract a huge entry from local trained horses, and two of the biggest and most successful trainers from 'headquarters' are top of the list: Henry Cecil and Michael Stoute. But Guy Harwood from Sussex, and Dick Hern from West Ilsley are next in the list, and good northern challengers are worth following

Leading jockeys: S. Cauthen, P. Eddery, W. Carson, W. Swinburn,
G. Starkey, T. Ives

Rowley Mile   2000 Guineas, Newmarket, late April/early May

First run over 1 mile 1 yard in 1809, the distance, always slightly over a mile, was varied twice in
the 19th century until standardised at a mile in 1902. The 2000 Guineas was originally open to
colts, geldings and fillies. From 1904 geldings were excluded, and then as now the race was open
only to 3-y-o colts and fillies. Colts carry 9 st, fillies 8 st 7 lb. In practice, these days, fillies
normally go for the 1000 Guineas, and leave the 2000 Guineas to the colts. A notable exception
this century was that great filly *Sceptre* in 1902 (see under *CLASSICS* in *Racing Alphabet* Chapter
One). *Garden Path* won in 1944 when (from 1940-1945) the war-time Guineas were run on the July
Course (the Rowley Mile course being occupied by the military). These have been the only fillies
to win this race so far this century. Since 1984 the race has been sponsored by General Accident.
In 1986 the prize to the winning owner was £129,312.

	Winner	Sire	Trainer	Jockey	Ran	Price
1960	Martial	Hill Gail	P.J. Prendergast (Ireland)	R. Hutchinson	17	18/1
1961	Rockavon	Rockefella	G. Boyd (Dunbar, E. Lothian)	N. Stirk	22	66/1
1962	Privy Councillor	Counsel	T. Waugh (Newmarket)	W. Rickaby	19	100/6
1963	Only For Life	Chanteur II	J. Tree (Beckhampton, Wiltshire)	J. Lindley	21	33/1
1964	Baldric II	Round Table	E. Fellows (France)	W. Pyers	27	20/1
1965	Niksar	Le Haar	W. Nightingall (Epsom)	D. Keith	22	100/8
1966	Kashmir II	Tudor Melody	M. Bartholomew (France)	J. Lindley	25	7/1
1967	Royal Palace	Ballymoss	N. Murless (Newmarket)	G. Moore	18	100/30 JF
1968	Sir Ivor	Sir Gaylord	M.V. O'Brien (Ireland)	L. Piggott	10	11/8F
1969	Right Tack	Hard Tack	J. Sutcliffe Jr (Epsom)	G. Lewis	13	15/2
1970	Nijinsky (Can)	Northern Dancer	M.V. O'Brien (Ireland)	L. Piggott	14	4/7F
1971	Brigadier Gerard	Queen's Hussar	W.R. Hern (W. Ilsley, Berkshire)	J. Mercer	6	11/2
1972	High Top	Derring-Do	B. Van Cutsem (Newmarket)	W. Carson	12	85/40F
1973	Mon Fils	Sheshoon	R. Hannon (Marlborough, Wiltshire)	F. Durr	18	50/1
1974	Nonoalco	Nearctic	F. Boutin (France)	Y. Saint-Martin	12	19/2
1975	Bolkonski	Balidar	H. Cecil (Newmarket)	G. Dettori	24	33/1
1976	Wollow	Wolver Hollow	H. Cecil (Newmarket)	G. Dettori	17	Evens F
1977	Nebbiolo	Yellow God	K. Prendergast (Ireland)	G. Curran	18	20/1
1978	Roland Gardens	Derring-Do	D. Sasse (U. Lambourn)	F. Durr	19	28/1
1979	Tap On Wood	Sallust	B. Hills (Lambourn)	S. Cauthen	20	20/1
1980	Known Fact*	In Reality	J. Tree (Beckhampton, Wiltshire)	W. Carson	14	14/1
	(*Nureyev (USA) by Nijinsky finished 1st. Disqualified)					
1981	To-Agori-Mou	Tudor Music	G. Harwood (Pulborough, Sussex)	G. Starkey	19	5/2F
1982	Zino	Welsh Pageant	F. Boutin (France)	F. Head	26	8/1
1983	Lomond	Northern Dancer	M.V. O'Brien (Ireland)	P. Eddery	16	9/1
1984	El Gran Senor	Northern Dancer	M.V. O'Brien (Ireland)	P. Eddery	9	15/8F
1985	Shadeed (USA)	Nijinsky (Can)	M. Stoute (Newmarket)	L. Piggott	14	4/5F
1986	Dancing Brave (USA)	Lyphard (USA)	G. Harwood, Pulborough, Sussex)	G. Starkey	15	15/8F

Well-backed horses have a good record over recent years, but the 1970s threw up some shock
winners in this first Classic. It is best to stick to the better-backed horses.

Trainers Four winners: Vincent O'Brien (Ireland). Two winners: Henry Cecil (Newmarket), F. Boutin (France), Guy Harwood (Sussex).
Jockeys Two winners each: Willie Carson, G. Dettori, Pat Eddery, Greville Starkey.

Rowley Mile   1000 Guineas, Newmarket, late April/early May

First run at 7 furlongs 178 yards in 1814; became 1 mile from 1902. Run on the July Course, Newmarket, during the war years 1940-45. Sponsored by General Accident since 1984. For 3-y-o fillies only, all carrying 9 st.

	Winner	Sire	Trainer	Jockey	Ran	Price
1960	Never Too Late II	Never Say Die	E. Pollet (France)	R. Poincelet	14	8/11F
1961	Sweet Solera	Solonaway	R. Day (Newmarket)	W. Rickaby	14	4/1JF
1962	Abermaid	Abernant	H. Wragg (Newmarket)	W. Williamson	14	100/6
1963	Hula Dancer	Native Dancer	E. Pollet (France)	R. Poincelet	12	1/2F
1964	Pourparler	Hugh Lupus	P.J. Prendergast (Ireland)	G. Bougoure	18	11/2
1965	Night Off	Narrator	W. Wharton (Newmarket)	W. Williamson	16	9/2F
1966	Glad Rags	High Hat	M.V. O'Brien (Ireland)	P. Cook	21	100/6
1967	Fleet	Immortality	N. Murless (Newmarket)	G. Moore	16	11/2
1968	Caergwrle	Crepello	N. Murless (Newmarket)	A. Barclay	14	4/1
1969	Full Dress II	Shantung	H. Wragg (Newmarket)	R. Hutchinson	13	7/1
1970	Humble Duty	Sovereign Path	P. Walwyn (Lambourn)	L. Piggott	12	3/1JF
1971	Altesse Royale	Saint Crespin	N. Murless (Newmarket)	Y. Saint-Martin	10	25/1
1972	Waterloo	Bold Lad	J.W. Watts (Richmond, Yorks)	E. Hide	18	8/1
1973	Mysterious	Crepello	N. Murless (Newmarket)	G. Lewis	14	11/1
1974	Highclere	Queen's Hussar	W.R. Hern (W. Ilsley, Berks.)	J. Mercer	15	12/1
1975	Nocturnal Spree	Supreme Sovereign	H.V.S. Murless (Ireland)	J. Roe	16	14/1
1976	Flying Water (Fr)	Habitat	A. Penna (France)	Y. Saint-Martin	25	2/1F
1977	Mrs McArdy	Tribal Chief	M.W. Easterby (Malton, Yorkshire)	E. Hide	18	16/1
1978	Enstone Spark	Sparkler	B. Hills (Lambourn)	E. Johnson	16	35/1
1979	One In A Million	Rarity	H. Cecil (Newmarket)	J. Mercer	17	Evens F
1980	Quick As Lightning	Buckpasser	J. Dunlop (Arundel, Sussex)	B. Rouse	23	12/1
1981	Fairy Footsteps	Mill Reef (USA)	H. Cecil (Newmarket)	L. Piggott	14	6/4F
1982	On The House	Be My Guest (USA)	H. Wragg (Newmarket)	J. Reid	15	33/1
1983	Ma Biche (USA)	Key To The Kingdom	Mme C. Head (France)	F. Head	18	5/2F
1984	Pebbles	Sharpen Up	C. Brittain (Newmarket)	P. Robinson	15	8/1
1985	Oh So Sharp	Kris	H. Cecil (Newmarket)	S. Cauthen	17	2/1F
1986	Midway Lady	Alleged (USA)	B. Hanbury (Newmarket)	R. Cochrane	15	10/1

Favourites Have about the same ratio of success as in the 2000 Guineas — 9 (34.6 per cent) — but fewer really big-priced winners than in the race open to colts as well as fillies. Longest priced winners in recent years are 35/1, 33/1. Once again, the best policy is to concentrate on the first few in the market.

As far as 2-y-o pointers are concerned, the Cheveley Park Stakes at Newmarket, and the Hoover Mile at Ascot which take place the previous autumn are excellent guides to the 1000 Guineas. In the five years to 1986, *Ma Biche* won both the Cheveley Park and the Guineas, *Pebbles* and *On The House* won the Guineas after being placed in the Cheveley Park, while *Favoridge*, *Desirable* and *Al Bahathri* were placed in both races. Since its introduction in 1978, the Hoover Mile, now elevated to Group status, has rapidly established itself as a guide to the following year's fillies' Classics. Both *Quick as Lightning* and *Oh So Sharp* won the Hoover Mile before their Newmarket success the following spring.

Trainers   Henry Cecil has the best record with three winners, while Newmarket stables have provided 50 per cent of the winners in the period.

Jockeys still riding   No dominant candidate, but Yves Saint-Martin from France has twice ridden the winner.

1 mile 1 furlong Hcp   The Cambridgeshire, Newmarket, October

First run 1839 and sponsored since 1978 by the William Hill Organisation.

	Winner (Draw)	Age	Wt.	Trainer	Jockey	Ran	Price
1960	Midsummer Night II (36)	3	7.12	P. Hastings-Bass (Kingsclere, Berkshire)	D. Keith	40	40/1
1961 (d-h) {	Henry The Seventh (26)	3	8.4	W. Elsey (Malton, Yorkshire)	E. Hide	27	100/8 2F
	Violetta III (25)	3	7.8	H. Wragg (Newmarket)	L.C. Parkes	27	33/1
1962	Hidden Meaning (40)	3	9.0	H. Leader (Newmarket)	A. Breasley	46	7/1F
1963	Commander-In-Chief (10)	4	8.0	E. Cousins (Tarporley, Cheshire)	F. Durr	23	100/7
1964	Hasty Cloud (21)	6	7.10	H. Wallington (Epsom)	J. Wilson	43	100/8JF
1965	Tarqogan (19)	5	9.3	S. McGrath (Ireland)	W. Williamson	30	100/8
1966	Dites (25)	4	7.4	H. Leader (Newmarket)	D. Maitland *5	34	33/1
1967	Lacquer (8)	3	8.6	H. Wragg (Newmarket)	R. Hutchinson	34	20/1
1968	Emerilo (30)	4	7.9	P. Allden (Newmarket)	M.L. Thomas	35	20/1
1969	Prince de Galles (6)	3	7.12	P. Robinson (Newmarket)	F. Durr	26	5/2F
1970	Prince de Galles (13)	4	9.7	P. Robinson (Newmarket)	F. Durr	27	6/12F
1971	King Midas (15)	3	7.9	D. Candy (Wantage, Oxon)	D. Cullen	29	10/1
1972	Negus (21)	5	9.0	D. Candy (Wantage, Oxon)	P. Waldron	35	16/13F
1973	Siliciana (32)	4	8.5	I. Balding (Kingsclere, Berkshire)	G. Lewis	37	14/13F
1974	Flying Nelly (29)	4	7.7	W. Wightman (Upham, Hampshire)	D. Maitland	39	22/1
1975	Lottogift (22)	4	8.2	D. Hanley (Lambourn)	R. Wernham *5	36	33/1
1976	Intermission (18)	3	8.6	M. Stoute (Newmarket)	G. Starkey	29	14/1
1977	Sin Timon (11)	3	8.3	J. Hindley (Newmarket)	A. Kimberley	27	18/1
1978	Baronet (15)	6	9.0	C.J. Benstead (Epsom)	B. Rouse	18	12/1
1979	Smartset (20)	4	8.8	R. Johnson Houghton (Blewbury, Oxon)	J. Reid	24	33/1
1980	Baronet (11)	8	9.3	C.J. Benstead (Epsom)	B. Rouse	19	22/1
1981	Braughing (5)	4	8.4	C. Brittain (Newmarket)	S. Cauthen	28	50/1
1982	Century City (12)	3	9.6	L. Cumani (Newmarket)	J. Mercer	29	20/1
1983	Sagamore (18)	4	7.8	F. Durr (Newmarket)	M.L. Thomas	30	35/1
1984	Leysh (7)	3	8.7	S.G. Norton (Barnsley, Yorkshire)	J. Lowe	34	33/1
1985	Tremblant (21)	4	9.8	R.V. Smyth (Epsom)	P. Eddery	31	16/1
1986	Dallas (16)	3	9.6	L. Cumani (Newmarket)	R. Cochrane	31	10/1

*Apprentice allowance claimed

Favourites   For the average backer, finding the winner of the Cambridgeshire is by far the harder problem of the two 'legs' of the Autumn Double. The race is invariably a death or glory charge of outsize proportions spread across the galloping expanses of the Rowley Mile in sunshine whose paleness is matched only by punters' faces at the finish. Unlike the Cesarewitch, it is *not* a race for the leading market fancies. Only two clear favourites have won since 1960, with one joint-favourite, and a similar number of 2nd and 3rd favourites. On the other hand, 33/1

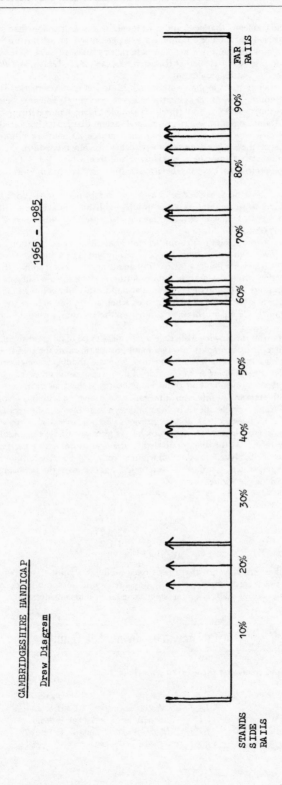

CAMBRIDGESHIRE HANDICAP

Draw Diagram

1965 - 1985

successes abound (no fewer than five) and even longer prices, and no less than 49 per cent of the winners in the period started at 20/1 or above — a percentage remarkably unchanged since the very earliest years of the century when the pattern was different, and there were several well gambled-on short price winners such as *Ballantrae, Hackler's Pride, Velocity,* and *Polymelus* (at 11/10 the shortest-priced favourite of them all).

Trainers Another contrast to the Ceasarewitch is the fact that Newmarket stables shine here on their home ground, 13 winners being trained here since 1960. The next best training area is Lambourn (six winners), then Epsom (three). No single trainer stands out.

Jockeys The Cambridgeshire is also an unusual race in that Lester Piggott never managed to ride the winner of it which helps to illustrate the fact that no one jockey dominates the race. Frankie Durr was on the winner three times as a jockey, has already saddled the winner once as a trainer, and is the nearest to being a specialist in the race, while 'Taffy' Thomas, whom Durr engaged for *Sagamore* in 1983, has twice been successful, just as he has in most big handicaps over the years.

Age 3-y-o used to be twice as successful as 4-y-o. Cambridgeshire victories are now more or less evenly divided between these two age groups, with few older horses winning (a notable exception being *Baronet* who won as a six-year-old *and* eight-year-old, thus becoming the oldest to win during this century).

Weight Winners are spread throughout the entire handicap range, but unlike most big betting handicaps, very low weights these days do not generally win. The feather-weight 6 st 3 lb carried by *Esquire* in 1945 is now no longer possible, but an all round upward shift of the handicap scale only partly explains why the Cambridgeshire, formerly dominated by horses weighted under 8 st, now has an unusual (compared with similar handicaps) number of winners weighted over 9 st. This is a handicap bracket not to be ignored when attempting to solve the Cambridgeshire puzzle. Eight winners (29.6 per cent) have come from this top most section of the handicap since 1960.

Draw The draw on the Rowley Mile is generally held to be of no great significance. The field for the Cambridgeshire often splits into two main groups (towards the stands side rails and far running rails) with sometimes a proportion running up the middle. These circumstances, added to marginal differences in going from one side of the course to the other, make it impossible to lay down any inflexible rule about the draw. Nonetheless, as the draw diagram (on p. 167) shows, those drawn with very low numbers on the stands rails have no winning record in the period under review. On the far rails, the three highest drawn were the dead-heaters *Henry The Seventh* and *Violetta III* as far back as 1961, and the previous year's winner *Midsummer Night II.* The best winning chance, in fact, appears to be held by horses from just under the middle of the draw to medium high numbers. As the diagram, based on the draw number as a percentage of the total field, shows, approximately two-thirds of all winners from 1965-85 came within the 40 per cent to 75 per cent bracket, which, translated into practical figures, gives the following draw numbers most likely to include the winner:

Field	Draw
20	8 to 15
25	10 to 19
30	12 to 23
35	14 to 26
40	16 to 30

It must be emphasised, however, that this is meant only as a guide to narrow the possibilities. Exceptions, as the records show, do occur and are bound to continue doing so, while the positioning of the starting stalls is a final factor to be taken into consideration.

2¼ mile Hcp   The Cesarewitch, Newmarket, October

First run, 1839 and sponsored since 1978 by the Tote.

	Winner	Age	Wt.	Trainer	Jockey	Ran	Price
1960	Alcove (f)	3	7.8	J.F. Watts (Newmarket)	D. Smith	20	100/30F
1961	Avon's Pride	4	7.11	W. Hern (W. Ilsley, Berkshire)	E. Smith	27	100/8 3F
1962	Golden Fire**	4	7.11	D. Marks (Winkfield, Berks.)	D. Yates *5	25	25/1
	Orchardist (5 lb†)	3	8.2	C.J. Benstead (Epsom)	W. Williamson		25/1

1963	Utrillo	6	8.0	H.R. Price (Findon, Sussex)	J. Sime	25	100/8 2F
1964	Grey of Falloden (3 lbt)	5	9.6	W. Hern (W. Ilsley, Berkshire)	J. Mercer	26	20/1
1965	Mintmaster (5 lbt)	4	7.9	A. Cooper (Malton, Yorks.)	J. Sime	18	13/2 2F
1966	Persian Lancer	8	7.8	H.R. Price (Findon, Sussex)	D. Smith	24	100/7
1967	Boismoss	3	7.1	M.W. Easterby (Malton, Yorkshire)	E. Johnson *3	23	13/1
1968	Major Rose	6	9.4	H.R. Price (Findon, Sussex)	L. Piggott	33	9/1F
1969	Floridian	5	7.3	L. Shedden (Wetherby, Yorkshire)	D. McKay *5	23	20/1
1970	Scoria	4	7.0	C. Crossley (Neston, Wirral)	D. McKay	21	33/1
1971	Orosio	4	8.2	H. Cecil (Newmarket)	G. Lewis	18	5/12F
1972	Cider With Rosie	4	7.11	S. Ingham (Epsom)	M.L. Thomas	21	14/1
1973	Flash Imp	4	7.8	R.V. Smyth (Epsom)	T. Cain *5	29	25/1
1974	Ocean King	8	7.7	A. Pitt (Epsom)	T. Carter	27	25/1
1975	Shantallah	3	8.10	H. Wragg (Newmarket)	B. Taylor	17	17/13F
1976	John Cherry (USA) (6 lbt)	5	9.13	J. Tree (Beckhampton, Wiltshire)	L. Piggott	14	13/2 2F
1977	Assured (6 lbt)	4	8.4	H. Candy (Kingston Warren, Berkshire)	P. Waldron	11	10/1
1978	Centurion	3	9.8	I. Balding (Kingsclere, Berks.)	J. Matthias	17	9/2F
1979	Sir Michael	3	7.8	G. Huffer (Newmarket)	M. Rimmer *5	11	10/1
1980	Popsi's Joy	5	8.6	M. Haynes (Epsom)	L. Piggott	27	10/12F
1981	Halsbury	3	8.4	P. Walwyn (Lambourn)	J. Mercer	30	14/1
1982	Mountain Lodge (f) (4 lbt)	3	7.10	J. Dunlop (Arundel, Sussex)	W. Carson	28	9/12F
1983	Bajan Sunshine	4	8.8	R. Simpson (Epsom)	B. Rouse	27	7/1JF
1984	Tom Sharp	4	7.5	W. Wharton (Melton Mowbray, Leicestershire)	S. Dawson *5	26	40/1
1985	Kayudee	5	8.1	J. Fitzgerald (Malton, Yorks.)	A. Murray	21	7/12F
1986	Orange Hill (f)	4	7.9	J. Tree (Beckhampton, Wiltshire)	R. Fox	25	20/1

(f) filly   † penalty carried   * apprentice allowance claimed

**In 1962, *Orchardist* beat *Golden Fire* by a neck, but on an objection for boring was disqualified and placed second. David Yates, then an apprentice, admitted afterwards that he would not have objected had not someone suggested it to him in the weighing room.

Favourites   The Cesarewitch is not a race usually won by an outsider. In the period examined four favourites (prices 100/30 to 9/1) won, seven 2nd favourites (prices 5/1 to 100/8), and two 3rd favourites (prices 7/1 and 100/8).

This makes a total of one in every two winners coming from the first three in the betting. Further, 80 per cent of winners were well-backed horses, and in general, in making a Cesarewitch choice, it need not be necessary to look beyond the first half dozen in the market. The remaining 20 per cent of winners started at 20/1, 25/1 × 3, 33/1, and 40/1. Despite the extreme distance of the race, penalised horses do well. *John Cherry*'s record 9 st 13 lb and *Grey of Falloden*'s 9 st 6 lb included penalties, but *Centurion* (9 st 8 lb) and *Major Rose* (9 st 4 lb) were the only other horses to have won carrying 9 st or over during the period; in fact, including these four, only half a dozen have won in this handicap bracket during the entire century so far.

Changes in the minimum handicap rating make it difficult to draw any useful conclusion about likely winning weights, but the handicap range between 7 st 11 lb and 8 st 2 lb (penalties included, but *not* overweight or apprentice allowances) provided 35 per cent of winners from 1960 onwards.

Relatively fresh horses are worth looking at for the Cesarewitch (a principle held by, once again, Ryan Price, whose success bears witness to it. *Persian Lancer* had a fairly busy pre-race preparation, but *Major Rose*, runner-up in 1967 and winner in 1968 had only three previous outings, and two, respectively, during those seasons).

Others: 1985 *Kayudee* 2 runs; early Oct (5th) and early (Sept) (unplaced)

　　　　 1984 *Tom Sharp* 2 runs; early Oct (unplaced) and mid-Aug (unplaced)

1976 *John Cherry* 4 races previously
1973 *Flash Imp* 5 races previously
Jeremy Tree's programme for *John Cherry*, 13/2 Second Favourite for the race when he won in 1976 is a good example of a well spaced run-up to the Cesarewitch:

April	1 m 7 f	Lingfield, Unplaced.
May	2 m 2 f	Chester Cup. Won
June	2 m	Sandown Henry II Stakes. Unplaced.
Sept	2 m	Newbury Autumn Cup. Won.

Trainers   There have been no outstanding trainers since the late Ryan Price sent out three winners in the 1960s. Dick Hern trained two winners in the same decade, but has had none since. There are two salient points to observe, however: first that this race is one which big stables do not monopolise; and second Newmarket yards do not have the success that might be expected in a 'local' race — they have had only four successes since 1960. In the same period, the number of winners from Epsom (six) with fewer runners, and the Lambourn area (six) should be noted. At the same time there has been a marked decline in the fortune once enjoyed by Yorkshire yards in the Cesarewitch — between 1945 and 1969 they were no fewer than nine winners down south. *Kayudee* in 1985 was the sole winner from the north since then.

Jockeys   The value of a good claiming apprentice is underlined in this race as their six winning rides represent 23 per cent of the total during the period. Among the senior jockeys, no one at present looks to be a candidate for matching the extraordinary success of the Smith brothers. In 32 seasons up to 1966, Eph Smith (four) and Doug Smith (six) rode just under a third of all the Cesarewitch winners! Of present jockeys, Dennis McKay rode winners in successive years 1969-70, and a final point worth noting is that senior jockeys put up overweight on six occasions during the period, and their horses still won.

Age   No firm pattern emerges from a study of ages of winners. More 4-y-o are successful than any other age group, but this is simply because the number of 4-y-o entered relative to other ages. On a comparison between entries and number of winners from a particular age group, 3-y-o have a slight edge (26 per cent of total winners against 23 per cent proportion of entries). A good improving 3-y-o too, is a likely Cesarewitch candidate because he keeps ahead of the (human/computer) handicapper. *Centurion* provides an example: running in and winning maiden races mid-season, then winning three other races before the Cesarewitch, and keeping his form to win that, thanks to the skill of his trainer, Ian Balding. Having said that, veterans should not be ignored. They are a relatively small proportion of the total entry, but the victories of the 8-y-o *Ocean King* and *Persian Lancer* are there in the records, the latter a particular training triumph for Ryan Price.

SANDOWN PARK   Right-hand   Flat and National Hunt

Draw: Round course, no advantage. Straight course, if soft, high numbers are best.

Sandown, near Esher in Surrey, was the first racecourse in the country to be entirely enclosed. It opened in 1875, and was immediately popular, with a frequent train service bringing racegoers from London in 20 minutes. The original stands lasted for almost a century on the top of a hill and gave a marvellous vantage point for seeing every detail of the running. The new stands, opened in 1973 by HM The Queen Mother whose chasers have won many races at the course, incorporate an entirely enclosed betting hall with Tote and SP facilities, and the view from them is as good as ever though lacking entirely the faded Edwardian charm of the old buildings. The oval circuit, which is crossed by a 5 furlong straight across the middle, has fairly easy gradients, but a very stiff uphill finish (for both tracks) which makes Sandown a tough course, demanding on stamina, and favouring the horse which likes to stride out. Equally, the fences are stiff for the jumpers, and, coming in fairly rapid succession in the back straight beside the railway, allow no room for indifferent performers or inexpert riding. Some main races: Flat — Sandown has a fair share of Pattern and listed races through-out the season, with its most important event the Eclipse Stakes, sponsored at present by Joe Coral. This is a 1¼ mile 'semi-Classic' first run in 1885, and the list of its past winners is a Turf roll-call of honour. Outstanding horses to have won it most recently include *Pebbles* and *Dancing Brave*; its illustrious past includes the names *Diamond Jubilee*, *Persimmon*, *Ard Patrick* and *Bayardo* up to *Blue Peter*, *Tulyar*, *Royal Palace*, *Mill Reef* and *Brigadier Gerard*. Other races include the Trusthouse Forte Mile, Guardian Classic Trial (3-y-o over 1¼ mile), Westbury Stakes, Esher Cup, Brigadier Gerard Stakes, Henry II Stakes (stayers), Temple Stakes (sprinters), National Stakes (2-y-o) and Solario Stakes (2-y-o over 7f) which is a race which produces its share of subsequent Classic winners, including in recent years *Oh So Sharp* and *To-Agori-Mou*.

An outstanding National Hunt programme includes the Anthony Mildmay and Peter Cazalet Memorial Chase, named after the great amateur rider Lord Mildmay, who performed wonders for National Hunt sport, and his trainer Peter Cazalet to whom the Queen Mother first sent horses. Its first running, in 1952, was won appropriately by *Cromwell*, a favourite horse of Lord Mildmay's whom he had so nearly ridden to victory in the 1948 Grand National. To the inspiration of another great supporter of jumping, Colonel Whitbread, is owed one of the earliest great sponsored chases, the Whitbread Gold Cup, run in the spring, and the Imperial Cup, now sponsored by the William Hill organisation, is, by contrast, one of the oldest established (first run in 1907) hurdle events in the calendar. Sandown, too, is also the home of the Grand Military Meeting and Royal Artillery Meeting.

Leading trainers: *Flat* M. Stoute (Newmarket), G. Harwood (Pulborough, Sussex), C.E. Brittain (Newmarket), H. Cecil (Newmarket), W.R. Hern (W. Ilsley, Berkshire)

National Hunt J. Gifford (Findon), F. Winter (Lambourn), T.A. Forster (Wantage), D. Elsworth (Fordingbridge)

Leading jockeys: *Flat* Pat Eddery, W. Carson, S. Cauthen, G. Starkey, W. Swinburn, T. Quinn

National Hunt S. Smith Eccles, R. Rowe, H. Davies

YORK   Left-hand   Flat only

Draw: When the going is soft or heavy, low numbers are best on the straight course.

York has widely been referred to as 'the Ascot of the North,' which is an insult as far as Yorkshire people are concerned, since they regard Ascot as 'the York of the South'. Records of racing at York go back as far as 1530, and Charles I is known to have watched a horse race on Acomb Moor in 1633, but according to an article in *The British Racehorse* by Patricia Smyly, racing was transferred from Clifton Ings to the present site on the Knavesmire after the floods of 1731. The first grandstand went up a quarter of a century later, and today the facilities at York are among the best in the country, with a quality of racing to match. The 2 mile course is wide, completely flat, with easy sweeping turns. The 7 furlong straight joins the round course just under 5 furlongs from home, and the entire course provides an extremely fair test for the thoroughbred. The main meetings take place in May and August, the latter commonly known as the 'Ebor' Meeting when the big handicap of that name takes place as well as the Gimcrack Stakes for 2-y-o, commemorating the game little grey horse *Gimcrack* of the 18th century whose popularity led to the foundation of the Gimcrack Club at York, said to be, after the Jockey Club, the second oldest race club in the land. Other top class races at this meeting are the Group One events, the Benson and Hedges Gold Cup, with well over £100,000 prize money, the William Hill Sprint Trophy and Yorkshire Oaks. At the main spring meeting the valuable Oaks and Derby trials, the Musidora Stakes and Mecca-Dante Stakes, are run as well as the Yorkshire Cup. In addition there are four other first class meetings throughout the season at which the big feature races include the William Hill Trophy, the John Smith's Magnet Cup and Hong Kong Marlborough Cup. Big crowds come to the Knavesmire to enjoy the high grade racing and facilities and the strong betting markets.

Leading trainers: J. Dunlop (Arundel, Sussex), W.R. Hern (W. Ilsley, Berkshire), J. Tree (Beckhampton, Wiltshire), H. Cecil (Newmarket), M. Stoute (Newmarket), G. Wragg (Newmarket)

Leading jockeys: Pat Eddery, W. Carson, S. Cauthen, T. Ives, W. Swinburn

---

1¾ mile Hcp   Ebor Handicap, York, August

First run in 1843, 12 years after racing at York first took place on the Knavesmire. Sponsored since 1976 by the Tote. The prize to the winner in 1986 was £42,860.

	Winner	Age	Wt.	Trainer	Jockey	Ran	Price
1960	Persian Road	5	8.4	J. Tree (Beckhampton, Wiltshire)	G. Moore	21	18/1
1961	Die Hard	4	8.9	M.V. O'Brien (Ireland)	L. Piggott	21	11/2F
1962	Sostenuto	4	8.10	W. Elsey (Malton, Yorkshire)	D. Morris	18	9/1
1963	Partholon	3	7.8	T. Shaw (Ireland)	J. Sime	22	100/6
1964	Proper Pride	5	7.11	W. Wharton (Newmarket)	D. Smith	20	28/1
1965	Twelfth Man	4	7.5	H. Wragg (Newmarket)	P. Cook	25	6/1F
1966	Lomond	6	9.2	R. Jarvis (Newmarket)	E. Eldin	23	100/8

1967	Ovaltine	3	7.0	J.F. Watts (Newmarket)	E. Johnson	22	100/8
1968	Alignment	3	7.8	W. Elsey (Malton)	E. Johnson	20	9/1
1969	Big Hat	4	7.3	D. Hanley (Lambourn)	R. Still *3	19	40/1
1970	Tintagel II	5	8.5	R.C. Sturdy (Shrewton, Wiltshire)	L. Piggott	21	6/1F
1971	Knotty Pine	5	8.7	M. Jarvis (Newmarket)	F. Durr	21	9/2F
1972	Crazy Rhythm	4	8.6	S. Ingham (Epsom)	F. Durr	21	19/2
1973	Bonne Noel	4	9.2	P.J. Prendergast (Ireland)	C. Roche	20	4/1F
1974	Anji	5	7.8	J. Sutcliffe Jnr (Epsom)	T. McKeown	18	20/1
1975	Dakota	4	9.4	S. Hall (Middleham, Yorks.)	A. Barclay	18	7/1
1976	Sir Montagu	3	8.0	H.R. Price (Findon, Sussex)	W. Carson	15	11/4F
1977	Move Off	4	8.1	J. Calvert (Thirsk, Yorkshire)	J. Bleasdale *5	14	9/1
1978	Totowah	4	8.1	M. Jarvis (Newmarket)	P. Cook	22	20/1
1979	Sea Pigeon (USA)	9	10.0	M.H. Easterby (Malton, Yorkshire)	J.J. O'Neill	17	18/1
1980	Shaftesbury	4	8.5	M. Stoute (Newmarket)	G. Starkey	16	12/1
1981	Protection Racket (USA)	3	8.1	J. Hindley (Newmarket)	M. Birch	22	15/2
1982	Another Sam	5	9.2	R. Hannon (Marlborough, Wiltshire)	B. Rouse	15	16/1
1983	Jupiter Island	4	9.0	C. Brittain (Newmarket)	L. Piggott	16	9/1
1984	Crazy (Fr)	3	8.13	G. Harwood (Pulborough, Sussex)	W. Swinburn	14	10/1
1985	Western Dancer	4	8.6	C. Horgan (Wokingham, Berkshire)	P. Cook	19	20/1
1986	Primary (CAN)	3	8.7	G. Harwood (Pulborough, Sussex)	G. Starkey	22	6/1

* Apprentice allowance claimed

Favourites   This popular stayers handicap at the York August Meeting started as the Great Ebor, and was the only race at the meeting then worth more than £100 added prize money. In 1986 there was £50,000 added under Tote sponsorship, the most prize money that can be added in a handicap. In the past 25 years five winners have, appropriately, come from Yorkshire training establishments, two of them trained by Bill Elsey (whose father, Captain Charles Elsey, also trained two in the post-war period) and one of them the record age and weight carrier better known as Champion Hurdler *Sea Pigeon*, trained by Peter Easterby near Malton.

A record of six (23 per cent) winning favourites, and 53.8 per cent of winners from the first four in the betting make the Ebor an excellent race for backers. Penalised horses also do well, despite the long distance — five in the past 12 years.

Trainers   Both Michael Jarvis (Newmarket) and Vincent O'Brien (Ireland) have had two winners.

Jockeys   Paul Cook has also been successful with three winners but it is not an outstanding race for apprentices.

Weight   It is difficult to draw a useful conclusion. 53 per cent of winners came from the 7 st 8 lb – 8 st 7 lb bracket, but this may simply be a function of the total handicapped within that range. Horses with high weights also do well — 19 per cent carried over 9 st when they won.

4½ miles   The Grand National, Aintree, March/April

Sponsored since 1984 by Seagram.

	Winner	*Age*	*Wt.*	*Sire*	*Trainer*	*Jockey*	*Ran*	*Price*
1960	Merryman II	9	10.12	Carnival Boy	N. Crump (Middleham, Yorks.)	G. Scott	26	13/2F
1961	Nicolaus Silver	9	10.1	Nicolaus	T.F. Rimell (Kinnersley, Worcs.)	H. Beasley	35	28/1
1962	Kilmore	12	10.4	Zalophus	H.R. Price (Findon, Sussex)	F. Winter	32	28/1

	Winner	Age	Wt.	Sire	Trainer	Jockey	Ran	Price
1963	Ayala	9	10.0	Supertello	K. Piggott (Lambourn)	P. Buckley	47	66/1
1964	Team Spirit	12	10.3	Vulgan	F. Walwyn (Lambourn)	G.W. Robinson	33	18/1
1965	Jay Trump (USA)	8	11.5	Tonga Prince	F. Winter (Lambourn)	Mr T. Smith	47	100/6
1966	Anglo	8	10.0	Greek Star	F. Winter (Lambourn)	T. Norman	47	50/1
1967	Foinavon	9	10.0	Vulgan	J. Kempton (Compton, Berks.)	J. Buckingham	44	100/1
1968	Red Alligator	9	10.0	Magic Red	D. Smith (Bishop Auckland, Co. Durham)	B. Fletcher	45	100/7
1969	Highland Wedding	12	10.4	Question	G.B. Balding (Weyhill, Hants.)	E. Harty	30	100/9
1970	Gay Trip	8	11.5	Vulgan	T.F. Rimell (Kinnersley, Worcs.)	P. Taaffe	28	15/1
1971	Specify	9	10.13	Specific	J. Sutcliffe Sr (Epsom)	J. Cook	38	28/1
1972	Well To Do	9	10.1	Phébus	T. Forster (Wantage, Oxon.)	G. Thorner	42	14/1
1973	Red Rum	8	10.5	Quorum	D. McCain (Southport, Lancashire)	B. Fletcher	38	9/1JF
1974	Red Rum	9	12.0	Quorum	D. McCain Southport, Lancashire)	B. Fletcher	42	11/1
1975	L'Escargot	12	11.3	Escart	D. Moore (Ireland)	T. Carberry	31	13/2
1976	Rag Trade	10	10.12	Menelek	T.F. Rimell (Kinnersley, Worcs.)	J. Burke	32	14/1
1977	Red Rum	12	11.8	Quorum	D. McCain (Southport, Lancashire)	T. Stack	42	9/1
1978	Lucius	9	10.9	Perhapsburg	G. Richards (Greystoke, Cumbria)	B.R. Davies	37	14/1
1979	Rubstic	10	10.0	I Say	S.J. Leadbetter (Denholm, Roxburghshire)	M. Barnes	34	25/1
1980	Ben Nevis	12	10.12	Casmiri	T. Forster (Wantage, Oxon.)	Mr C. Fenwick	30	40/1
1981	Aldaniti	11	10.13	Derek H	J. Gifford (Findon, Sussex)	R. Champion	39	10/1
1982	Grittar	9	11.5	Grisaille	F. Gilman (Morcott, Leicestershire)	Mr C. Saunders	39	7/1F
1983	Corbiere	8	11.4	Harwell	Mrs J. Pitman (Lambourn)	B. de Haan	41	13/1
1984	Hallo Dandy	10	10.2	Menelek	G. Richards (Greystoke, Cumbria)	N. Doughty	40	13/1
1985	Last Suspect	11	10.5	Above Suspicion	T. Forster (Wantage, Oxon.)	H. Davies	40	50/1
1986	West Tip	9	10.11	Gala Performance	M. Oliver (Droitwich, Worcs.)	R. Dunwoody	40	15/2

The Grand National — Fate of the Favourites

1977	15/2F	**Andy Pandy** 8-10.7	(Had won Grand National Trial at at Haydock in February)	Fell at Becher's Brook 2nd circuit when in clear lead
1978	8/1F	**Rag Trade** 12-11.3	(Winner in 1976)	Tailed off and pulled up before 21st fence

1979	13/2F	Alverton 9-10.13	(Had won Cheltenham Gold Cup earlier in month)	Fell at Becher's 2nd circuit, and was killed
1980	8/1F	Rubstic 11-10.11	(Winner previous year)	Fell at 15th fence (The Chair)
1981	8/1F	Spartan Missile 9-11.5	(4th in Cheltenham Gold Cup previous month)	2nd
1982	7/1F	Grittar 9-11.5	(Previous month had won 3 mile Hcp Chase at Leicester under top weight, then finished remote 6th in Cheltenham Gold Cup. Runner-up in February in Whitbread Trial Chase at Ascot)	Won
1983	6/1F	Grittar 10-11.12	(Winner previous year)	5th
1984	9/1F	Greasepaint 9-11.2	(Runner-up previous year)	2nd
1985	13/2JF	Greasepaint 10-10.13	(Runner-up previous 2 years)	4th
	13/2JF	West Tip 8-10.1	(Had won four longer distance Chases in a row, including the Mildmay-Cazalet Memorial Chase at Sandown in January and the Ritz Club National Hunt Hcp Chase at Cheltenham in March)	Disputing lead and going well when fell at Becher's Brook 2nd circuit
1986	13/2F	Mr Snugfit 9-10.7	(Runner-up previous year)	4th

Shortest price favourite: 2/1F *Golden Miller* in 1935. This great steeplechaser, winner of the National the previous year, and already winner of the Cheltenham Gold Cup four times in a row (to be followed by a further victory in 1936), was top of the handicap with 12 st 7 lb. First time round, however, he jumped badly at the fence after Valentine's and unseated his rider, Gerry Wilson. The race provided the first of *Reynoldstown*'s two successive victories. 27 ran.

Shortest price winning favourite: *Poethlyn* 1919 at 11/4, 22 ran.

Longest price favourites: 1964: 100/7 Joint-Favourites: *Time* (fell four fences from home), *Pappageno's Cottage* (finished 10th), *Flying Wild* (fell at the first fence) and HM The Queen Mother's *Laffy* (fell at the 4th fence). The race went to *Team Spirit*, then 12-years-old, who was winning on his fifth attempt at Aintree. (33 ran.)

As far as the general public are concerned, the Grand National provides the biggest annual flutter of all, more popular even than the Derby. Bookmakers' and Tote turnover on that day in early April easily tops seven figures, with punters undaunted by the cold statistics furnished by the race. The Grand National field averages 38 starters, of which only a dozen will complete the course; 15 will fall, two will be brought down, two will unseat their riders, three will refuse to jump a fence at some stage of the race, and four will be pulled up before the finish. At least, these are the average figures, rounded up or down, over the past decade. Here are the full statistics on which the figures are based:

	1977	1978	1979	1980	1981	1982	1983	1984	1985	1986	TOTALS
Runners	42	37	34	30	39	39	41	40	40	40	382
Completed the course	11	15	7	4	12	8	10	23	11	17	118
	(26.2%)	(40.5%)	(20.6%)	(13.3%)	(30.6%)	(20.5%)	(24.4%)	(57.5%)	(27.5%)	(42.5%)	(30.9%)
Fell	19	18	13	12	17	19	13	10	15	12	148
	(45.2%)	(48.6%)	(38.2%)	(40.0%)	(43.6%)	(48.7%)	(31.7%)	(25.0%)	(37.5%)	(30.0%)	(38.7%)
Brought down	4	Nil	7	1	1	2	Nil	Nil	Nil	4	19 (5.0%)
Unseated rider	1	1	1	2	1	4	5	3	3	2	23 (6.0%)
Refused	4	1	Nil	5	7	4	9	1	3	Nil	34 (8.9%)
Pulled up	3	2	6	6	1	2	4	3	8	5	40 (10.5%)
State of going	Good	Firm	Good	Heavy	Good	Good	Soft	Good	Good to soft	Good to soft	

Nine year olds are the most successful age group, closely followed by ten-year-olds as the figures below show:

Age	Total No of Starters	Total Finishers*	Total Winners	Total others Placed	Percentage of age-group Win and Place
7-y-o	5	2	Nil	Nil	Nil
8-y-o	47	10 (21.3%)	1	3	8.5%
9-y-o	102	39 (38.2%)	3	13	15.7%
10-y-o	97	34 (35.1%)	2	8	10.3%
11-y-o	70	16 (22.9%)	2	4	8.5%
12-y-o	49	18 (36.7%)	2	2	8.2%
13-y-o	12	1	Nil	Nil	Nil

*Percentages are the percentage of that age group to finish.

The percentages confirm the superiority of 9-y-o, with 38.2 per cent of the age group completing the course, and 15.7 per cent of them being at least placed. But statistically, the veteran 12-y-o stand out as a good age group for getting round Aintree, with an average chance of winning or being placed.

With the outstanding exception of that popular Aintree hero *Red Rum*, winning the National is not a guarantee of success in subsequent years, as the following demonstrates:

Grand National Table (age in brackets)
1973 RED RUM (8) won. L'Escargot (10) 2nd.
1974 RED RUM (9) won. L'Escargot (11) 2nd.
1975 Red Rum (10) 2nd. L'ESCARGOT (12) won. Rag Trade (9) last of 10 to finish.
1976 Red Rum (11) 2nd. RAG TRADE (10) won.
1977 RED RUM (12) won.
1978 Red Rum (13) withdrawn last minute. Rag Trade (12) pulled up.
1979 RUBSTIC (10) won. Ben Nevis (11) brought down, remounted, pulled up.
1980 Rubstic (11) fell 15th. BEN NEVIS (12) won.
1981 Rubstic (12) 7th. ALDANITI (11) won.
1982 GRITTAR (9) won. Aldaniti (12) fell 1st.
1983 Grittar (10) 5th. CORBIERE (8) won.
1984 Grittar (11) 10th. Corbiere (9) 3rd. HALLO DANDY (10) won.
1985 Corbiere (10) 3rd. Hallo Dandy (11) fell 1st. LAST SUSPECT (11) won. West Tip (8) fell 22nd.
1986 Corbiere (11) fell 4th. Hallo Dandy (12) 12th. Last Suspect (12) pulled up. WEST TIP (9) won.

Despite the reputation of the National for providing extremely long priced winners, a blind £1 each way on the favourite over the past 10 years would have resulted in a loss of only 75 pence before tax, while a similar amount on the second favourite would have made a profit (untaxed) of £17.62 for the £20 outlay (three winners at 9/1, 10/1, and 15/2, plus five placed horses).

The Grand National, the future of which was recently for so long in the balance, is assured now to give its annual spectacle of courage, skill, narrow escapes and hard luck, triumph and tragedy. No amount of plain statistics, nor proliferating valuable jumping races can rob the race of its place still close to the heart of the National Hunt sport. It still remains, too, a summit of owners', trainers', and riders' ambitions, and a huge attraction, in which television has played an important part, to a public far greater than that which normally goes racing on a cold winter's afternoon. In the past, when the Grand National dominated the chasing scene, a horse (for example *Golden Miller*, or *Freebooter*) would be said to be 'an Aintree type'. These days, the ability to jump well still remains paramount, but greater need seems to be required for a turn of foot on the long run-in than just stamina to last it out. Such is the variety of good opportunities for staying chasers these days that there are no longer outstanding 'key' races leading to the National, although those horses who do well at Haydock Park are still worth following at Aintree, and if they have class, so much the better. Seagram deserve great credit for underpinning the success of the National with their sponsorship, and in 1987 increased the prize money to more than £100,000.

CHAPTER TEN

Trainers and Jockeys

A fool can train a racehorse, but two wise men can't.

This utterance illuminates the fact that no two men or women will agree on how best to train a racehorse. A good trainer may make a better horse out of a moderate one; a bad trainer, equally, is capable of turning a potentially good performer into a poor creature who is useless on the racecourse. Likewise, one of the marks of a good trainer is that he or she is able to get a horse to maintain winning form and run up a sequence of firsts, a feat usually beyond the abilities of an indifferent trainer, for whom a horse's one win, if any, signals the end of the line. To gain an idea as to which trainers are the most successful it is necessary to study the form books and the various statistical compilations concerning trainers' performance (see Chapter Five) to which reference should be made.

It is beyond the scope of this book or knowledge of the author to deal with the kaleidoscopic variations of methods of training racehorses, but some appreciation of the business is necessary for anyone who goes racing and/or has a bet, not least as a help to understanding what a trainer may say to the press after a race. Jack Leach (in *Sods I Have Cut On The Turf*) defines the one object of training as: '... to produce the animal fit, well, and feeling as if it could lick creation on the day of the race'. Exactly how this object was achieved in the past was the subject of much secrecy, leading to a common supposition that racehorse training was no more or less than a black art. Fortunately, today, there are books in existence which partially lift the veil, and two I would particularly recommend: *The Brigadier* by John Hislop which gives much enlightenment on the details of how *Brigadier Gerard*, one of racing's heroes, was prepared for his astonishing career of 18 races in which he was beaten only once; and *My Greatest Training Triumph*, edited by John Hughes (an outstanding modern Clerk of the Course) and Peter Watson. This book provides a remarkable spy hole on the previously arcane world of training, with 24 of today's leading trainers, both on the flat and over jumps, writing about their hopes, despairs, problems, methods, and much else besides. One extract is quoted here in order to give some idea of the immense amount of care, thought and detail which go into making a winner; in this case, another champion of not so long ago (as well as *Brigadier Gerard*'s great rival) *Mill Reef*. This is what his trainer, Ian Balding, wrote about his preparation for the Prix de l'Arc de Triomphe, the little colt's great victory in the autumn of 1971, following his performance in one of this country's great prestige races, the King George VI and Queen Elizabeth Stakes at Ascot that July, when *Mill Reef* left his opponents standing and won by half a dozen lengths with Geoff Lewis looking round and easing him at the finish:

'Now it was decision time. Did we aim for the St Leger or the Arc or both? Up to now, the races had almost picked themselves and the preparation of the horse had been relatively straightforward. I felt that my real test as a trainer was only just starting.

Mr Mellon and I were both very keen to win the Arc; we felt it was not just the most valuable and prestigious race of the year in Europe, but also the ultimate test for the true middle-distance champion. Much as I would love to have won the St Leger — and I was quite certain *Mill Reef* could have won it had we let him run — I did not feel it fitted into his programme if we wanted to win the Arc. Admittedly, we were not chasing the Triple Crown as *Nijinsky* had been the previous year, but it was still a difficult decision to make, to deliberately miss a Classic in which our horse would have started about 8-1 on!

There were ten weeks between the King George and the Arc and I felt it was vital to give him a four-week rest after Ascot which thus allowed him a six-week build-up for the big race at Longchamp. If one had considered using the St Leger as a preparatory race for the Arc, it would have given us only three weeks to train *Mill Reef* for what was after all a Classic; also the distance of $1\frac{3}{4}$ miles was, in my opinion, hardly suitable as a stepping stone for the $1\frac{1}{2}$ miles test three weeks later. Ideally, I would have liked a race over $1\frac{1}{4}$ miles about two weeks before the Arc and an easy confidence-building race at that. There was nothing suitable at that time, so we took him to Newbury racecourse for a decent work-out with *Morris Dancer* and *Bright Beam* over $1\frac{1}{4}$ miles. Although there was no prize money, it seemed ideal.

Now about his four-week rest period after Ascot: what exactly does one mean by rest? One cannot suddenly turn out into a paddock a fit, fresh, three-year-old colt worth several million pounds as one might do with a filly. Nor can one afford to "let him down" in condition as one does for example during the winter months. I considered that a break, mentally as well as physically was needed and more than anything perhaps a change in routine. Consequently, I sent him off with my great stable servant *Aldie*, a grand horse, for light exercise on their own. It was here that the beauty of Kingsclere as a training establishment with its vast variety of gallops helped. Instead of going to the Downs twice a week, the two of them would go for a jog and steady canter on the winter gallops we had not used for six months, or wander round the farm right away from the main string. Then every evening, John Hallum would take him out for a long lead and pick of grass instead of being tied up and rigorously groomed at evening stables. All this time, however, Bill Palmer scarcely had to cut down on his feed at all. We did just enough exercise with him to stop him getting too fresh for safety, but always right away from the main summer gallops.

All seemed to go smoothly, but in spite of my careful planning, I still had an uneasy feeling that perhaps the horse might just have gone over the top. His work after the Newbury gallop seemed to lack sparkle and I could just begin to detect his coat losing a little of its summer bloom. Geoff shared my anxiety and I must say those last two weeks became somewhat testing for us all.'

On the gallops

Some horses thrive on work, and others don't need much; some trainers believe in a lot of work — Sir Jack Jarvis was renowned in Newmarket for the prodigious amount of work he gave his horses; others favour a less strenuous approach. Josh Gifford (in *My Greatest Training Triumph*) says, 'We're lucky with the ground at Findon [Sussex]: if it pours with rain for twelve hours, the horses cut through the grass on to the flints; but we know that if we don't get any more rain for twenty-four hours, it dries up and we've got perfect ground the following day. You don't have to work just for the sake of it. The younger horses have to be taught to gallop — you've got to be working them; but the older horses know how to gallop and jump and you can do just as much work with them trotting up and down the hills.' But the whole question of how much work, like much else in training, is a matter of opinion. In the 18th and early 19th centuries the business of training expanded and flourished, but trainers were then what would be called today 'private trainers', i.e. they were in charge of the horses of one particular individual. There are still a few private trainers today. The only big private stable until 1986 was Manton, where Robert Sangster installed Michael Dickinson with nearly 50 of his horses, mostly two-year-olds. But most are what are known as 'public trainers', i.e. they charge fees to train the horses of any number of individuals and in 1986 Barry Hills, who is a public trainer, took over at Manton.

The 'public trainer' has been a feature of the racing scene for not much more than a century, and when they first appeared there were still some fairly rudimentary (as well as cruel and ineffective) techniques commonly employed. One of these was bleeding a horse, in the way that physicians cupped humans as a cure-all. Fortunately, this medieval practice has long since disappeared, together with 'sweating' — exercising horses by subjecting them to long and punishing gallops in heavy rugs. Since those unenlightened times, training has taken great strides forward and modern techniques include, in some big stables, the practice of weighing horses (the theory being that, like human athletes, they have a physical weight at which they race best). There are covered rides for use in times of frost and snow, as well as all-weather gallops, and equine swimming pools (for which a Certificate of Approval has to be issued by the Jockey Club) in which horses can exercise and enjoy themselves at the same time. A look into a modern Flat racing stable is provided by this extract from an article in *The Sporting Life* on John Dunlop's extremely successful establishment at Arundel (Sussex) by Simon Holt:

'There are nigh on 200 horses housed here and in the trainer's overflow yard at Findon, the largest string of racehorses in the country. Yet, when arriving on a blistering hot afternoon recently, I was immediately struck by the peace and tranquility of the place. The horses, their heads peering dreamily out of the boxes, averted their sleepy eyes in bored nonchalance as I entered the yard. Only a cock crowing disturbed the peace.

But many of these horses and their predecessors have been the subjects of crescendoes of noise on the racecourse — for John Dunlop has sent out nearly 1,300 winners, taking in virtually every major race you can name since the ex-royal Ulster Rifle subaltern had his first successes in 1966. Remember such names as dual Derby hero *Shirley Heights*, the flying *Habibti*, Eclipse winner *Scottish Rifle*, the grand stayer *Ragstone* and classic winning fillies *Quick As Lightning* and *Circus Plume*; *Posse*, *Awaasif*, *Balmerino*, *North Stoke*, *Wassl* etc; the list could go on and on . . .

Dunlop is, to use a well worn cliché, at the top of the tree. No mean achievement considering that on completing his National Service, he started from absolute scratch in trying to get into racing. He explained: "I put an advertisement in *The Sporting Life*'s situations wanted column, saying: 'Young man requires a job in racing. Limited practical experience but great enthusiasm.'"

"My mother and father were both keen racegoers and I was always fascinated. My father was a founder member of Chepstow but we had no real contacts from a professional point of view."

To his great surprise, Dunlop received several replies and joined Neville Dent, who trained jumpers at Brockenhurst. After two years he moved to the present stables where Gordon Smyth was training at the time and, such was his progress, in another two years was in charge himself. That early enthusiasm remains and, having just passed his 47th birthday, he admits to still loving it and "enjoying the continual challenge".

An exceptionally busy man, he has a sharp brain which seems constantly active. He is alert and articulate and has a thorough, business-like attitude.

The scale of the Arundel operation is enormous. Dunlop employs between 100 and 120 staff, which include: three charming secretaries, two professional assistants, three other pupil assistants of varying experience, four head lads and their deputies and four travelling head lads. Turnover in outgoing bills or gross income alone is about £1.5 million.

Was it always the plan to run such a large show with so many horses? He replied: "Well, I've always felt that this is a percentage business. A very small number are good horses, a much greater number are moderate. It is often difficult to know at the outset which is which. For example, I have a horse this year called *Tommy Way* — Italian foaled, bred and owned. He was first refused for the select scale at Milan and then went to the October sale at Newmarket with a reserve of £10,000 which he didn't make. Well it's not the sort of horse you would take if you were limiting the number in your string but he is one of the leading three-year-old money winners in Europe this season."

Cleaning up abroad is a Dunlop trademark. *Tommy Way,* who was beaten in a minor event at Haydock earlier this season, has gone on to win the Group One Derby Italiano, Group One Gran Premio di Milano and Group Two Grosser Hansa Preis at Hamburg — netting, £193,339 in winning prize money.

The trainer continued: "There is an economic argument for having more horses and that concerns the maintenance and construction of gallops, particularly all-weather gallops, which are very expensive. If you have 200 horses which are paying a gallop fee towards it, then it is obviously more viable than if you have 40 horses. With a small stable, it is very difficult to recover the normal everyday overheads."

Running such a large stable, Dunlop can only be in one place at a time and must inevitably rely heavily on good staff, which he thinks himself lucky to have.

Obviously he inspires loyalty: "We've got several people who have been here 30 or 40 years — before I came. Stable lads tend to be a floating labour force but as a rule they do stay with us. We're greatly helped by having nearly 30 cottages here, so we do have a nucleus of married men who are obviously more stable."

The place looked spotless on my visit and all horses sent to the course bearing the words "trained J.L. Dunlop, Arundel" in the racecard always look a picture of health. Incredibly he can identify every horse in the yard and most likely its breeding too. He shrugs this ability aside modestly: "It would be very surprising if one couldn't recognise all the horses and remember their breeding. They're all very individual and one does see them every day. People always say that a shepherd can recognise every single sheep in a flock of 500, yet they are all the same colour with similar characteristics to the untutored eye.

"But horses are completely different. No, I don't think it's a particularly commendable attribute . . ."'

John Dunlop's remarks about the economic viability of smaller yards will be echoed by the professional trainers who run such establishments. For every trainer such as John Dunlop, Henry Cecil, Michael Stoute, Guy Harwood, Arthur Stephenson and others who count their horses in hundreds, there are scores of individuals who operate on a far more modest scale. (For details of their many problems and how they operate, the weekly features in *The Sporting Life Weekender* and *Raceform Handicap Book* offer a valuable insight, while the *Timeform* Black Book trainer interviews are excellent.) With many small yards, despite the all round increase in prize money, it is still of paramount importance to have a betting 'touch' from time to time. Such 'touches' can be regarded as usually beyond the clairvoyance of newspaper experts, although the market may sometimes give a clue to racegoers and betting shop habitués. With smaller yards, it is worth studying the previous form of any horse for whom a leading jockey has been engaged, although the fact of an unusual, high-powered riding arrangement is there for all to see, so the bookmakers will not be likely to be offering bargain prices, and more likely the reverse in the opening stages of the market.

In National Hunt racing, the yards tend to be much smaller than on the Flat. In addition to professional licensed trainers, a good number of whom run very small operations, there are well over 600 permit holders who annually apply for a permit from the Jockey Club in order to be able to train a family horse or horses for competition over hurdles and fences under rules. The big professional yards such as those of Josh Gifford and Fred Winter, and up north, Arthur Stephenson and G.W. Richards, may often dominate the prize money, but stables with only a few horses are numerically in a large majority, and send out their share of winners. A study of *Horses in Training* combined with *Trainers Review* will unearth the clues to such stables and the likelihood of their success; for example, the case of H. Wharton who has a mixed yard of under 20 horses at Middleham, Yorkshire. Scant success on the Flat was followed by a jumping season in which he saddled 10 winners from 54 runners, taking prize money of more than £20,000. Similarly J.S. Delahooke, whose percentage of success holds the overall record for the season, specialises in hunter chases. Two of his horses each won four out of five races, and *Jack Of All Trades* won one out of six, bringing in nearly £18,500 prize money and the astonishing percentage success rate of 56.3. *Ruff's Guide* lists approximately 600 *winning* trainers for the National Hunt season 1984-85. Only six per cent achieved double figures with their number of winning horses and, of the rest, a huge proportion (many of them permit holders) saddled only one winner. In addition, *Trainers Review* provides nearly 15 depressing pages of trainers who saddled no winners whatsoever during the season (and by no means all of them were permit holders).

How many trainers, then, are there? *Horses in Training* for 1986 lists about 565 licensed trainers on the Flat and over jumps, or both (including some in France and Ireland). That may seem a large number, but, in fact, the total number given has declined in the past 20 or so years — the 1965 edition listed 750. By contrast, today's trainers are in charge of a far larger number of horses. The racehorse population explosion is matched in human terms only by the Third World. Around the beginning of this century there were an estimated 3,000 or so racehorses. In 1946 (after an inter-war increase and a drop during the Second World War) the number was still only 4,000+, a guide by which to compare the mid-sixties figure of 9,000. Only 20 years later, it was still climbing, and stood at 14,000.

At the same time, there are in the United Kingdom only about 6,500 races on the Flat and over jumps to be won, so quite apart from a horse's ability and a trainer's skill, or lack of it, statistics alone dictate that a considerable number of disappointments, both equine and human, are inevitable. Many of those disappointments, sad to say, happen to the very small establishments, and with no disrespect to National Hunt permit holders and their often splendid success with a single much loved animal, and to the one-off yards, which, if well chosen can provide good betting opportunities, the most consistent success comes to the bigger yards. That does not mean, however, that they necessarily provide betting value with the same consistency. The 1986 edition of *Trainers Record* gives the basis for some useful advice, dividing stables into four categories:

1   **The On-Course Gambling Stable:** Easy to identify in weak markets where the price shifts are out of all proportion to the actual money put on a horse. Who is putting the money on is more important as a factor, moreover, than the money itself, an instance of bookmakers 'betting to faces'. False prices and poor value are often involved here, and the stables themselves likewise have a bad ratio of winners to runners.

2   **The Off-Course Gambling Stable:** Inspired stable money is placed through commission agents and other 'putters-on' with a view to disguising the source of the bet. This type of stable is difficult to distinguish from the non-betting stable but a general lack of complete outsiders in their record may give a clue, and the money is worth following.

3   **Non-Gambling Stables:** Only the biggest stables can afford not to gamble. Even if the guv'nor is not a betting man the lads and other connections often produce the same effect. The non-gambling stable is typified by long odds winners, apparently unfancied animals beating well supported stable companions, and a good profitability figure.

4.   **Stables with a Big Public Following:** These are the big stables which get widely reported in the media and often have the top jockeys riding for them. Their exposure in the press often means false favourites, so take a careful look at the number of horses made favourite from the big yards and especially those which show level stakes losses. They can be expensive to follow.

Successful Stables

To help identify by statistics the most successful stables, the following lists have been compiled with the aid of *Ruff's Guide* and *Trainers Review*. They show the top (in terms of total number of winners) trainers for the Flat seasons 1976-1985, and the National Hunt seasons 1976-77 to 1985-86, together with the current number of horses in training with each trainer. In addition, there is a list of trainers whose winning totals are, overall, on the upgrade for the past five years, and some extra statistics useful for assessing the jumps, where, unlike the Flat, smaller yards tend to have more success.

Top 20 Flat Trainers: Record over 10 years 1976–1985

	Horses in Training 1986		Total Winners	1985 Percentage Winners/Runners
Henry Cecil	169	Newmarket	997	38.0%
Michael Stoute	142	Newmarket	877	26.1%
Guy Harwood	137	Pulborough, Sussex	772	24.5%

John Dunlop	192	Arundel, Sussex	744	12.9%*
Barry Hills	131	Lambourn	660	13.1%
Peter Walwyn	108	Lambourn	627	10.9%
Major Dick Hern	102	W. Ilsley, Berkshire	617	17.5%
Paul Cole	107	Wantage	508	14.7%
Peter Easterby	81	Malton, Yorkshire	452	9.2%
Ian Balding	114	Kingsclere, Berkshire	444	15.1%
Clive Brittain	115	Newmarket	431	11.5%
Reg Hollinshead	100	Rugeley, Staffordshire	428	6.8%
Bill Watts	69	Richmond, Yorkshire	412	12.2%
Jeremy Hindley	53	Newmarket	411	18.4%
Gavin Pritchard-Gordon	68	Newmarket	388	12.7%
Fulke Johnson Houghton	59	Blewbury, Oxfordshire	380	8.7%*
Richard Hannon	75	Marlborough, Wiltshire	368	8.0%
Luca Cumani	112	Newmarket	340	12.3%
Harry Thomson Jones	104	Newmarket	333	16.1%
Michael Jarvis	80	Newmarket	319	7.6%

*These are not typical figures. Equine virus affected the 1985 runners, and John Dunlop's stable was virtually closed down during the middle of the season.

On the Upgrade	Winners				
	1981	*1982*	*1983*	*1984*	*1985*
Kim Brassey (Lambourn)	—	12	19	23	25
Luca Cumani (Newmarket)	30	25	35	50	60
Geoff Huffer (Newmarket)	18	22	26	27	30
Steve Norton (Barnsley, Yorkshire)	19	29	41	43	35
Matt McCormack (Wantage)	3	13	11	16	22

Trainers for Courses

Much more detailed information on this important specific point is available in the daily tables published in *The Sporting Life*, and in *Trainers Review* and *Trainers Record*. Meanwhile, here are a few highlights:

Leading Trainers sending to the Midlands and North (see North v South below)

Ian Balding	Leicester
Henry Cecil	Newcastle, Thirsk, York
John Dunlop	Leicester
Major Dick Hern	Wolverhampton
Michael Stoute	Newcastle, Redcar
Harry Thomson Jones	Beverley, Thirsk, Redcar

Leading Trainers on other Courses

Ian Balding	Bath (a lot of winners, but many favourites), Windsor
Henry Cecil	Newbury
Richard Hannon	Brighton and Epsom
Sally Hall, Peter Easterby and Bill Watts	Runners sent from Yorkshire to Grade One Southern courses such as Ascot
Geoff Lewis	On his 'home' course at Epsom
Major Dick Hern	Goodwood
Harry Thomson Jones	Ascot, Brighton, Chepstow

Trainers for Races

John Sutcliffe is a notable absentee from the top 20 (in fact, he comes 30th with a total of 206 winners in 10 years), but this shrewd trainer, who excels at placing his horses should always be noted in big handicaps (see Chapter Nine, Big Race Analysis) and also does very well in selling races.

Jeremy Tree, the Master of Beckhampton, is usually thought of as a highly successful trainer of top class horses in top class races, and not as a handicap trainer. Nonetheless, he has a first class record in handicaps at Ascot when he has engaged a leading jockey (notably Pat Eddery).

Top 25 National Hunt Trainers: Record over 10 years 1976-77 to 1985-86

		Total Winners	1985-86 Percentage Winners/Runners		No of Older Horses in yard
			Hurdle	Chase	
Fred Winter	Lambourn	750	11.0	17.9	66
Dickinson family (Mrs Monica Dickinson since 1984)	Harewood, Yorkshire	714	22.6	32.2	38
Arthur Stephenson	Bishop Auckland, Co. Durham	679	11.0	17.9	86*
Josh Gifford	Findon, Sussex	577	14.0	16.3	66
G.W. Richards	Penrith, Cumbria	518	9.9	23.8	47*
Peter Easterby	Malton, Yorkshire	504	16.7	16.4	42*
The late Fred Rimell/ Mrs Mercy Rimell	Kinnersley, Worcestershire	468	13.5	20.0	36
Fulke Walwyn	Lambourn	448	18.2	23.7	30
Capt. Tim Forster	Wantage, Oxfordshire	405	14.9	23.1	58
David Nicholson	Stow-on-the-Wold, Gloucestershire	386	9.2	12.8	42
Les Kennard	Taunton, Somerset	327	17.2	14.7	28
Stan Mellor	Lambourn	300	10.6	15.4	50*
David Gandolfo	Wantage, Oxfordshire	294	6.8	12.3	35
Nick Henderson	Lambourn	291	16.8	28.0	56
John Jenkins (1979 on)	Epsom	291	18.8	26.0	58*
John Edwards	Ross-on-Wye, Herefordshire	281	6.1	26.2	41
Martin Pipe	Wellington, Somerset	245	18.6	20.3	57*
Neville Crump	Middleham, Yorkshire	225	12.5	17.0	17
Denys Smith	Bishop Auckland, Co. Durham	225	9.8	12.9	68*
Jimmy Fitzgerald	Malton, Yorkshire	209	10.1	26.5	62*
Mrs Jenny Pitman	Lambourn	205	15.9	23.9	61
Nick Gaselee	Lambourn	198	13.1	20.2	36
Martin Tate	Kidderminster, Worcestershire	180	5.8	—	22
John Webber	Banbury, Oxfordshire	196	4.2	13.4	43
Roger Fisher	Ulverston, Cumbria	191	11.1	10.5	35*

*Mixed National Hunt and Flat yard

In addition, D. Elsworth, Fordingbridge, Hampshire, has trained 173 winners since 1978-79, and *Ruff*'s has no record of O. Sherwood (Lambourn) because before 1985-86 he did not quality for the list. In that season, however, he sent out 48 winners.

On the Upgrade	Total winners	1981-82	-83	-84	-85	-86
J.A.C. Edwards		37	27	19	22	40

D. Elsworth	24	25	26	32	37
J.R. Fitzgerald	16	28	35	41	28
J.R. Jenkins	21	42	69	76	65
M.C. Pipe	20	23	32	51	80
Mrs J. Pitman	8	20	18	41	46

Top Ten National Hunt Trainers 1985-86*

(Based on Total Number of Winners)

No of Runners		Total Winners
424	M.C. Pipe	80
489	W.A. Stephenson	71
336	J.R. Jenkins	65
330	G.W. Richards	56
358	J. Gifford	55
187	O. Sherwood	48
234	T. Forster	47
240	N.J. Henderson	46
253	Mrs J. Pitman	46
274	F. Winter	41

(Based on percentage Winners/Runners in Hurdles and Chases)

	Success as percentage	Total No of Runners
Mrs M. Dickinson (Harewood, Yorkshire)	27.3%	121
O. Sherwood (Lambourn)	25.7%	187
F. Walwyn (Lambourn)	21.1%	142
T. Forster (Wantage)	20.1%	234
P. Mitchell (Epsom)	20.5%	78
J.R. Jenkins (Epsom)	19.9%	326
S. Christian (Newbury, Berkshire)	19.2%	78
M.C. Pipe (Wellington)	18.9%	424
Mrs J. Pitman (Lambourn)	18.2%	253

*Trainers with more than 75 runners only

Women Trainers

How women finally forced the Jockey Club into granting them trainers' licences is a depressing saga of male hypocrisy and stone age attitudes to women. The story is well told by Caroline Ramsden in her book *Ladies In Racing*. Norah Wilmot had trained from 1930 onwards; Mrs Florence Nagle had saddled her first winner *Thoroughwort* at Lingfield in 1947; and Helen Johnson Houghton (twin sister of Fulke Walwyn, mother of the present trainer Fulke Johnson Houghton, and eventually, at last, made a member of the Jockey Club) on the tragic death of her husband in 1952, took over the string and trained not only Dorothy Paget's *Nucleus* to win several high class races at Ascot and Newmarket, and to be runner-up to *Meld* in the St Leger, but also *Gilles de Retz*, winner of the 1956 2000 Guineas. Some records have now been suitably amended, but as originally published, they name 'C. Jerdein' as the trainer, and in this lies the clue to the two faced way in which women trainers were then treated. The Jockey Club was perfectly aware that women were *de facto* trainers but refused to recognise them as such — a man had to hold the licence. So, the head lads of Mrs Johnson Houghton, Mrs Nagle, Norah Wilmot, Auriol Sinclair and others became literally 'front men', while in the case of Mrs Rosemary Lomax (later, when licensed, she trained the Ascot Gold Cup winner, *Precipice Wood*) her husband held the licence. It took a long and hard campaign, an exchange of some bitter but pertinent letters and, finally, a high court judgement before the Jockey Club caved in, thus ending in 1966 a situation which was Gilbertian in every extreme except humour. Today, the veteran Mrs Dingwall, Sally Hall, Mrs Dickinson, Mrs Jenny Pitman, and Mercy Rimell, who took over the yard on the untimely and sad death of her husband Fred, are among those who have turned out several hundred winners between them, and who are successfully showing the flag for women in training.

Newmarket v The Rest

It has already been amply demonstrated that Newmarket is the centre of the Flat racing world. Upwards of 2,300 racehorses are trained there on the acres of Jockey Club gallops; in addition there is the racecourse itself, or, to be more accurate, two racecourses, a great number of stud farms, equine research establishments and other facilities, as well as the Jockey Club rooms. As far as jumping goes, however, the Downs in Berkshire, Oxfordshire and Wiltshire, with the village of Lambourn as the focal point, is now the biggest training area for National Hunt racing. It also constitutes the second most important Flat training area with a total number of horses in training for both kinds of racing exceeding even that at Newmarket. The two powerful Sussex stables of Guy Harwood and John Dunlop make another training area that has grown immensely in importance; and the various Yorkshire centres, chiefly Malton and Middleham, although they have fallen on hard times recently are still numerically the third biggest training area in the UK.

Across the water, in Tipperary, Vincent O'Brien's establishment regularly has an important influence on the English racing scene, while the exploits of other Irish stables, many of them on the Curragh, at Cheltenham in particular, need little introduction. From France, Francois Boutin is a frequent contender for big English prizes, and horses from his 168-strong stable at Lamorlaye often give good each way value, a fact which is just as often ignored by the average English backer. But Newmarket remains the name most synonymous with Turf activities in this country. Its drawback, from a backer's point of view, is that many of its runners, particularly those from the biggest and most publicised stables, offer minimum value.

Henry Cecil, who is the outstanding trainer of his generation, both stepson and son-in-law of the most outstanding trainers of *their* day, respectively Captain Cecil Boyd-Rochfort and Sir Noel Murless, had an astonishing season in 1985, beating all his own previous records. Approximately two-thirds of all his runners finished in the first three in their races, while his percentage of winners/races run, at 38 per cent was remarkable by any standards. Selective backing of his horses might have produced a reasonable profit for the backer, but the fact remains that a £1 bet on every one of his 347 runners would have yielded a profit of only £26.09, and that before deduction of tax. £347 'invested' for a return of less than 7½ per cent is not only hard work, but of no interest to the average punter.

With the talented Henry Cecil and Michael Stoute to the fore, Newmarket produces a higher proportion of odds-on favourites than anywhere else, an illustration of which is given by the following statistics concerning 2-y-o in the month of July, 1985: Newmarket won 58 of the 152 2-y-o races (38.2 per cent) but 31 of these winners were made favourite, and of these 17 were odds-on. Henry Cecil, in particular, had winners which were virtually unbackable for the ordinary punter. Of his 10 winners, eight were favourites (seven heavily odds-on — at 1/5, 1/4 (twice), 2/9, 4/11, 4/9, and 1/2) and the other two were second favourites at 5/2 and 9/4.

Of Michael Stoute's eight winners, five were favourites (four odds-on, at 1/3, 4/11, 4/6 and 4/5) and of Harry Thomson Jones's six successes, five were favourites, although only one of them won at a shade of odds-on, the rest being odds against. Forty-five of Newmarket's winners started at odds of 4/1 or shorter (28 of them 4/1 down to even money, and 17 odds-on down to 1/5). The shining exceptions, from the backer's viewpoint, were G. Huffer's Yarmouth success at 40/1, John Winter's at 20/1, Mrs Reavey at 16/1, in the long price bracket; and, in the medium range, L. Cumani (10/1), Bruce Hobbs (9/1), M.A. Jarvis (8/1), R.J. Williams (9/1 and 7/1), M.J. Ryan (11/1), Gavin Pritchard-Gordon (12/1 and 5/1), M.F. Morley (6/1) and Mrs Reavey (no longer training at Newmarket) again, (6/1).

10 winners:	H. Cecil
8 winners:	M. Stoute
6 winners:	H. Thomson Jones
5 winners:	G. Huffer
3 winners:	G. Pritchard-Gordon, R.J. Williams
2 winners:	W. Jarvis, J. Hindley, B. Hanbury, Mrs Reavey, M.A. Jarvis, L. Cumani, A.P. Jarvis.
1 winner each:	C. Brittain, B. Hobbs (retired at end 1985), B. Hanbury, P. Kelleway, M.F.D. Morley, M.J. Ryan, R. Sheather, A.C. Stewart, J. Winter, G. Wragg.

Lambourn and surrounding area won 45 of the 152 2-y-o races (29.6 per cent). Lambourn itself produced 22 winners out of those 45. The total is next best to that of Newmarket, but in contrast, although there were 16 favourites, only *four* were odds-on, with the better known and most powerful establishments, particularly that of Ian Balding, providing a majority of short priced winners. In addition, there were nine winning second favourites, and, in general, the prices for Lambourn winners were far better than those for any other area, Newmarket in particular.

Lambourn	6 winners	B. Hills	(5/4f, 15/8f, 7/2 2f, 9/2, 2f, 6/1, 13/2)
	3 winners	K. Brassey	(4/6f, 5/1, 33/1)
		P.F. Cole	(2/1f, 3/1 2f, 8/1)
		P. Walwyn	(3/1 2f, 11/2, 15/2)
	2 winners	C. Nelson	(13/2, 20/1)
	1 winner	M. Blanshard	(14/1)
	each	M.E.D. Francis	(7/1 2f)
		W.W. Haigh	(11/2)
		D.R. Laing	(7/4 2f)
		M.D. Usher	(20/1)
Wantage	3 winners	H. Candy	(evens f, 5/2 2f, 11/2)
	1 winner	J.D. Bethell	(6/1)
	each	R.F. Johnson Houghton	(11/10f)
		M. McCormack	(5/2 2f)
W. Ilsley	6 winners	W.R. Hern	(4/6f, 4/5f, 11/4f, 9/2 2f, 9/1, 10/1)
Kingsclere	6 winners	I. Balding	(4/9f, evens f, 5/4f, 11/10f, 13/8f, 100/30)
Newbury	1 winner	P. Cundell	(evens f)
	each	C. James	(7/4f)
Marlborough	1 winner	R. Hannon	(7/1)
	each	D. Sasse	(20/1)
		J. Tree	(5/2 jf)

Yorkshire Stables   The Yorkshire contribution was the third best area total — 29 (19.1 per cent) — and although the numbers dropped from previous months, with many more southern stables winning on Yorkshire courses, Middleham's share of winners increased as against Malton and district. Favourites (only two odds-on), second favourites, and winners at longer prices were divided in roughly equal proportion.

Malton and district	3 winners	M.H. Easterby	(11/10f, 14/1, 16/1)
	2 winners	M.W. Easterby	(5/2f, 4/1 2f)
		C. Tinkler	(9/4 2f, 7/2 2f)
		N. Tinkler	(2/1f, 3/1 2f)
	1 winner	C.B. Booth	(11/2)
	each	K. Stone	(10/1)
York	1 winner	M. Brittain	(15/2)
Middleham	3 winners	G.M. Moore	(11/10f, 3/1f, 5/2 2f)
	2 winners	Miss S. Hall	(4/5f, 9/2)
		C.W. Thornton	(6/4f, 8/1)
	1 winner	W. Bentley	(20/1)
	each	T. Fairhurst	(13/2)
		R.W. Stubbs	(2/1f)
Richmond	3 winners	J.W. Watts	(5/6f, 5/2 jf, 9/1)
Barnsley	3 winners	S.G. Norton	(2/1 2f, 5/2 2f, 5/1 2f)
Doncaster	1 winner	R. Thompson	(15/8f)

Summary — Winners of 2-y-o races, July 1985 (152 races)

	Total Winners	Percentage of total 2-y-o Races	No of Winning Favourites	(Odds-on Favourites)	Percentage Favourites in Winning Area Total	No of 2nd Favourites	No of Winners at Longer Prices
Newmarket	58	38.2%	31	(17)	53%	13	14
Lambourn area	45	29.6%	16	(4)	35.5%	9	20
Yorkshire area	29	19.1%	11	(2)	37.9%	8	10

The remaining 13.1% of races were won by Epsom stables (6.6%), Lancashire, Sussex and Midlands.

North v South

Ayr, Doncaster, Haydock Park, Liverpool, Newcastle and York provide some of the best racing in Britain, but the plight of many northern trainers is one of the sad aspects of today's racing scene, particularly on the Flat (over the jumps, without the huge financial investment required for consistent success, the northern stables are far better able to hold their own). Industrial decline in the north of England is one of the reasons. There are few local owners with enough money to compete with the rich southern training scene, now dominated and subsidised by Arab investment and interest (the decline can be noted in more detail in the Big Race analyses in Chapter Nine). Far fewer big handicaps, and fewer Classics, are now won by the north. Joint ownership and projects such as Full Circle have gone some way to meeting the problem, but it still remains. At the same time, there is justifiable resentment in the north at the southern 'raiders' who go to northern tracks, be it Beverley or Hamilton Park, Thirsk or Pontefract, Carlisle or Ripon, and return home with a lot of the best prizes from this rich variety of mostly modest but attractive courses. The graphic overleaf, reproduced from *The Times*, illustrates the story.

Early Birds

A few horses, year after year, shine in the spring in particular; some, however, do not produce their best form until the autumn. An example of the latter is *Naftilos* who, after a busy but unsuccessful early season in 1985, won three times within six weeks over long distances between the end of August and mid-October. Older fillies, however, can be very unpredictable at this time of year, and lose their form entirely. A look through the index of past form books will show, each year, which horses fall into which categories, and they are often well worth following at the appropriate time.

Correspondingly, some trainers regularly have their horses, especially two-year-olds, more forward in condition than those of other trainers (it is rare for trainers such as Henry Cecil, Michael Stoute, Ian Balding, Dick Hern and Jeremy Tree, for example, to have a two-year-old runner before May).

SOUTHERN RAIDERS

A comparison between the top ten in the north and the top ten in the south

Trainer	Prize £	Wins
R. Hollinshead	£197,493	54
S. Norton	£186,756	43
M. H. Easterby	£134,828	30
J. Watts	£131,535	28
J. Fitzgerald	£111,629	21
D. Chapman	£95,804	34
M. W. Easterby	£73,419	24
D. Plant	£68,643	14
J. Berry	£67,505	30
T. Fairhurst	£66,351	17

Total No. trainers with runners – 353

Total win + place prize money – £15,536,959

1984 Flat Season – top six trainers

Trainer	Prize £	Wins	%	% of trainers
H. Cecil	£748,338	108	4.8	0.3
G. Harwood	£709,158	93	9.4	0.6
J. Dunlop	£675,388	89	13.7	0.85
M. Stoute	£631,890	96	17.8	1.1
R. Hern	£599,799	56	21.7	1.4
B. Hills	£549,638	58	25.2	1.7
L. Cumani	£464,587	50		
C. Brittan	£360,968	33		
P. Cole	£329,337	61		
H. Wragg	£320,646	22		

Produced for *The Times* by Racing Research, publishers of Computer Racing Form.

Those who, winter weather permitting, get their horses ready for an early campaign, include:

Training area

Yorkshire: P. Rohan, N. Tinkler, M. Brittain
Newmarket: R.Boss, W. O'Gorman, P. Kelleway
Marlborough: R. Hannon
Lancashire: J. Berry
Lambourn: D.R. Laing, P. Cole, M. McCormack

Staying Power

There is an increasing dearth of stayers and today there are no trainers specialising in the handling of long distance horses. George Todd, the former master of Manton, once said, 'If I wanted to prepare a horse for the Cesarewitch, I should want him for at least two years'. Time and economics do not permit such preparations these days. The pressure of bigger prize money at shorter distances means, too, that stayers in the yard are almost a luxury, and the list of trainers who have proved themselves good with stayers is dominated by those with big yards. Henry Cecil comes near the top of the list, if nothing else for his inspired training of *Le Moss* to win two Ascot Gold Cups, Goodwood Cups, and Doncaster Cups in successive years, as well as another cup winner in *Ardross*, thus following in the footsteps of 'The Captain', his step-father, who had an unrivalled record with stayers. Here is a short list of trainers of stayers who have excelled, not all of them with the most powerful strings: Ian Balding, Henry Candy, Henry Cecil, Luca Cumani, John Dunlop, Jimmy Fitzgerald, Guy Harwood, Major Dick Hern, Barry Hills, Michael Stoute, Jeremy Tree, Peter Walwyn.

Jockeys

The best advice about jockeys is to follow the ones in *Form*. Lists of promising apprentices, and even promising young riders who have lost their allowance, soon lose their value, and riding arrangements change with bewildering rapidity. At the present time both Lester Piggott and Joe Mercer have quit the Flat racing scene, and John Francome the National Hunt, leaving gaps that may not be filled for a long time. Lester Piggott followed Fred Archer, Steve Donoghue and Sir Gordon Richards as the most polished performer in the saddle of his time, while John Francome can be described in the same terms over the jumps.

Trainers Review gives a first class guide to where jockeys shine, and the advice implicit in their statistics should be taken, along with the various assessments in table form which appear in the sporting press. So, with Pat Eddery, Willie Carson, Steve Cauthen (joined this year by another leading American, Cash Asmussen), Walter Swinburn, Tony Ives, Richard Quinn and Ray Cochrane to the fore on the Flat, the younger ones have it all to prove. Fortunately, with support being given to apprentice training and the more enlightened trainers giving boys and girls rides whenever possible, and keeping old horses for them to learn on, the standard of jockeyship among the young today is higher than it has ever been in general terms. Correspondingly, the value of a claiming apprentice in a good class race must be stressed today as of more importance than it was even 20 years ago, and this chapter can be appropriately rounded off with some proof of how successful claiming apprentices were in the 1985 season.

Overleaf is a list of the most valuable handicaps won by apprentices in the 1985

Flat season, in which their allowance was a crucial factor in winning the race:

Course	Dist.	Race (Value)	Winner	Age	Wt.	Apprentice & (Allowance Claimed)	Won By	Ran	Start. Price
Doncaster	2¼m	Town Plate (£7,882)	Relkisha	4yr	7-6	N. Adams (5)	neck	14	16/1
Epsom[1]	1¼m	City and Suburban* (£9,598)	Redden	7yr	7-4[2]	C. Rutter (5)	½l	15	25/1
York	1m1f	Wings Holiday Hcp (£5,049)	Chance in a Million	3yr	8-5	D. Leadbitter (5)	neck	12	13/2
York[2]	6f	Wm Hill Trophy Hcp (£19,150)	Si Signor	3yr	8-9(7x)	M. Lynch (7)	1l	12	9/4F
Royal Ascot[3]	1m	Royal Hunt Cup (£20,224)	Come on the Blues	6yr	8-2(7x)	C. Rutter (5)	1½l	27	14/1
Newcastle	2m	Northumberland Plate** (£22,089)	Trade Line	4yr	7-10	T. Williams (3)	¾l	13	17/2
Newmarket[4]	7f	Bahrain Trophy (£8,220)	Domynga	3yr	7-5[1]	S. Dawson (3)	neck	13	20/1
Haydock Park	1¼m	Southport Hcp (£5,208)	Wild Hope	4yr	9.2	G. Carter (5)	1l	20	6/1
Newbury	1m1f	Mail on Sunday Autumn Hcp (£14,958)	Shellman	3yr	7-6	G. Carter (5)	neck	12	12/1
Doncaster	1m	A.T. Cross Jockeys' Championship (£6,391)	Well Rigged	4yr	7-10	G. Carter (5)	½l	20	11/4F

Notes   In two cases the apprentice, because of the allowance he claimed, had to put up overweight, since the allowance took him below his natural riding weight. The amount of overweight is indicated in square brackets next to (and is included in) the weight actually carried.

1   C. Rutter, because of overweight, could effectively claim only 3 lb of his allowance. It was still enough to give him a vital 'pull' in the handicap.

2   Si Signor's original handicap weight was increased by a 7 lb penalty for a success in his previous race, which came after the weights were published for the William Hill Trophy. M. Lynch's allowance cancelled the penalty exactly, and gave enough in hand for a good win at this sprint distance. [The penalty is indicated by (7x).]

3   Similar to Note 2.

4   Similar to Note 1. S. Dawson was able to claim only 2 lb of his 3 lb allowance, but it was enough to give Domynga a narrow victory.

CHAPTER ELEVEN
Breeding Pointers to Performance

Our English racehorses differ slightly from the horses of every other breed; but they do not owe their difference and superiority to descent from any single pair, but to continued care in selecting and training many individuals during many generations

Charles Darwin *On the Origin of Species* 1859

Darwin was writing within a century of Sir Charles Bunbury's notable reforms under the *aegis* of the Jockey Club to alter the demands of English racing upon the thoroughbred. A blend of speed and stamina was always necessary to win races; with shortened races, as well as younger contestants, speed became of more importance. Today, more than a century after Darwin propounded his controversial theories, speed has overtaken stamina in the majority of our racehorses, at the same time with a loss of versatility, and, with less strenuous racing careers, a lessening of toughness in many animals. Even in Victorian times there were horses such as *Plaisanterie, Foxhall* and *Rosebery* who were capable of winning both the Cesarewitch and Cambridgeshire in the same season, within a fortnight. No horse in training today could do that, and some of the longer distance races are being shortened. The Great Metropolitan, which used to wind its way in the spring over the Downs at Epsom not so long ago and rejoin the racecourse proper, is now, instead of a 2¼ mile spectacle, down to 1½ miles. The Brown Jack Stakes, named after that wonderful and greatly-loved Ascot stayer, used to share with the race he won so many times, the Queen Alexandra Stakes, the title of the longest race in the calendar; it has now been shortened to 2 miles. The oldest and longest Classic, the St Leger, over 1¾ miles, is no longer supported in the way it used to be, partly because fewer horses these days stay that distance than even 50 years ago, and partly because of competition from rich races taking place in Europe and America, notably the Prix d l'Arc de Triomphe at 1½ miles. No longer is the Derby winner automatically trained for Doncaster.

The influence of American-bred horses in all this is difficult to assess. The first four home in the 1986 Derby were all American bred. The fact remains that in the late 19th century the distance of their Triple Crown races were: Kentucky Derby 1½ miles until 1895, Preakness Stakes 1½ miles until 1888, Belmont Stakes 1 mile 5 furlongs until 1873. The 1986 distances are, respectively, 1¼ miles, 1 mile 1½ furlongs, and 1½ miles. Against this, American horses tend to be a tough breed, well tried on their racecourses, but with 1½ miles being the extreme limit required of their stamina the ultimate effect in the UK is easy to predict. In practical terms, the tables which follow tell the whole sad story. They have been compiled with the intent of giving some indication of what names to look for as sires at different distances. The dearth of staying sires, or more accurately those transmitting staying power to their progeny, and to dams of winners, can be contrasted at leisure with the legion of those who get speedy, short runners.

Selected Sires of Stayers (1 m 6 f plus) 1985

Where winners are given, the dam's sire is included in brackets, as is sire's maternal grandsire.

Blakeney
  3 winners at 14 f-21 f
Blushing Groom (Fr) 1974 by Red God — Runaway Bride (Wild Risk)
  2 winners including *Spicy Story* (Nijinsky) Doncaster Cup winner.
Busted 1963 by Crepello — San Le Sou (Vimy)
  4 winners at 14 f-16 f
Bustino 1971 by Busted — Shipyard (Doutelle)
  5 winners, none over more than 14 f, including 2 Hcp wins by *Rakaposhi King* (Shantung)
Captain James 1974 by Captain's Gig — Aliceva (Alcide)
  1 Hcp winner × 3 races at 15 f-16 f
Caro 1967 by Fortino II — Chambord (Chamossaire II)
  1 Hcp winner × 4 races at 15 f-19 f
Dancing Champ 1972 by Nijinsky (Can) — Mrs Peterkin (Tom Fool)
  1 Hcp winner × 3 races 16 f-18 f
Grundy 1972 by Great Nephew — Word from Lundy (Worden II)
  3 winners at 16-20 f
High Line 1966 by High Hat — Time Call (Chanteur II)
  9 winners at 14 f-16 f including *Tale Quale* (Vienna) Jockey Club Cup winner, and *Trade Line* (Javelot) winner of (Hcp) Northumberland Plate.
Lombard (Ger) 1967 by Agio — Promised Lady (Prince Chevalier)
  2 winners at 14 f-16 f including *Destroyer* (Sahib) Henry II Stakes winner.
Julio Mariner 1975 by Blakeney — Set Free (Worden II)
  4 winners at 14 f-19 f
Mill Reef (USA) 1968 by Never Bend — Milan Mill (Princequillo)
  1 winner × 3 races at 16 f-20 f:— *Meadowbrook* (Harken), Ascot Stakes winner.
Orchestra 1974 by Tudor Music — Golden Moss (Sheshoon)
  2 winners at 16 f
Reliance II 1962 by Tantieme — Relance III (Relic)
  2 winners × 5 races at 14 f-18 f, including *Morgan's Choice* (Alcide), (Hcp) Chester Cup Winner.
Relko 1960 by Tanerko — Relance III (Relic)
  3 winners at 16 f-18 f including *Floyd* (Honeyway), winner of (Hcp) Queen's Prize.
Rheingold 1969 by Faberge II — Achene (Supreme Court)

3 winners × 5 races at 14f-20f, including *Gildoran* (Lyphard), winner of Ascot Gold Cup.

The Minstrel (Can) 1974 by Northern Dancer — Fleur (Victoria Park)
2 winners × 4 races at 14f-16f each, including *Wassl Merbayeh* (Arturo A), winner of Queen's Vase

Troy 1976 by Petingo — Lamilo (Hornbeam)
3 winners × 5 races at 14f-16f, including *Ilium* (Riverman USA) winner of Yorkshire Cup, and *Inde Pulse* (Javelot).

Val De L'Orne (Fr) 1972 by Val de Loir — Aglae (Armistice)
Sire of *Valuable Witness* (Northern Dancer) unbeaten in 4 races in 1985 from 14f-22.2f, wins including the Goodwood Cup and Queen Alexandra Stakes, longest race in the Calendar.

Warpath 1969 by Sovereigh Path — Ardreaskan (Right Royal II)
3 winners × 6 races at 15f-18f, four of them won by the good staying handicapper *Path's Sister* (Gyr) (USA).

Welsh Pageant 1966 by Tudor Melody — Picture Light (Court Martial)
2 winners at 14f-16f, notably *Longboat* (Reliance II) winner of the Monosagaro Stakes (and in 1986 of the Ascot Gold Cup, Goodwood Cup and Henry II Stakes).

Selected Sires of Middle-Distance Performers 1985

Alias Smith (USA), Alleged (USA), Auction Ring (USA), Blakeney, Blushing Groom (Fr), Brigadier Gerard, Busted, Bustino, Camden Town, Captain James, Caro, Cawston's Clown, Dominion, Ex-Directory, Free State, Great Nephew, Green Dancer, Grundy, High Line, High Top, Imperial Fling, Kris, Mill Reef, Nijinsky, Niniski, Northern Dancer, Persian Bold, Posse, Radetzky, Relko, Roberto, Sexton Blake, Shirley Heights, Star Appeal, The Minstrel, Top Ville, Transworld, Troy, Vaguely Noble, Vitiges (Fr), Welsh Pageant.

Selected Sires of 7f Horses, Milers, and 1¼ mile Performers, 1985

Absalom, Ahonoora, Alias Smith (USA), Alleged (USA), Auction Ring (USA), Bay Express, Be My Guest (USA), Bellypha, Blue Cashmere, Blushing Groom (Fr), Bold Lad, Bold Owl, Brave Shot, Brigadier Gerard, Camden Town, Cawston's Clown, Comedy Star, Connaught, Dance In Time, Danzig, Derrylin, Dominion, Final Straw, Forli (Arg), Formidable, General Assembly, Great Nephew, Gunner B, Habitat, He Loves Me, Hello Gorgeous, Home Guard, Ile de Bourbon, Import, Jazzeiro (USA), Kala Shikari, Kampala, Kris, Lord Gayle, Lyphard (USA), Mr Prospector,

Northfields (USA), Nureyev, Palm Tack, Persian Bold, Piaffer, Pitskelly, Posse, Prince Tenderfoot (USA), Pyjama Hunt, Quiet Fling (USA), Rapid River, Record Token, Reform, Relkino, Rio Carmelo (Fr), Riverman (USA), Run The Gantlet (USA), Rusticaro (Fr), Sexton Blake, Sharpen Up, Sir Ivor, Stanford, Thatch (USA), Thatching (USA), Top Ville, Tower Walk, Town and Country, Tromos, Troy, Tyrnavos, Vaigly Great, Welsh Pageant, Windjammer, Young Generation.

Sprinters Table A
Sprinting Sires 1985   Sires of winners, 3-y-o and up, at 6f and 5f

Abwah 1969 (7.2)
African Sky 1970 (6.9)
Air Trooper 1973 (6.8)*
Alydar (USA) 1975 (9.1)*
Balidar 1966 (6.6)* aa
Banquet Table (USA) 1974 (8.3)*
Batonnier (USA) 1975 (7.0)
Be Friendly 1964 (7.5) A, D
Birdbrook 1961 (6.9)
Blue Cashmere 1970 (7.0)* B
Bold Bidder 1962 (9.0)* a
Bold Lad 1964 (7.4) aaaa
Brave Shot 1976 (8.4)*
Caruso 1962 (6.0)
Cawston's Clown 1974 (8.1)*
Celtic Cone 1967 (7.6)*
Certingo 1967 (6.0)
Coded Scrap 1973 (5.5)
Comedy Star (USA) 1968 (8.2)* a
Crooner 1966 (9.4)
Daring March 1974 (6.3)*
Dawn Review 1969 (6.0)
Decoy Boy 1967 (7.1)
Dragonara Palace (USA) 1971 (8.1)*
Drone (USA) 1966 (6.5)
Dubassoff (USA) 1969 (10.0)*
Faraway Times 1974 (7.0)
Final Straw 1977 (8.2)*
Forlorn River 1962 (7.7) C
Frimley Park 1975 (5.1)
Godswalk (USA) 1974 (7.2)* A
Gold Stage (USA) 1977 (6.2)

Golden Dipper 1964 (7.1)
Goldhills Pride 1974 (6.0)
Good Counsel (USA) 1968 (10.6)
Habat 1971 (7.1)*
Habitat 1966 (7.8)* aaaaaa
He Loves Me 1974 (8.6)*
High Top 1966 (10.0)*
Hittite Glory 1973 (8.0)*
Home Guard (USA) 1969 (8.4)* a
Homing 1975 (9.9)*
Hot Spark 1972 (7.1)
Hotfoot 1966 (9.7)*
Import 1971 (7.1)*
Indianira (USA) (5.0)
Jellaby 1973 (7.8)*
Jimmy Reppin (8.6)*
J.O. Tobin (USA) 1974 (6.5)*
Kala Shikani (7.2)
King Emperor (USA) 1966 (9.0)
Kings Bishop (USA) 1969 (11.1)
Le Johnstan 1968 (7.8)*
Lochnager 1972 (6.3) B, C
London Bells (Can) 1977 (7.0)*
Lt Stevens 1961 (7.8)
Lucky Wednesday 1973 (6.5)*
Mandrake Major 1964 (7.0)*
Mansingh (USA) 1969 (6.7)*
Marshua's Dancer (USA) (8.3)
Martinmas 1969 (8.2)*
Miami Springs 1976 (8.9)*
Monsanto (Fr) 1972 (9.9)*
Most Secret 1968 (6.3)*

Mr Redoy (USA) 1974 (7.0)*
Mummy's Pet 1968 (6.4)* a
Music Boy 1973 (6.6)*
Nonoalco 1971 (8.7)*
Nureyev (USA) 1977 (8.6)*
On Your Mark 1964 (8.4)* a
Our Native 1970 (8.2)*
Owen Dudley (USA) 1970 (9.0)
Pals Passage 1964 (9.7) a
Parade of Stars 1969 (5.7)
Persian Bold 1975 (9.7)
Pitskelly 1970 (9.1)*
Poker 1963 (6.2)
Realm 1967 (7.4) C
Record Token 1972 (8.2)* D
Red Alert 1971 (7.6)
Roi Soleil 1967 (8.2)*
Roman Warrior 1971 (7.0)*
Royben 1968 (5.5)
Rupert Bear 1971 (6.0)
San Feliou (Fr) 1976 (6.0)
Saritamer (USA) 1971 (7.1) C
Scottish Rifle 1969 (9.9)*

Shack (USA) 1976 (7.3)
Sharpen Up 1969 (7.5)*
Shecky Greene (USA) 1970 (6.1)
Skyliner 1975 (7.0)*
Stradavinsky 1975 (8.5)*
So Blessed 1965 (8.3)* B, C
Song 1969 (6.0) A
Sonnen Gold 1977 (8.6)*
Space King 1959 (10.4)*
Steel Heart 1972 (6.4)
Swing Easy (USA) (7.1)* A, B
Topsider (USA) 1974 (7.0)
Torsion (USA) 1970 (7.8)
Touch Paper 1969 (8.4)*
Tower Walk 1966 (7.9)* B
Tumblewind (USA) 1964 (7.9)
Welsh Captain 1974 (9.8)*
Whistlefield 1973 (6.6)
Whistling Deer 1973 (6.6)
Workboy 1969 (8.4)*
Young Emperor 1963 (8.4)
Young Generation 1976 (7.7)

Notes
Italic — winners of
A Kings Stand Stakes, 5f Royal Ascot, June
B William Hill Spring Championship, formerly the Nunthorpe Stakes, 5f York, August
C July Cup, 6f Newmarket, July Meeting
D Vernons Sprint Cup, 6f Haydock Park, September
a indicates also grandsire of sprint winners as well as sire, with number of stallions indicated by
number of a's.
Years are years when foaled.
Numbers in brackets indicate the stamina index or average winning distance of progeny.
*indicates that the sire has got winners during the season at longer than sprint distances. (Where
there is no asterisk stamina index indicates capability or otherwise of siring longer-distance
winners.) (Stamina indices by permission of *The Statistical Record*.)

Sprinters Table B
Sires of Dams of winners (Maternal grandsires) if not mentioned in Table A as
Sires of Winners
3-y-o and up winning in 1985 at 5f, 6f & 7f

Abernant 1946 (7.3) by Owen Tudor A, Bx2, Cx2
Amber Rama 1967 (8.7) by Jaipur
Arch Sculptor 1973 (7.5) by Habitat
Atan 1961 (6.5) by Native Dancer

Bay Express 1971 (6.3) by Polyfoto
Bold Ruler 1954 (7.8) by Nasrullah
Bounteous 1958 (8.3) by Rockefella
Bullrush 1959 (5.6) by Matador
Burglar 1966 (6.1) by Crocket
Chebs Lad 1965 (8.4) by Lucky Brief
Constable 1953 (6.4) by Panorama
Crocket 1960 (9.7)* by King of the Tudors
Delta Judge 1960 (8.0) by Traffic Judge
Falcon 1964 (9.3)* by Milesian
Goldhill 1961 (7.5) by Le Dieu d'Or A
Gratitude 1953 (6.6) by Golden Cloud B
Hard Sauce 1948 (8.1) by Ardan
Jukebox 1966 (7.4) by Sing Sing
Kings Leap 1959 (8.6)* by Princely Gift
Kings Troop (8.6)* by Princely Gift
Klairon 1952 (9.4)* by Clairon II
Klondike Bill 1958 (8.2)* by Golden Cloud
Lear Jet 1966 (8.2) by King's Troop
Manacle 1964 (7.5)* by Sing Sing
Mountain Call 1965 (7.4)* by Whistler
Native Prince 1964 (6.8) by Native Dancer
Palestine 1947 (8.6) by Fair Trial
Quorum 1954 (9.3)* by Vilmorin
Raise a Native 1950 (9.7)* by Native Dancer
Red God 1954 (7.6)* by Nasrullah
Ridan 1959 (8.4) by Nantallah
Runnymede 1961 (7.1)* by Petition
Sing Sing 1957 (6.6) by Tudor Minstrel
Skymaster 1958 (7.9)* by Golden Cloud
Thirteen of Diamonds 1949 by Mustang
Track Spare 1963 (8.5)* by Sound Track
Tudor Grey 1960 (5.1) by Tudor Minstrel
Tyrant (USA) 1966 (7.2) by Bold Ruler
Vilmorin 1950 (6.0) by Gold Bridge
Weepers Boy 1961 (6.5) by Whistler
Whistling Wind 1960 (8.4)* by Whistler
Windjammer (USA) 1969 (9.0)* by Restless Wind

In addition, the following names for farther back in sprinting pedigrees not in Table A or B should also be noted:

Althrey Don	Golden Vision
Ballyogan	Hook Money
Bebe Grande	Pappa Fourway
Golden Lion	Right Boy

Sammy Davis	The Bug
Set Fair	Tin King
Sky Gipsy	Tin Whistle
Stephen Paul	Vilmoray

The National Hunt scene

It is a widely-held notion that the breeding of a jumper does not matter a great deal. The contrary is proved by sires such as *Vulgan* who dominated the scene for many years and not only because of the great number of mares he covered (the dam, incidentally, of the 1986 Grand National winner, *West Tip*, was by Vulgan). Similar proof is given by the present top National Hunt sire, *Deep Run*. The second list below indicates some of the present sires who are important not merely on the basis of prize money won by their progeny. The foaling date is included in order to show how many of these are near or past their zenith as sires, bearing in mind that it is nearly ten years from birth before a National Hunt sire can show any results. Some, including *Menelek* and *Master Owen*, are now dead, so their influence is bound to decline. But a list of those who seem likely to make a name in the future is appended (with position in prize money table in brackets where applicable).

Jumping Sires 1985-86

(Order according to prize money won)

	Sire	Grandsire	No of Winners	No of Races Won	Prize Money Earned	1984-85 Performances			
1	Deep Run*	Pampered King	40	80	303,642	(39	65	139,921)	(1)
2	Master Owen*	Owen Tudor	7	19	79,817	(15	28	53,069)	(9)
3	Idiot's Delight	Silly Season	11	21	77,072	(8	14	33,146)	(28)
4	Gala Performance (GN) (USA)	Native Dancer	5	7	73,489	(4	9	42,978)	(14)
5	The Parson	Aureole	11	18	72,473	(8	15	28,167)	(34=)
6	Precipice Wood	Lauso	16	25	62,713	(15	29	110,687)	(3)
7	Menelek	Tulyar	19	28	61,116	(24	46	111,818)	(2)
8	Celtic Cone	Celtic Ash	19	25	59,274	(11	14	22,329)	(47)
9	Brave Invader (USA)	Ribot	8	14	57,997	(14	24	33,425)	(26)
10	Raise You Ten*	Tehran	7	13	53,678	(10	21	44,623)	(13)
11	Spartan General	Mossborough	6	14	53,444	(11	12	33,607)	(50)
12	Grey Mirage	Double-U-Jay	5	17	52,198	(5	7	11,843)	
13	Royal Palace	Ballymoss	2	3	47,728	(5	9	54,274)	(8)
14	Auction Ring*	Bold Bidder	3	6	45,848	(4	4	6,499)	
15	Mandamus*	Petition	10	18	42,362	(7	9	18,016)	
16	Politico (USA)	Right Royal V	8	18	42,047	(6	11	17,176)	
17	Little Buskins	Solar Slipper	6	13	41,649	(9	15	41,964)	(15)
18	Busted*	Crepello	7	13	39,920	(6	12	15,834)	
19	Cantab	Cantaber	6	11	36,451	(11	20	45,327)	(12)
20	Lucky Brief	Counsel	4	7	35,065	(4	5	24,111)	(44)
21	Broxted*	Busted	3	5	32,881	(		)	(—)
22	Giolla Mear	Hard Ridden	12	23	31,337	(9	11	16,998)	
23	Pitpan	Pampered King	10	18	30,011	(6	8	11,890)	

	Sire	Grandsire	No of Winners	No of Races Won	Prize Money Earned	1984-85 Performances			
24	Normandy	Vimy	4	9	29,583	(4	9	26,783)	(38)
25	Dance In Time	Northern Dancer	5	12	29,571	(6	15	25,703)	(40)

*Cheltenham prize money included
(GN) Grand National prize money included

Most Prolific Sires of National Hunt Winners 1985-86

(On the basis of siring at least 10 winning horses and/or horses who between them won at least 15 races.)

	Relative Order in prize-money table	Sire	Foaled	Grandsire	No of Winners	No of Races Won	Prize Money Earned in £s
1	(1)	Deep Run	1966	Pampered King	40	80	303,642
2	(7)	Menelek	1957	Tulyar	19	28	61,116
3	(8)	Celtic Cone	1967	Celtic Ash	19	25	59,274
4	(6)	Precipice Wood	1966	Lauso	16	25	62,713
5	(22)	Giolla Mear	1965	Hard Ridden	12	23	31,337
6	(3)	Idiot's Delight	1970	Silly Season	11	21	77,072
7	(5)	The Parson	1968	Aureole	11	18	72,473
8	(15)	Mandamus	1960	Petition	10	18	42,362
9	(23)	Pitpan	1969	Pampered King	10	18	30,011
10	(2)	Master Owen	1965	Owen Tudor	7	19	79,817
11	(67)	New Brig	1956	Solar Slipper	11	14	18,607
12	(17)	Little Buskins	1957	Solar Slipper	9	15	41,964
13	(27)	Scottish Rifle	1969	Sunny Way	9	15	29,234
14	(39)	Tycoon II	1962	Tamerlane	9	15	24,870
15	(48)	Hotfoot	1966	Firestreak	10	13	22,448
16	(16)	Politico	1967	Right Royal V	8	18	42,047
17	(81)	Free State	1973	Hotfoot	8	15	15,615
18	(12)	Grey Mirage	1969	Double-U-Jay	5	17	52,198
19	(36)	Godswalk (USA)	1974	Dancer's Image	6	15	25,196

The following should also be noted:

Thatch 1970 (84), Crash Course 1971 (71), Averof 1971 (66), Le Bavard (Fr) 1971 (82), Oats 1973 (76), Relkino 1973, Julio Mariner 1975 (90), Remainder Man 1975, Dominion 1972 (40), Sunyboy 1970, Netherkelly 1970, General Ironside 1973.

CHAPTER TWELVE
Systems

Follow a winning two-year-old until it gets beaten, and then back the one that beats it.

There was a time when the affable face of Ralph Freeman used to look out from the advertisements in *Ruff's Guide*. He would be smoking a big cigar, and proclaimed not only that he had laid and paid the owner of *Mill House* £50 each way at 200/1 for the Cheltenham Gold Cup (which the horse had won, SP 7/2 Fav) but 'Large or Small. Ralph Freeman Ltd will operate Any Systems'. I know of no comparable advertisement today, which is a little odd, because as Jack Leach (author of the advice at the head of this chapter) wrote in *Sods I Have Cut On The Turf*: 'Systems? Bookmakers love them'.

Systems fall under three main headings:

1. Those which involve blind backing irrespective of a study of form or other considerations on the part of the backer. They are the horseracing equivalent of roulette systems and include all blind backing of favourites, second favourites etc, jockeys' mounts, trainers, newspaper naps, top weights in nursery handicaps, low/high numbers in the draw, forecast betting involving the favourite to beat or be beaten by the field, second favourite each way in fields of eight runners, 12-to-follow bets, and so on. The intrinsic flaw in such systems is that they do not offer the precise mathematical odds involved in winning or losing in a casino. The first factor contributing to this is the horse itself which, unlike the roulette wheel, can have moods, pull a muscle, feel off colour, or, if a filly, come unexpectedly into season just before a race. Then again, the system also compels backing a horse regardless of whether it likes hard going or heavy ground; whether it is ridden by a Steve Cauthen or an apprentice having his or her first ride in public; on a suitable galloping course, or an unsuitable sharp track; or with no chance whatsoever on the form book. Systems involving favourites further suffer from and frequently founder on the surfeit of short prices inseparable from the operation. Favourites do best when the going is good or good to firm, and enough form is available of a consistent variety, but in general backing favourites doesn't pay in the long run, nor does blind backing of jockeys, trainers, or newspaper naps. Systems involving these inevitably strike long losing runs from time to time; some jockeys show sizeable profits at some courses but far more show colossal losses to a level stake wagered on them every time they have a ride.

2. These 'systems' could perhaps best be called limited systems. They all involve a degree of selectivity and judgement on the part of the backer arising from a study of form and other factors. They are, essentially, an amendment of category one systems. For example, instead of backing every favourite

irrespective of any factor other than it being the favourite, it is decided to limit the system to 'only on good or good to firm going, and only if ridden by one of the six most successful jockeys'.

3. The third category is not really a system as such, but is so-called as in the phrase, 'I've got a system', meaning, 'I've got a method of finding winners which seems to work'. Into this category comes following the market, following in-form trainers and jockeys, beaten favourites dropped in class, horses carrying penalties for easy wins on their previous outing and so on.

Since two-year-olds run more consistently than older horses it is worth a brief look at systems involving them. Below is a table showing how two-year-old favourites, second favourites and others fared up to August in the Flat season, 1985.

	March	April	May	June	July*	August*
Number of 2-y-o races	11	46	91	115	152	160
Number of winning favourites and percentage	6 (54.5%)	23 (50%)	39 (42.8%)	46 (40%)	68 (44.7%)	58 (36.25%)
Number of winning 2nd favourites and percentage	5 (45.5%)	11 (23.9%)	17 (18.7%)	23 (20%)	34 (22.4%)	42 (26.25%)
Number of long priced winners and percentage	Nil	12 (26.1%)	35 (38.5%)	46 (40%)	50 (32.9%)	60 (37.5%)

*Non-handicap only

If a level stake £1 had been wagered on every two-year-old favourite in March and April 1985, profits of £12.90 and £7.92 would have been realised in those months respectively, but by the end of May the system would have shown a loss, continuing throughout the rest of the season. The main reason is that by this time the two-year-old form is beginning to be exposed, resulting in shorter priced favourites, and the bigger stables, notably those of Henry Cecil, Michael Stoute, Guy Harwood, Ian Balding and John Dunlop are starting to bring out their good two-year-olds on to the racecourse. The likelihood of success has almost always gone before them on the winds of rumour and gallop reports, and some very short priced winners are often the result. Altogether, from May onwards, because of the high proportion of odds-on (sometimes heavily so) and other short priced two-year-old favourites plus betting tax, this is no system for the moderate backer, though two-year-old favourites at any time of the year and however short the price, will always, despite the tax, provide opportunities for those with enough money to risk. To reinforce the argument, here are some figures for July 1985 a time when form was well settled and good ground gave an encouraging proportion of winning favourites of all kinds:

Two-year-olds, July 1985

Races (excluding nursery handicaps):	152
Winning favourites:	68 (44.7%)
Winning second favourites:	34 (22.35%)

} 67%

Winners other than first or second favourites:

at SP between 5/2 and 8/1:	27 (17.77%)
at SP between 9/1 and 14/1:	11 (7.24%)
at SP between 16/1 and 100/1:	12 (7.89%)

Prices of Winning Favourites (Total 68)

Odds greater than 2/1 against:	12 (from 5/2 to 4/1)
Even money to 2/1 against:	29
Odds-on down to 2/1 on:	18
Odds shorter than 2/1 on:	9

It can be seen, therefore, that no less than 82.4 per cent of winning two-year-olds favourites during the month were returned at an SP of 2/1 or shorter, and that approximately 40 per cent were odds-on. Some of the odds-on prices were quite impossible for the smaller punter, and included 5/1 on, 9/2 on, and 4/1 on, twice.

A breakdown by area of where the heavily odds-on winners were trained is also illuminating, as well as where they ran:

July 85 Winning 2-y-o favourites	*Newmarket*	*Lambourn and* *surrounding area*	*Yorkshire/North*
	31	16	11
Heavily odds-on	7*	1**	None

*5/1 on	Mr C.A.B. St George's *Ghika*, Yarmouth (Henry Cecil) won by 3/4l. 6 ran.
4/1 on	Mr Stavros Niarchos' *Faustus*, Nottingham (Henry Cecil) 4l. Made all the running. 8 ran.
4/1 on	Mr P. Burrell's *Tussac*, Warwick (Henry Cecil) 8l. Made all. 8 ran.
9/2 on	Sheikh Mohammed's *Mazaad*, York (Henry Cecil) 2l. 2 ran.
3/1 on	Mr R.C. Clifford Turner's *Good Lord*, Nottingham (Michael Stoute) 3l. Made all. 10 ran.
11/4 on	HH Aga Khan's *Katayla*, Sandown (Michael Stoute) s.h. Made all. 5 ran.
9/4 on	Mr P. Burrell's *Water Cay*, Newbury (Henry Cecil) 6l. Made all. 6 ran.
**9/4 on	Mr G. Strawbridge's *Measuring*, Windsor (Ian Balding) 2l. 6 ran.

The salient point which arises from this summary is that all but three of the winners were entered to outclass the opposition at second class tracks, all being from big stables. Such runners, and there are many throughout the season at similar prohibitive odds in two-year-old races, are no value for the smaller punter, and have to be ignored as betting opportunities.

Top-weights in Nursery Handicaps

In 1985, if every top-weight in every nursery handicap had been backed to a £1 level stake, a handsome profit of £36.52 after tax would have been shown. There were 25 winning top-weights in the total of 116 nurseries. In 1986, however, a similar bet would have shown an equally impressive loss — of £34.80. Only 15 top-weights won from a total of 120 nurseries — which seems as good an illustration as any of the swings and roundabouts of system betting.

Forecast Betting

Any systems based on forecast betting are not to be recommended from the outset, whether Tote Dual Forecast or the Bookmakers Computer Straight Forecast (see Chapter Six).

Systems involving fields of four, five and six runners have been tested. None of them pay off, and in fields beyond these small numbers of runners, when dividends may be higher, the outlay is too great to justify a system. Below are the results of various systems based on four-runner races throughout the 1985 Flat season. The columns are self-explanatory, and show that after an enormous outlay an average of 34 per cent winning bets yielded a gross loss on the year of £103.82. The fact that the final column shows a profit of £100+ is largely the result of a lucky dividend in one race only.

Computer straight forecast in 4-horse races*

Column 1 Each month shows ratio winning bets to number of races.
Column 2 Shows monthly profit/loss for each type of bet (to £1 level stake)

Bet	Fav. to beat the field (£3)		Fav. to be 2nd to the field (£3)		Fav. unplaced All other combinations (£6)		Fav./2nd fav. reversed (£2)		2nd Fav. to beat the field (£3)		2nd Fav. to be 2nd to the field (£3)	
(stake per race)												
Mar./Apr.	1/4	−£7.99	1/4	−£8.56	2/4	+£14.03	0/4	−£8.00	2/4	+£6.73	0/4	−£12.00
May	3/6	−£10.51	2/6	−£5.90	1/6	−£22.33	3/6	−£1.97	1/6	−£13.05	3/6	+£0.85
June	7/14	−£13.45	2/14	−£31.31	5/14	+£90.53	8/14	−£2.95	4/14	−£14.75	8/14	+£130.33
July	7/11	−£6.16	2/11	−£22.15	2/11	−£33.51	6/11	+£1.23	2/7	−£10.15	5/11	+£6.77
August	2/7	−£14.73	4/7	+£17.31	1/7	−£36.43	1/7	−£12.03	0/7	−£21.00	2/7	−£13.46
Sept.	3/6	−£7.06	0/6	−£18.00	3/6	+£5.80	2/6	−£13.46	2/6	+£15.23	3/6	−£4.79
Oct./Nov.	2/2	+£1.21	0/2	−£6.00	0/2	−£12.00	1/2	−£1.07	0/2	−£6.00	1/2	−£3.07
	25/50 =		11/50 =		14/50 =		21/50 =		11/50 =		22/50 =	
TOTALS	50% winners		22% winners		28% winners		42% winners		22% winners		44% winners	
	Loss £58.69		Loss £74.61		Profit £6.09		Loss £38.25		Loss £42.99		Profit £104.63	

*Except those with joint favourite/joint 2nd favourites

Twelve-to-follow, seven-to-follow

This is a harmless and often pleasantly rewarding way of betting in small stakes. Before the Flat season begins, and again in November when the jumps come into their own, newspaper and magazine racing correspondents often publish the names of their 'horses to follow'. The best lists contain a mixture of more or less obvious selections based on observation and form from the previous season, together with some likely winners which migh turn up at outside prices. A level stake to win or each way is wagered on the horses in the list every time they run, or it can be stipulated 'stop at a winner'. Most credit bookmakers will operate such systems for individual backers, wins and losses being automatically credited/debited to the weekly account.

Second favourite each way in fields of eight runners

This system cannot be operated 'blind' i.e. with unnamed second favourites, since bookmakers will not take bets on such selections except win only. The system depends therefore on observation of the market. Backing second favourites each way in fields of eight runners gives three chances of some success to five chances of failure. This was highly profitable in the days when bookmakers paid a quarter of the odds a place in fields of eight runners, and there was no tax. Today it is less so, because bookmakers pay only one-fifth of the odds a place in such fields, and there is tax to pay as well. So, an 11/2 place horse is required to break even, and far fewer second favourites start at that price than at 4/1, which was the old break even figure.

To illustrate how bookmakers have closed down on what used to be a 'knocking' bet, these are the results from one summer month in the days when good profits could be expected by backers using the 'system':

22 placed second favourites (July 1962)

Prices 6/1, 11/2, 5/1 × 3, 9/2, 4/1 × 9, 7/2 × 3, 11/4, 15/8, 7/4, 6/4

Resulting at a quarter of the odds a place: six marginal winners, nine break even, seven losers.

But today at one-fifth the odds, these figures would become: one marginal winner, one break even, 20 losers.

Today this system can still be expected to be profitable, though not as handsomely as before. However observation of the market in itself presents an occasional danger that the wrong 'second favourite' will be chosen. Last-second shifts in the betting might make what appears to be a firm second favourite into a favourite (particularly in a weak market). Alternatively it might be displaced out to third favourite, but this does not happen often enough to invalidate the general strategy.

Following the Market

(See Chapter Four)

Two-year-old selling races

This a good medium for following the market. For example in the Aboyeur (S) Stakes for 2-y-o on 1 April, 1985 at Nottingham, *Auntie Bobbie*, third on her one previous outing (when hampered in a similar race at Doncaster just over a week before hand and placed third on an objection) was backed down from 7/1 to 13/8 second favourite in a four horse field. The favourite started at 5/4 on, but was beaten 2½ lengths by *Auntie Bobbie* at level weights, who made all the running. A good example showing two-year-old reliability, and a market move in favour of the winner.

Here's how the betting opened: Favourite *Miss Magnolia*, 7/2 *Miss Maggie*, 7/1 *Auntie Bobbie*, 8/1 *Bonny Reef*

The SP was: 4/5 *Miss Magnolia*, 13/8 *Auntie Bobbie*, 11/2 *Miss Maggie*, 14/1 *Bonny Reef*

Finally, outside all the categories come some systems which, without putting a single coin on a horse, might avoid losses, and thus be judged to turn in a consistent profit. Negative systems such as these will make no appeal to the majority of punters, who, like Oscar Wilde, can be relied on to resist anything but temptation. Nonetheless the following methods have stood the test of time in helping to avoid an examination in bankruptcy:

Odds-on favourites

These do not generally appeal to small backers, but the prices of the next best in the market often do, irrespective of merit of the horses concerned. The system here is not to oppose an odds-on favourite because the next best is 5/1 against. Better no bet than a 5/1 loser, backed on the previous principle that the favourite's odds are too short to warrant an interest. In any case, remembering for example *Brigadier Gerard*'s odds-on victories, it was pleasure enough just to see him win.

The eight horse card

Normally there are six races on a card, often there are seven, when races have to be divided, and sometimes eight. Eight betting opportunities, it seems, but, in fact, there may be none at all. The system here is not to have a bet in every race simply for the sake of it, and in recognition that the opportunity is there.

The getting out Stakes

Traditionally the last race on the card, when every fancied runner has gone down in the previous five races; the bookmakers are as near to dancing on their boxes as they ever will be; the floor of Tattersalls' Ring is knee deep in lost hopes in the shape of torn-up losing tickets, and punters turn to the last race as the final desperate resort. The winning system here is to remember the song: 'There's Always Tomorrow'.

APPENDIX A
Rules on Betting

(As authorised by Tattersalls' Committee on 8 February, 1886, and last revised on 15 November 1982)

1. Tattersalls' Committee have authority to settle all questions relating to bets, commissions for bets and any matters arising either directly or indirectly out of wagers or gaming transactions on horseracing, to adjudicate on all cases of default, and *at their discretion*, to report defaulters to the Jockey Club. If a defaulter is a partnership or limited company all or any of the partners or their agents and all or any of the shareholders, directors, officers or agents of the defaulting company may be reported to the Jockey Club.

Upon an application being made to the Committee in any case to admit or hear further evidence, the Committee may at its discretion decide to re-hear such case and upon such re-hearing may admit such further evidence and uphold, reverse or amend its original decision or adjudication as it may think fit.

2. In all bets there must be a possibility to win when the bet is made.

3. No betting first past the post will be recognized by the Committee.

4. All bets are PP — play or pay — with the following exceptions:

(A) Single ante post bets, being made before the day on which the race is run, will be void if the race is abandoned, declared void, or if the conditions of the race are altered after bets are made, or on a horse balloted out under Jockey Club Rule 125, but in any such circumstances accumulative ante post bets (win or place) will stand and be settled at the ante post price(s) laid on the remaining horse(s).

(B) Bets other than ante post bets will be void if the race is abandoned, declared void or postponed to another day, or if they are on a horse which does not come under starter's orders. Bets 'on the distance' are void if the first or second horse is disqualified, or the placings are reversed.

(C) In the case of bets made at a price on the day of the race before it has been officially notified that a horse has been withdrawn before coming under starter's orders, the liability of a layer against any horse remaining in the race, win or place, will be reduced in accordance with the following scale depending on the odds current against the withdrawn horse at the time of such official notification:

(a)	3/10 or longer odds on by 75p in the £.
(b)	2/5 to 1/3 by 70p in the £.
(c)	8/15 to 4/9 by 65p in the £.
(d)	8/13 to 4/7 by 60p in the £.
(e)	4/5 to 4/6 by 55p in the £.
(f)	20/21 to 5/6 by 50p in the £.
(g)	Evens to 6/5 by 45p in the £.
(h)	5/4 to 6/4 by 40p in the £.
(i)	13/8 to 7/4 by 35p in the £.
(j)	15/8 to 9/4 by 30p in the £.
(k)	5/2 to 3/1 by 25p in the £.
(l)	10/3 to 4/1 by 20p in the £.
(m)	9/2 to 11/2 by 15p in the £.
(n)	6/1 to 9/1 by 10p in the £.
(o)	10/1 to 14/1 by 5p in the £.
(p)	If over 14/1 the liability would be unchanged.
(q)	In the case of two or more horses being withdrawn before coming under starter's orders, the total reduction shall not exceed 75p in the £.

Bets made at starting price are not affected, except in cases where insufficient time arises for a fresh market to be formed, when the same scale of reductions will apply. In the event of the withdrawal of one or more runners in circumstances which would lead to only one runner and therefore a 'walkover', all bets on the race will be void. The race will be considered a 'walkover' for the purpose of settling bets.

For the purposes of this rule, the non-appearance of the number of a declared runner in the number board shall be held to be an official notification of the withdrawal of such horse before coming under starter's orders.

(D) In the event of an announcement being made that the provisions of Rule 4(c) do not apply on the grounds that no market had been formed at the time of withdrawal of a declared runner or in the event of the number of a declared runner not appearing in the number board, all bets (other than ante post bets) made at a price prior to either eventuality shall be settled at starting price.

(E) In the event of a horse or horses being withdrawn under Jockey Club Rule No. 125 (limitation of the number of runners in a race), all ante post bets on such horse(s) shall be void and the liability of a layer against any horse(s) remaining in the race, win or place, will be reduced in accordance with a rate to be announced before the race by Tattersalls' Committee, dependent on the odds current against the withdrawn horse(s) at the time of such official withdrawal.

5. When the all right signal has been hoisted over the number board as provided for in Rule 162 of the Rules of Racing, or such other rule being in identical terms which may be substituted for it, the bets go to the horses as officially shown on the board, and no objection or disqualification made subsequent to the hoisting of such signal shall disturb the destination of the bets.

6. Bets made on one horse against another or that one horse beats another, are determined if either of them *should win*. Bets made between horses 1, 2, 3 are determined by the places assigned by the judge. Unless agreed by the parties it is not indispensable that both horses should start.

7. In the event of a dead-heat, and in 'double events' if *either* is decided in the backer's favour and the other results in a dead-heat, the money betted must be put together and equally divided, except in the event of a dead-heat in a match in which case bets are void. In 'double-events' if both horses backed run dead-heats the money betted must be put together and divided in the proportion of one-fourth to the backer and three-fourths to the layer.

8. If a bet is made on one of the horses that runs a dead-heat against a beaten horse the backer of the horse that ran the dead-heat wins half his bet. If odds are laid on one horse against another 1, 2, 3 and they run a dead-heat for any of such places, the money betted must be put together and equally divided.

9. If odds are laid without mentioning the horse, the bet must be determined by the state of the odds at the time it was made. Bets made after a race that a horse will be disqualified, stand, even if no objection be made.

10. Any bet made from signal or indication when the race has been determined, shall be considered fraudulent and void.

11. Subject to Rule 4(a) accumulative bets are not determined until the last event has been run.

12. Bets made on horses winning any number of races within the year shall be understood to mean between 1 January and 31 December, both dates inclusive.

13. In the event of a race being ordered to be run over again, or of a false start or breakaway, starting price bets shall be regulated by the price current at the time of the original 'off', false start or breakaway. All bets in favour of any horse which started on the first but did not go to the post on the second occasion in the case of a race run over again, or in favour of any horse not returning to the post (by permission) in the case of a false start or breakaway are lost, except when such a horse has not come under starter's orders.

14. No bet can be declared off except by mutual consent but on any allegation of fraud or corrupt practice, the Committee may investigate the case and may declare the bet void. Either of the bettors may demand stakes to be made on proving to the satisfaction of the Committee, or any two of them, that he has just cause for doing so, and, *if ordered*, the bets must be covered or sufficient security given within the time specified in such order, in default whereof the bets will be off.

15. The Committee will not *necessarily* enforce the full settlement of a compromised account. Before giving a decision they may require the books of the debtor and a statement of his accounts to be submitted to them; and they may order the account to be settled if they think a reasonable offer is made, and on such terms as they may decide.

16. All bets made after a photo finish has been signalled shall be settled in the same way as if they had been made on the result of the race.

17. If any extraordinary occasion should arise, or in cases of notorious and palpable fraud, any of the before-mentioned rules may be suspected by the Committee, and any of the before-mentioned rules may be altered or added to by a simple majority of the whole Committee.

How to Read Raceform

In order of appearance

The Official Going, shown at the head of each meeting, is recorded in the following stages: Hard, Firm; Good to firm; Good; Dead; Good to soft; Yielding; Sticky; Soft; Holding; Heavy.

Going Assessed on Time shown in parentheses, after going allowance at meeting: Hard (H); Firm (F); Good (G); Yielding (Y); Soft (S); Heavy (Hvy).

Wind is included for EVERY UK meeting. Apart from 'nil', 'almost nil' and 'squally', wind conditions are shown in degrees of 'against', 'across' and 'behind'.

Visibility is Good unless stated.

Starting Stalls are shown in the form 'Stalls high' or 'Stalls low', indicating that (looking from the Stands) the stalls are POSITIONED on the high (left) or low (right) side of the course. All races are started by stalls unless otherwise stated.

Race Numbers are the same as those in Raceform Note-Book. Some Irish and French races are exclusive to the Note-Book so gaps will occur in Raceform race numbers. All race numbers for foreign and Irish meetings carry the suffix 'a'.

Distance of Race. On courses that have two tracks of the same distance (st) indicates straight course and (rnd) indicates round.

The Figures on the left of each horse's name represent the number of the race in which it last ran. An asterisk indicates win, and a small figure (^{2}, ^{3}, ^{4}) second, third or fourth in its previous appearance.

Blinkers shown after runner's name thus (bl), Hoods thus (h), Hood and blinkers are shown (h & b).

Trainer is shown in italics after every runner and does not appear in the index.

Weights shown are actual weights carried. Small figures against weight denotes overweight carried in lbs.

(7x) = including 7 lb extra for win after publication of weights.

‡^{3}, ‡^{5}, ‡^{7} = apprentice allowance deducted.

Apprentice Allowances

The holders of apprentice jockeys' licences under the provisions of Rule 60(iii) are permitted to claim the following allowances in Flat races:
7 lb until they have won 10 Flat races run under the Rules of any recognised Turf Authority; thereafter 5 lb until they have won 50 such Flat races; thereafter 3 lb until they have won 75 such Flat races.

These allowances can be claimed in the Flat races set out below, with the exception of races confined to apprentice jockeys:
(a) All handicap and all selling races
(b) All other races with guaranteed prize money of not more than £3,500.

The Draw for places at the start is shown after each jockey's name.

The Official Distances between the first six horses are shown on the right-hand side immediately preceding their position at the finish.

Distances beyond sixth place may be shown after inspection of race-finish photographs. Unknown positions are shown in saddle-cloth number order.

Withdrawn horses, that fail to come under orders after entering the parade ring, are included in the Index to past racing (with W after the race number); side reference, odds and reason for withdrawal (if known) are shown in italics below the bottom horse of the race.

Stewards' Enquiry, except in special circumstances, is included only if it concerns a prize winner(s).

Tote price includes £1 stake. Dual Forecast dividends are shown in parentheses.

Owner of the winner is shown immediately after the Tote; then the winning trainer's location; then the breeder of the winner.

Race Times in Great Britain (except official times which are electrically recorded and shown to 100th of a second) are clocked by our own watch-holders. Figures in parentheses following the time show the number of seconds slower than standard for the course distance. Times equal to and faster than standard are shown as (equals standard) and (U1.8). Record times are shown either referring to the 2-y-o record (1 under 2y best) or the overall record (1 under best).

Speed Figures The numbers at the end of each race indicate the speed figures of the first six after each horse has been brought to 9 st and calculations made for going, wind and distances behind winner. These are shown strictly in 'past the post' order. Example: SF—100/96/94/80/77/74. To find speed figures for future races add 1 point for each 1 lb weighted below 9 st and deduct 1 point for each 1 lb above 9 st. Highest resultant figure is best.

Foreign Racing Principal French races and races abroad in which British horses take part are not received in time to insert in strict date order. Irish coverage is limited to only the top-class races. Starting this season (1985) all Group 1 and Group 2 French races will carry commentaries.

Index to Flat Racing — Please note that names of horses are indexed strictly as spelt and include country codes, e.g. Elect (USA) comes after Electro.

Abbreviations
Most of the contents explain themselves but to save space the following abbreviations are frequently used:

The Parade Ring
Classification of horses on looks:

b = bandaged fore	lt-f = light-framed	t = tubed
b.bind = bandaged hind	lw = looked very fit	unf = unfurnished: not furnished to frame
bkwd = backward in condition	nice c = nice colt: very good sort	v nice c = very nice colt; outstanding in looks
cmpt = compact	nt grwn = not grown	wl grwn = well grown: furnished to frame
gd sort = well made: above average on looks	scope = scope for development	w'like = workmanlike
h.d.w. = has done well: improved in looks	str = strong	
	swtg = sweating excessively	

The Running

a = always	bhd = behind	chal = challenge(d)
abt = about	bk = back	chsd = chased
a.p. = always prominent	blkd = baulked	circ = circuit
appr = approaching	bmpd = bumped	cl = close
awrdd = awarded	bnd = bend	cld = claimed
b.b.v. = broke blood vessel	btn = beaten	clr = clear
b.d. = brought down	bttr = better	comf = comfortably
bdly = badly	c = came	crse = course
bef = before	cd = could	ct = caught
bel = below	ch = chance	disp = disputed

disq = disqualified
dismntd = dismounted
dist = distance (240y from finish)
div = division
drvn = driven
dwlt = dwelt
edgd = edged
effrt = effort
ent = entering
ev ch = every chance
ex = extra
f = furlong
fdd = faded
fin = finish(ed)
fnd = found
fnl = final
fr = from
gd = good
gng = going
grad = gradually
grnd = ground
½-wy = half-way
hd = head
hdd = headed
hdwy = headway
hi = hill
hld = held
hmpd = hampered
hrd rdn = hard ridden
imp = impression
ins = inside
jnd = joined
jst = just
kpt = kept
l = length
lckd = lacked
ld = lead
ldr = leader
lft = left
lkd = looked
ltl = little
m = mile
mde = made
mid div = mid division

m.n.s. = made no show
n.d. = no danger
n.g.t. = not go through
nk = neck
n.m.r. = not much room
no ex = no extra pace
no imp = no impression
nr = near
nrr = nearer
nrst fin = nearest at finish
nt = not
nvr = never
one pce = one paced
out = from finish
outpcd = outpaced
pce = pace
pl = place
plcd = placed
plld = pulled
press = pressure
prog = progress
prom = prominent
p.u. = pulled up
qckn = quicken
qckly = quickly
r = race
racd = raced
rch = reach
rcvr = recover
rdn = ridden
rdr = rider
reard = reared
ref = refused
rm = room
rn = ran
rnd = round
rng = running
r.o. = ran on
rr = rear
rn wl = ran well
rspnse = response
rt = right
s = start
sddle = saddle

s.h. = short head
shkn = shaken
shld = should
shwd = showed
s.i.s. = slowly into stride
slt = slight
sme = some
sn = soon
spd = speed
s.s. = started slowly
st = straight
stdy = steady
s.u. = slipped up
stdd = steadied
str = strong
strtnd = straightened
styd = stayed
swtchd = switched
swvd = swerved
tch = touch
th = there
thro = through
thrght = throughout
ti = until
tk = took
t.n.p. = took no part
t.o. = tailed off
trble = trouble
trbld = troubled
uns = unseated
u.p. = under pressure
uphl = uphill
v = very
w = with
wd = wide
whn = when
wknd = weakened
wl = well
wnr = winner
wnt = went
w.r.s. = whipped round start
wt = weight
wy = way
y = yards

Select Bibliography

Betting
Alex Bird with Terry Manners. *The Life and Secrets of a Professional Punter* Queen Anne Press, 1985
Charles Sidney. *The Art of Legging* Maxline International, 1976

Breeding
Paola Ciechanowska. *Le Pur Sang Français* J.A. Allen 1969
Keylock's *Dams of Winners* Various edns. Knapp, Drewett.
Sir Charles Leicester. *Bloodstock Breeding* J.A. Allen 1964
Peter Willett. *An Introduction to the Thoroughbred* Stanley Paul 1966
Peter Willett. *The Classic Racehorse* Stanley Paul 1981

Historical
Asa Briggs. *A Social History of England* Weidenfeld 1983
Dennis Craig. *Horse-Racing* J.A. Allen 1963
Roger Mortimer. *The History of the Derby Stakes* Michael Joseph 1973
Richard Onslow. *Headquarters: A History of Newmarket and Its Racing* Great Ouse Press 1983
Vincent Orchard. *The Derby Stakes (1900-1953)* Hutchinson 1954
Caroline Ramsden *Ladies in Racing* Stanley Paul 1973
Alan Ross *The Turf* Small Oxford Books 1982
Alexander Scott. *Turf Memories of Sixty Years* Hutchinson 1924

Horses
John Fairley. *Great Racehorses in Art* Phaidon Press 1984
Clive Graham. *Great Horses of the Year 1954-55* McGibbon & Kee 1954
John Hislop. *The Brigadier* Secker and Warburg 1973
David Livingstone-Learmonth & John Hislop. *Famous Winners of the British Turf 1949-55* Hutchinson 1956
Roger Mortimer. *Twenty Great Horses* Cassell 1967
Vincent Orchard. *The British Thoroughbred* Ariel Press 1966

Jockeys
Edgar Britt. *Post Haste* Muller 1967
Dick Francis. *Lester, the Official Biography* Michael Joseph 1986
John Francome. *Born Lucky* Pelham 1985
Jack Leach. *Sods I Have Cut On The Turf* Gollancz 1961
M. Seth-Smith. *Knight of the Turf* (biog. Sir Gordon Richards) Hodder & Stoughton 1980
John Welcome. *Fred Archer, His Life and Times* Faber 1967
Tommy Weston. *My Racing Life* Hutchinson 1952

Journalism
Quintin Gilbey. *Fun Was My Living* Hutchinson 1970
Brough Scott. *On and Off The Rails* Gollancz 1984

National Hunt
Michael Ayres and Gary Newbon. *Over The Sticks* David & Charles 1971
David Hedges. *Mr. Grand National* (biog. Fred Winter) Pelham Books 1969
Alan Lee. *Cheltenham Racecourse* Pelham Books 1985
Richard Pitman, John Oaksey, Gerry Cranham. *The Guinness Guide to Steeplechasing* Guinness Superlatives 1979
Fred and Mercy Rimell. *Aintree Iron* (Autobiog.) W.H. Allen 1977
Michael Seth-Smith, Peter Willett, Roger Mortimer, John Lawrence. *The History of Steeplechasing* Michael Joseph 1966

Statistics
John Randall and Tony Morris. *Horse Racing: The Records* Guinness Books 1985

Training
Ed. John Hughes and Peter Watson. *My Greatest Training Triumph* Michael Joseph 1982
Hon George Lambton. *Men and Horses I Have Known* J.A. Allen 1963

Turf Politics
Tim Fitzgeorge-Parker. *The Spoilsports* Deutsch 1968

Periodicals, Annuals, Newspapers
The British Racehorse
Cope's Racegoers Encyclopaedia
Horse and Hound
Ladbroke's Flat Racing Companion
Pacemaker International
Playfair Racing Annual
Raceform Handicap Book
Racing and Football Outlook
Racing Post
Ruff's Guide to the Turf
The Sporting Life
The Sporting Life Weekender
Timeform Black Book and Annuals
Tote Racing Annual
Trainers Record
Trainers Review

NOTE

As this book went to press, on-course betting tax of 4 per cent was abolished in the 1987 Budget.

INDEX